Islamic charities and Islamic humanism in troubled times

Manchester University Press

HUMANITARIANISM

This series offers a new interdisciplinary reflection on one of the most important and yet understudied areas in history, politics and cultural practices: humanitarian aid and its responses to crises and conflicts. The series seeks to define afresh the boundaries and methodologies applied to the study of humanitarian relief and so-called 'humanitarian events'. The series includes monographs and carefully selected thematic edited collections which will cross disciplinary boundaries and bring fresh perspectives to the historical, political and cultural understanding of the rationale and impact of humanitarian relief work.

Calculating compassion: Humanity and relief in war, Britain 1870–1914 Rebecca Gill
Humanitarian intervention in the long nineteenth century Alexis Heraclides and Ada Dialla

Islamic charities and Islamic humanism in troubled times

Jonathan Benthall

Manchester University Press

The right of Jonathan Benthall to be identified as the author of this work has been asserted by him in accordance with the Copyright, Designs and Patents Act 1988.

Published by Manchester University Press
Altrincham Street, Manchester M1 7JA
www.manchesteruniversitypress.co.uk

British Library Cataloguing-in-Publication Data
A catalogue record for this book is available from the British Library

Library of Congress Cataloging-in-Publication Data applied for

ISBN 978 1 784 99308 5 hardback
ISBN 978 0 719 09972 4 paperback

First published 2016

Typeset by Out of House Publishing
Printed in Great Britain
by CPI Group (UK) Ltd, Croydon, CR0 4YY

For my grandchildren Violet, Alexander and Julia

Contents

Acknowledgements

I am grateful to the following for help in various ways over the last ten years: Akbar Ahmed, Michael Barnett, Jérôme Bellion-Jourdan, Jean-Nicolas Bitter, Kaja Borchgrevink, Erica Bornstein, Martin van Bruinessen, Benoît Challand, Bruno De Cordier, Didier Fassin, Michael Feener, Philip Fountain, Kay Guinane, Karin von Hippel, Jacob Høigilt, Gustaaf Houtman, Levi McLaughlin, Marie Juul Petersen, Mayke Kaag, Robert Lacey, Christian Lekon, Raphaël Liogier, Brian Pratt, Peter Redfield, Lawrence Rosen, Rupert Shortt, Janice Stein and Bertrand Taithe; as well as to the trustees and staff of many charities whose work I have tried to understand. Emanuel Schaeublin has been a particularly congenial colleague and constructive critic. Thanks also to the Department of Anthropology, University College London, for appointing me to an honorary research fellowship. The usual disclaimers apply.

Thanks are due to the publishers who have allowed material to be reproduced. The places of first publication are listed as follows.

Chapter 1: from *Understanding Islamic Charities*, edited by Jon Alterman and Karin von Hippel (Washington: CSIS Press), 2007.

Chapter 2: *Anthropology Today* 22: 4, August 2006 (London: Royal Anthropological Institute).

Chapter 3: *Journal of Humanitarian Assistance*, https://sites.tufts.edu/jha, 26 June 2008.

Chapter 4: The Graduate Institute of International and Development Studies, Geneva, an Occasional Paper published in 2008 by the Institute's Program for the Study of International Organization(s), which was dissolved in the same year.

Chapter 5: from *Gulf Charities and Islamic Philanthropy in the 'Age of Terror' and Beyond*, edited by Robert Lacey and Jonathan Benthall (Berlin: Gerlach Press), 2014, resulting from a paper delivered at the Gulf Research Meeting at the University of Cambridge, July 2012.

Chapter 6: UCLA *Journal of Islamic and Near Eastern Law* 10, 2010–11, pp. 1–10.

Chapter 8: *Asian Journal of Social Science* 42: 1–2, 2014 (Leiden: Brill).

Chapter 9: *Asian Ethnology*, originally prepared for a special issue scheduled to appear in the second issue of 2016.

Chapter 10: *Anthropology Today* 21: 1, February 2005 (London: Royal Anthropological Institute).

Chapter 11: *Times Literary Supplement*, 1 June 2012.

Chapter 12: *Times Literary Supplement*, 10 September 2014.

Chapter 13: *Times Literary Supplement*, 12 October 2012.

Chapter 14: *Times Literary Supplement*, 29 January 2014.

Chapter 15: *Anthropology Today* 29: 4, August 2013 (London: Royal Anthropological Institute).

Chapter 16: 'Qaradawi, Yusuf Al-', in *Oxford Encyclopedia of Islam and Politics*, vol. 2, edited by Emad El-Din Shahin and Peri J. Bearman, 2014 (New York: Oxford University Press), pp. 294–7.

Chapter 17: *Times Literary Supplement*, 10 December 2014.

Finally, my thanks to Manchester University Press and all who have contributed their skills at the various stages in the publication process.

A note on omissions and transliteration

Omissions to avoid repetition are marked [...].

Arabic words and phrases have been transliterated except when words, including proper names, have become familiar in English. This leads to some unavoidable inconsistencies.

Introduction

Few topics are as contested today as contemporary Islam. This book concentrates on some of its more attractive and positive features, without lapsing into a roseate view. All the chapters have been published previously. The first two thirds (Part I) are devoted to Islamic charities and humanitarianism, are mainly grounded in original research, and are fairly up to date with the state of scholarship in this field. The last third of the book (Part II) gives attention to what I have called Islamic humanism. Here (with the exception of Chapter 10) the emphasis is more on reviewing the work of other authors and should be read as tentative and provisional. I am well aware of the delicacy and complexity of the issues raised.

This Introduction has the dual role of providing a guide to the contents and of updating the book's coverage. A new prefatory note has been added before each chapter, mainly to bring it up to date since first publication, but also sometimes to explain the circumstances in which it was written.

Part I, Chapters 1 to 9: Islamic charities

Turbulent times

I began to explore Islamic charities over twenty years ago. The origin of my interest was as follows. I had organized conferences on 'the refugee experience' and 'societies in acute crisis' in the early 1980s as director of the Royal Anthropological Institute, and for some fifteen years had sat as a volunteer on a number of committees of Save the Children UK. It was the over-hasty remark of the chairman of its overseas committee one day in 1991, when we were faced by an accumulation of humanitarian crises – 'Journalists are parasites on human suffering' – that provoked the writing of a book called *Disasters, Relief and the Media* (Benthall 1993). This was a study of the symbiosis between humanitarian organizations and the media, including marketing techniques. In the preface to a second edition published much later (2009), I made more explicit the model – inspired by Sidney Mintz's studies of global commodities – of a 'stable system', a 'disaster–media–relief chain', whereby representations of misery are exported from the 'South' to the 'North' as consumables, under the control of an oligopoly of media organizations and aid agencies, in return for aid flows. The stability is occasionally disturbed by a mega-disaster such as the 2004 Indian Ocean tsunami or the 2010 Haitian earthquake, then returns to normal. (In other cases, such as the forced migration resulting from the Syrian civil war since 2011, the system fails to engage with the scale and gravity of the emergency.) The book included snapshots of the cultures of three major agencies that made sophisticated use of the media: the International Committee of the Red Cross, Médecins Sans Frontières (plus its French offshoots), and World Vision; it also included an analysis of the logos and promotional devices used by the major aid agencies.

In 1996, given a six months' sabbatical by the Institute, I decided to explore why some thirty countries use the red crescent rather than the red cross as their emblem – a problem, dating back to the Serbo-Turkish war of 1876, which remains delicate even today for the International Red Cross and Red Crescent Movement. This led to field research in Jordan, the Palestinian Territories, Oman and, later, Algeria to investigate the extensive Islamic literature on zakat, originally the Islamic tithe; ṣadaqa, optional charity; and *waqf* (plural *awqāf*), the equivalent of the European charitable foundation. Shortly afterwards, I met a French political scientist, Jérôme Bellion-Jourdan, who had done complementary research in Sudan, Pakistan and Bosnia, and we pooled our resources to publish a jointly authored book, *The Charitable Crescent: Politics of aid in the Muslim world* (2003). We agreed not merely to present our conclusion that the extent of Islamic charity had been underestimated in the 'West', but also to make use of the classic anthropological manoeuvre of 'decentring' – the unsettling of preconceptions. Our book anatomized modern Islamic charity since its efflorescence after the 1970s, with its various strengths and weaknesses and with an emphasis on its political aspects in such fraught contexts as Afghanistan and Israel–Palestine; but we went on to glance obliquely at the universalistic values of Western humanitarianism. The book also summarized the histories of the *waqf* and of Islamic finance and economics as they relate to charity, and it explored the origins of zakat and allied concepts in foundational Islam.

Perhaps we would have had difficulty in finding a publisher on a topic previously regarded as marginal, but for 9/11 and the allegations (though they were never proved) that those suicide attacks had been partly funded through the abuse of Islamic charities. The justification for publishing such a book on contentious aspects of contemporary aid and humanitarianism was simple. Our intervention was designed not only to add to the sum of knowledge but also more pragmatically to help voluntary donations of money and other resources by Muslims to achieve optimum benefit for the ultimate recipients; but we also underlined the risks that the privileges of charities may be abused. True, one can be accused of either whitewashing nefarious activities or, on the contrary, unjustly tarnishing good reputations, but all one can do is draw on the widest spread of evidence available and keep an open mind.

We may think of the principles underlying Islamic humanitarianism as being like a system of springs that feeds a river. This upstream system can be studied in itself, but the present-day realities when the river is observed downstream are of a different order. Others may dismiss the river as an essentially disruptive force. I prefer to see the consequences of 9/11 and other international crises as being like weighty rock-falls that alter the river's flow. There is no doubt that, owing to a refusal to recognize the special responsibilities of charities, lax management or criminal intent (or a combination of those reasons), some Islamic charities were used as conduits to fund military hostilities before 2001.[1] But if we set aside the exceptions of Pakistan and Kuwait – both considered later in this Introduction – the blame attached to the sector for the funding of violent extremism since 2001 has almost certainly been exaggerated. Smuggling, extortion, kidnapping, drug trafficking, raids on banks, and oil sales seem to be the major sources of revenue for violent Islamist extremists, as well as remittances from private individuals who may wear a cloak of humanitarianism. Abuse of the privileges of organized charities occurs everywhere from time to time. The remedy must be to establish systems of accountability, regulation and monitoring, which can minimize abuse though never totally eliminate it.

In the small, immensely rich and deliberately contrarian state of Qatar (Dorsey 2015), attempts were made in the early 2000s to bring control of the charity sector up to international standards, but they seem to have seriously faltered.[2] The Syrian civil war, in particular, provoked individuals in some of the Gulf states to arrange for financial remittances to the patchwork of opposition groups, sometimes through charitable structures. In the case of Kuwait, as noted below, the war had the ripple effect of inflaming the Sunni–Shia divide among Kuwaitis.

Some important monographs on different aspects of Islamic charities have been published since 2003 (Clark 2004; Singer 2008; Fauzia 2013; Juul Petersen 2015), and increasingly numerous articles, briefing papers and reports. A workshop concentrating on Gulf charities was held at the University of Cambridge in the summer of 2012, which resulted in a collection of sixteen articles, plus an introduction and afterword, that set out to summarize the current state of knowledge (Lacey and Benthall 2014).

Summary of the chapters

Since 2003, I published a number of overview articles, one of which is republished here as Chapter 1. I carried out some limited fieldwork with branches of British Islamic charities in Mali and in Aceh, Indonesia – both deliberately chosen as a contrast with hotspots, because the political temperature was at the time cool in both places and Islamic charities were functioning with some success. The results, documented here in Chapters 2 and 3, are a contribution to the literature on the question of 'cultural proximity': does a confessional NGO have privileged access when working in regions where most of the population shares its religion? Chapter 4, which covers the zakat committees in the Palestinian West Bank during the 'Oslo period' (1993–2007), harked back to fieldwork in Jordan and Palestine during 1996, but also benefited from my experience of two kinds of professional, no longer strictly academic, activity which I did not anticipate when *The Charitable Crescent* was published, but which were made possible by the political salience of Islamic charities since 2001.

One of these activities was an advisory role with the Swiss Federal Department of Foreign Affairs, Political Division IV, concerning its project to help remove unjustified obstacles from Islamic charities, an exercise in political mediation or 'track two diplomacy' which unfortunately never succeeded in surmounting all the challenges it faced. My personal account of this experience is given in Chapter 5. I argue in this chapter that there is a need for all Islamic charities, from the petrodollar states in particular, to be brought more fully into the international aid system subject to agreed procedures of regulation and monitoring.

We are faced today with a 'humanitarian deficit' – almost unprecedented suffering and poverty experienced by Muslims in many countries, despite the potential of more materially fortunate Muslims to bring relief – exacerbated by the pressures on the overseas aid budgets of major Western nations. Equally important, a 'humanitarian vacuum' is created in complex zones of conflict, where for political reasons reputable Islamic charities have a much reduced presence, leaving a space open for violent extremist groups to bring a measure of succour to victims, or at least to pretend to be doing so. This issue was coming to a head in early 2015, when the so-called 'Islamic State' (ISIS), in control of some 3.6 million living under the 'caliphate', was accused of 're-branding' cardboard boxes marked World Food Program, full of aid supplies. ISIS, unlike other jihadi groups, set out to create a functioning Islamic state with its own simulacrum of a zakat system.[3]

The other extra-academic activity was serving as an adviser and expert witness in a number of legal cases, both criminal and civil, relating to Islamic charities. Confidentiality clauses preclude me from writing about the more important of these cases, but Chapter 6 – written for a law journal, describing a publicly documented civil case in the United States that hinged on the status of Palestinian zakat committees – benefited from my involvement in some other cases where the same issues arose. Chapter 7, with its introductory explanation, gives an account of another legal incident with similar content, though paradoxically it is clear that the gravamen of the case was quite different: the attempt by the US government to exclude a prominent European Muslim, Professor Tariq Ramadan, from American soil on ideological grounds. Upon reconsideration, however, it eventually changed its mind and allowed him the non-immigrant visa that he had applied for.

Chapter 8 goes a little way to compensating for the book's emphasis on the Middle East, Europe and America, republishing a review of Amelia Fauzia's monograph on Islamic philanthropy in Indonesia.

Chapter 9, 'Puripetal force in the charitable field', is the most theoretical and speculative in the book and may be seen as a link to the second part, devoted to 'Islamic humanism'. It sets out to clarify the wide range of relationships between religions and humanitarian traditions as ideological movements, taking Islam as an instance. It postulates that the concept of the 'sacred', which is culturally restricted, is a special case of boundary maintenance or 'purism'. Metaphorically, 'puripetal force' is defined as a tendency common to all ideological systems, a resistance to social entropy or anomie. The importance of purity in Islamic doctrine is well attested, but within that wider sphere we may identify the specially puritan version of Islam known as 'Wahhabi-Salafism'. As for humanitarianism and philanthropy, these occupy in the West a 'space' protected by special laws and conceived of as untainted in principle by politics and economics. Within the wider sphere of humanitarianism we may locate a more concentrated form which has underpinned the world-view and habitus of the International Committee of the Red Cross, represented by its main founder, Henry Dunant. The chapter outlines how the policies and programmes of various Islamic charity and welfare organizations – originating in Britain, Indonesia and Saudi Arabia – interact differentially with, on the one hand, Islamic doctrines and, on the other hand, humanitarian traditions. Meanwhile, US government policy towards charities sometimes seems dominated by an urge to peer into purity of motives. Finally, it is suggested that this explanatory model could equally be applied to Christian and other religious traditions, with the concluding thought that the common ground between the institutions of international humanitarianism and religious traditions is currently expanding.

Some recurrent themes

In any collection of previously published material, there is a risk of undue repetition, which can be irritating for the reader. I have omitted some brief material – signalling this by means of [...] – but have decided not otherwise to tamper with the original texts, except to correct a few misprints and other minor errors, and to apply some spelling and style consistencies for the purpose of this book. Where repetitions remain, it is because they relate to some important running themes.

Faith Based Organizations and 'cultural sensitivity'
I see Islamic charities as belonging to the wider category of Faith Based Organizations (FBOs), though this is a contested term because 'faith', in itself an equivocal concept, can inspire or authorize non-profit organizations in many different ways (Clarke and Jennings 2008; Fountain 2013a). A turning point in the recognition of the importance of religion in development – in particular, the immense extent of religious networks as ready-made forms of 'civil society' with the potential to bypass corrupt political structures – was the faith and ethics initiative overseen at the World

Bank by Katherine Marshall between 2000 and 2006, under the presidency of James Wolfensohn (Marshall 2011b; 2013; see also Fountain 2013a; 2013b). Marshall's personal contribution to enhancing this awareness worldwide has been permanent, but in 2006 she moved to the Georgetown-based Berkley Center for Religion, Peace, and World Affairs, heading its programme on Religion and Global Development. It appears that within the World Bank itself a gruelling battle was lost, for in 2015 there were no signs of its survival in the Bank's policies. Marshall is opposed to lumping FBOs together: her preference is to 'focus instead on specific groups of institutions, on countries, and on specific issues' (Marshall 2011a: 200).

The aid world is generally agreed on the need for 'cultural sensitivity', the effort to avoid imposing metropolitan assumptions when working with local communities, though there is dissent on some specific issues such as the gender roles, reproductive rights and the economic contribution of children. (Homosexuality in particular is a 'taboo' subject for all mainstream Islamic charities, as noted by Khan 2012: 106). The substantive issue of 'cultural proximity' is at least as old as the Serbo-Turkish war of the 1870s, as mentioned above. The issue as currently defined has arisen mainly in the context of work in the Muslim world, and 'cultural' here becomes a euphemism for 'religious'. An earlier debate about 'comparative advantage', dating back to the 1970s, focused on whether it could be shown that NGOs (of all types) performed better than governments in service provision. This developed into an ideological debate in the 1980s about states vis-à-vis civil society, where NGOs represent the alternative to the rollback of the state.

'Communitarian aid' has clearly been practised by all religious groups for centuries. It is still legal and acceptable in most Western countries to set up a charity for the exclusive benefit of adherents of a particular religion or for proselytizing purposes. I have attempted elsewhere a comparison in more detail between the work of Christian and Islamic aid agencies today, examining the issues of 'cultural proximity' that they raise (Benthall 2012b).

Islamic Relief Worldwide
Islamic Relief Worldwide (IRW), formerly just Islamic Relief, is the largest Islamic relief and development agency, founded in 1984 by the charismatic Dr Hany El-Banna, then an Egyptian medical student in Birmingham, England, after he had visited refugee camps in Sudan. (It is not to be confused with the International Islamic Relief Organization, based in Saudi Arabia.) It has an impressive record of growth and acceptance by British and European authorities, largely avoiding political problems, as will be clear from many favourable references in this book. (Helpfully, it has been welcoming to researchers such as myself.[4]) It seems that it was El-Banna's own initiative, when developing Islamic Relief's policies in the 1990s, to allow funds that it collected as zakat contributions to be disbursed for the benefit of non-Muslims as well as Muslims, without seeking authorization from Islamic

scholars. Meanwhile some Islamic scholars were arriving at the same interpretation of the Qur'anic rules on zakat, and some other important Islamic charities followed Islamic Relief's lead. The rules pertaining to zakat are the subject of endless debates among Islamic scholars, and it is the cornerstone of Islamic humanitarianism, though in practice a typical Islamic charity may receive more donations as *sadaqa*, which allows it more flexibility as to how they are disbursed.

Even Islamic Relief, known for its scrupulous administration, found itself under attack towards the end of 2014 by the governments of Israel and the United Arab Emirates because of allegations that its work in the Palestinian Territories had indirectly supported Hamas. The UK Disasters Emergency Committee issued a statement confirming that it had reviewed an independent audit report and was not aware of any evidence that Islamic Relief had used funds inappropriately in Israel and the Palestinian Territories.[5] A similar episode had occurred in May 2006 when its head of operations in Gaza was detained by the Israeli authorities for three weeks and deported. The charity commented then that 'the allegations appear to be a mixture of confusion and malice' (McGreal 2006). Any historian of Islamic humanitarianism will need to record the indefatigable contribution of El-Banna, who founded not only Islamic Relief but a number of umbrella organizations including the Muslim Charities Forum, with members of most of the leading British Islamic NGOs that have operations overseas.

The West Bank zakat committees

The special conundrum of the West Bank zakat committees as they were organized between 1993 and 2007 recurs, because it brought together the conflict resolution or mediation efforts described above and numerous legal cases.[6] The allegation that these zakat committees were merely fronts for Hamas was still the subject of intense litigation in the summer of 2015. I remain sceptical about this allegation, but have always tried to maintain an open mind, conscious that at any moment 'smoking gun' evidence might be produced to substantiate the charge. The names of two charities recur in this Palestinian context: the Holy Land Foundation of Richardson, Texas – the fate of which is described in the introduction to Chapter 6[7] – and the London-based Interpal, which in the summer of 2015 remained a cause célèbre in London since the views of the British and US authorities were so divergent – the former giving it lukewarm support, for it was in good standing with the Charity Commission, but the UK Foreign and Commonwealth Office declining to challenge the US Treasury's determination to keep it on a blacklist as an alleged 'terrorist entity'. Specific attention is given to the Interpal question in Chapter 5. Until late 2014, it seemed that most of the substantial sympathy for Interpal in Britain came from the Left, but a turning point may have been reached with the publication in November of a supportive article in the centre-right *Telegraph*, co-authored by its chief political commentator at the time, Peter Oborne (Delmar-Morgan and Oborne 2014a).

Banking problems

The international banking system has become increasingly sensitive to the risks of having Islamic charities as clients, especially those that work in 'high risk areas' such as conflict zones, whereas regulatory authorities generally require charities to use the banking system rather than cash. This can become an almost insuperable difficulty when donors want to remit humanitarian funds legally to places such as Syria where people are dying in agony. One important reason for 'de-risking' by banks is the extent of civil litigation in the United States, on whose currency, the US dollar, all banks depend for international transactions and where they nearly all have branches, which makes them liable to be sued for massive sums in American courts as alleged accessories to terrorism (De Goede 2012; Keatinge 2014). In 2015, British Muslim charities were taking urgent steps to influence government to make it easier for them to operate bank accounts and so respond to almost unprecedented needs in the Middle East and elsewhere. They argued in a meeting in the House of Commons on 25 February 2015 that, though there was supposed to be an excellent understanding between the US Treasury and the British Treasury on policy issues in general, it was a one-way relationship in this case, in that the US Treasury appeared to be impervious to influence. In the meantime, frustration among British Muslims who wanted to send relief aid to high-risk areas such as Syria was almost certainly one of the drivers that impelled some of them to sympathize with violent extremism. A working paper published by the Overseas Development Institute's Humanitarian Policy Group in 2015 gave comprehensive coverage to the tensions afflicting UK humanitarian aid in the 'age of counter-terrorism', with a special emphasis on Muslim charities but also addressing wider risks, and perceptions of risks, from the viewpoints of international aid agencies, the financial services industry and governments (Metcalfe-Hough et al. 2015).

Towards a more complete description

Islamic charities operate in virtually all countries where there are either Muslim donors or Muslim recipients or both. Until recently these charities occupied a kind of parallel world, unrepresented in official statistics of aid flows and unrecognized in the Western media. A recently published collection of essays on Islam and development was given the subtitle 'Exploring the invisible aid economy' (Tittensor and Clarke 2014), though this understates the efforts made since the turn of century to make it more visible to the Western mainstream. So far, no comprehensive mapping of the sector has been prepared and I cannot claim that my book covers this rapidly expanding field with the balance that one would wish for.

In addition to Syria, Lebanon and Iraq, the Shia majority in Sunni-ruled Bahrain, substantial Shia minorities in Kuwait and the Eastern Province of Saudi Arabia, and the Houthi insurrection in Yemen, threaten Sunni regimes with the spectre of an extended 'Shia crescent'. This book is limited to Sunni Islam, thus overlooking the huge and highly controversial religious foundations in Iran and the equally strongly politicized Hizbullah charities in Lebanon. Shia believers are required to pay a religious tithe (*khums*) to their imam or *marja'*, equal to one fifth of their annual income after deduction of expenses. Shia philanthropy is little documented in Western publications, but it is likely to attract more academic attention in future.[8]

Regrettably, many debates about Islamic charities are highly politicized. I rely on my own research and on open-source publications, having no access to intelligence reports and thus no doubt missing out on some important information. But we need to be sceptical about the swirl of propaganda. The political turbulence of this century has facilitated the emergence of so-called 'counter-terrorist studies', which often seem to bypass normal peer review and scholarly conventions – partly by means of dissemination via think tanks and political assemblies rather than academic institutions and journals, and by means of the United States legal system of eliciting expert testimony in a partisan manner, which tends to present contentious issues as black or white whereas in real life disagreements there are nearly always shades of grey.

Pakistan

Pakistan today gives us the clearest example of a major national charity that is almost certainly a front for a banned terrorist organization – Lashkar e Taiba (Army of the Pure), which was responsible for the 2008 attacks on Mumbai and has been an illegal organization since 2002. This is Jamaat u Dawa (Assembly for Propagation), which is affiliated to the Falah e Insaniyat (Humanitarian Foundation). Its version of Islam, Ahl i-Hadith, is close to the Saudi Wahhabism (Candland and Khan Qazi 2012). It appears to have violent political objectives relating to Pakistan, India and Afghanistan, but not further afield. Its founder, Hafiz Muhammad Saeed, who was also the head of Lashkar e Taiba, had in 2015 been three times arrested by the Pakistani authorities under Indian pressure on charges of terrorism, but released on the grounds that there was not enough evidence. He continued to direct Jamaat u Dawa, though the USA had announced a \$10 million bounty on him. Jamaat u Dawa was a leading agency in the emergency aid to the victims of the 2005 earthquake, which left hundreds of thousands of people seriously injured or homeless; national and international agencies were at that time willing to cooperate with it because it was able to get unique access to remote areas. It was also active in emergency aid after the 2010 floods. The policy of the US government is that Jamaat u Dawa should simply be extirpated. It seems that Jamaat u Dawa's welfare and emergency services in Pakistan, including hospitals and ambulances, are so extensive that the government does not dare to close it down (Kohlmann 2006). The moral dilemma that such a case throws up, in contexts of acute humanitarian need, is examined here in Chapter 9.

By contrast, the Edhi Foundation (mentioned in Chapter 1), founded in Pakistan by a twenty-year-old refugee from Gujarat in India, in 2015 the country's best-known philanthropist, is one of the most remarkable Islamic charities. Coverage of it in *The Charitable Crescent* (Benthall and Bellion-Jourdan 2003: 18–19) was based only on published sources including the founder's own memoir (Edhi 1996). Now, however, Christopher Candland, an American political scientist, has filled in some valuable information. Abdul Sattar Edhi only registered his charitable activity as an association in 1983 after his wife's heart attack forced him to address the question of how his work would continue after he and his wife died. There is now a group of several associated Edhi foundations, which in 2015 he was continuing to run with his family. Together they manage in Pakistan numerous hospitals, 335 welfare clinics, many orphanages and dispensaries, and the de facto national ambulance service, among other things. They also have a presence in thirty-four countries, including the United Kingdom and Germany, attracting substantial donations from the Pakistani diaspora, and their international section provides extensive emergency relief services. It seems that – because many Pakistani Muslims still contend that only Muslims are entitled to benefit from zakat, yet the foundations serve anyone in need without regard to religion – they keep separate accounts for Muslim and non-Muslim beneficiaries.

Candland writes (forthcoming) of the 'high degree of respect and often a palpable loving atmosphere' surrounding Edhi, who 'is one of the more charming, appealing looking, and pleasant people one is likely to meet'. He and his family 'have devoted their entire lives – from dawn to dusk, from childhood to old age – to serving those in need'. Deeply rooted in religious morality, Edhi's achievement is one of the most convincing illustrations of the potential of Islamic charity, though situated in one of the world's most deviant religious polities. Edhi himself has observed 'Pakistanis give wholeheartedly. They just walk in and give … This is a good country. It's just run by bad people'. If Islamic philanthropy in some other countries, such as those in the Gulf, were to emulate Edhi's high ideals and earn through example the right to be allowed to function without political impediment, a surge of volunteering and charitable giving could be unleashed.

Turkey

A notable gap in this book's coverage is Islamic charities founded in Turkey, which is gaining an increasingly salient presence on the humanitarian scene. This country, which had been identified with Mustafa Kemal Atatürk's secularism since the abolition of the Ottoman Caliphate in 1922, came under the control in the early 2000s of the populist and pragmatically Islamist AKP (Adalet ve Kalkınma Partisi, or Justice and Development Party), which asserted an active foreign policy, sometimes called 'neo-Ottomanist', with a view to establishing the nation as a global power. These ambitions have been reflected in the work of the Turkish Red Crescent Society (mentioned here in Chapter 3), which like all components of the International Red Cross and Red Crescent Movement is legally non-confessional, but also in a major NGO, the IHH Humanitarian Relief Foundation. This was founded in 1992 at the time of the Bosnian war in the Balkans and is active in over a hundred countries suffering from poverty and the consequences of wars and natural disasters. I visited its headquarters in Istanbul in 2011 but otherwise am dependent on published sources.

IHH has a strongly Islamic character, for instance with its emphasis on giving for *qurbani*, the festive sacrifice at the end of the annual hajj pilgrimage, on Eid al-Adha or 'Id al-Kabir. As a proxy for this traditional animal sacrifice, donors may contribute funds to IHH to facilitate ritually prescribed slaughters for the benefit of poor people in such countries as Bosnia and Kyrgyzstan. The holy month of Ramadan, as with all other Islamic charities, is the prime season for fundraising: in 2011, 1.5 million people received food pack distributions for *iftar* (the Ramadan evening breakfast), clothes and educational assistance. Like every other Islamic charity I know of, it runs an orphan programme – 'orphan' being defined in the Muslim world as a child who has lost his or her father, that is to say the family breadwinner. The spiritual merit to be gained by helping orphans, a marked feature of Islamic moral teaching which dates back to the Prophet Muhammad's own upbringing as an orphan, is put to use by means of an online sponsorship scheme that, in 2011, was claimed to be supporting some 20,000 orphans in thirty-one countries including Turkey itself.

As a result of its experience in responding to earthquakes, IHH has on occasion carried out projects in earthquake-stricken regions where there are virtually no Muslims, such as Haiti and Japan. However, its efforts are normally almost entirely concentrated on assisting Muslims, including in regions such as Latin America where they are in a minority. 'The fact is that Islam is growing like a snowball in Latin America. Islam's message of rights and justice empowers the pro-revolution and rebellion Latin people who have long been repressed but who do not like this … Polite, sensitive, sympathetic and always-smiling Latin people want to get rid of Western clothes choking them for centuries.'[9]

IHH is best known internationally for its prominent participation, with the flagship *Mavi Marmara* and two other ships, in the multinational but non-governmental aid convoy that set out to breach the naval blockade of Gaza in May 2010. Israeli forces intercepted the flotilla in international waters and, as a result of violent clashes, nine Turkish activists were killed and seven Israeli commandos, as well as many activists, were wounded. A UN report, chaired by Sir Geoffrey Palmer, concluded in September 2011 that Israel was justified in intercepting the flotilla because of the real threat to its security if weapons were to enter Gaza from the sea, and that the attempt to breach the blockade was reckless. 'Serious questions' existed about the conduct and objectives of the flotilla organizers, particularly IHH. However, Israel's decision to board the vessels with substantial force at a great distance from the blockade zone was excessive and unreasonable, and there was also 'significant mistreatment' of passengers after the takeover of the vessels until their deportation.[10]

The incident contributed to deteriorating relations between Turkey and Israel, which had been cordial for some twenty years. In March 2013, Prime Minister Netanyahu apologized to his Turkish counterpart, Recep Tayyip Erdoğan, and some compensation by Israel to families of the deceased was negotiated. But Israeli–Turkish relations had not recovered by the summer of 2015. IHH is treated as a terrorist organization in Israel on account of its supposed cooperation with Hamas. However, my impression is that IHH as a whole is one of the most professionally administered Islamic NGOs, comparable in its effectiveness to Islamic Relief or Muslim Aid, though – unlike those British charities –refusing to renounce proselytism.

The other international Islamic relief agency that I visited in Istanbul in 2011 was Kimse Yok Mu ('Is there anybody there?'), mentioned in Chapter 9, which is affiliated to the well-established Gülen (or Hizmet) movement, though this is not advertised in its publicity. It was founded quite recently in 2002 and has grown rapidly to work in over 100 countries, claiming over 180,000 volunteers worldwide. It claims to deliver its assistance regardless of religion, language or ethnicity. I have no reason to doubt its professionalism, but, having studied many NGOs, I have never come across one so devoted to self-congratulation through the collection of testimonials, plaques and the like. On the other hand, it has experimented with a new way of establishing personal links between donors and beneficiaries – the Sister Family programme – whereby well-off families can apply to sponsor a family in need and help to alleviate its problems in practical ways, such as helping to find employment, as well as merely giving money.[11]

Fethullah Gülen, born in Anatolia in 1941 and now resident in a kind of exile in Pennsylvania, is an enigmatic figure who spans the two main themes of this book: charity and humanism. The political scientist Olivier Roy, one of the most perceptive commentators on contemporary Islam, has hailed him as 'a scholar of extraordinary proportions':

> In addition to his great contribution to the betterment activities of education in Turkey by encouraging people to open private schools, he is renowned for his painstaking endeavors for the establishment of mutual understanding and tolerance in society. His social reform efforts, begun during the 1960s, have made him one of Turkey's most well-known and respected public figures … His belief and feelings are profound, and his ideas and approach to problems are both wise and rational. (Roy 2004: 225)

Relations between the Turkish government and the Gülen movement were previously friendly, but since 2013 became embittered after corruption allegations against the ruling AKP. Prime Minister Erdoğan accused the movement of setting itself up as a 'state within a state' by infiltrating the police and judiciary, and in 2014 a Turkish court issued an arrest warrant for Gülen on the grounds that he was operating an armed terror group (Letsch 2014). Also in 2014, the government set out to revoke

Kimse Yok Mu's rights as a charity because of its affiliation with the Gülen movement and blocked its bank accounts. This move was criticized by opposition politicians, however, and it appears that the charity has been able to continue collecting funds.

Kuwait

As outlined in a Brookings briefing paper published in December 2013 (Dickinson 2013), the case of Kuwait is complex. The State of Kuwait was the first government in the Gulf to launch a development fund, as early as 1961: the Kuwait Fund for Arab Economic Development. Kuwait has been the largest non-Western humanitarian donor for the crisis in Syria, and the fourth largest donor overall. The International Islamic Charity Organization, in particular, is recognized as one of the most effective and experienced in the region (Juul Petersen 2015). Kuwait's regulation of charities has been less strict than that imposed in Saudi Arabia. This has facilitated the collection and transfer of funds with strictly humanitarian intent. There is evidence, however, that some of the money raised by Kuwaiti Sunnis was applied for military purposes and these remittances had the effect of encouraging both the fracturing of the military opposition to the Bashar al-Assad regime and the growth of Islamist extremism in Syria. These financial transfers were mainly organized by prominent individuals, often with the trappings of charity, but also through a few established charities such as Sheikh Fahad al-Ahmed Charity. Meanwhile, members of Kuwait's Shia minority were attempting to do the same in support of the Syrian regime. The Syrian war thus had the ripple effect of aggravating the Sunni–Shia divide which hitherto had been relatively free from tensions in Kuwait. Kuwaiti support for the Syrian opposition began to decline by the end of 2012 and the government pushed through new anti-money laundering laws in 2013.

The Revival of Islamic Heritage Society (RIHS, *Jamiaat Ihya' al-Turath al-Islami*) in Kuwait, an umbrella organization of Kuwaiti Salafis, was designated as a terrorist entity in 2008 by the US Treasury on account of its activities in Pakistan, Afghanistan and Bangladesh since 2005. However, in 2015 it was still functioning freely in Kuwait. Zoltan Pall has shown (Pall 2014) that a schism between 'purists' and 'activists' in this association is at the heart of the internal dynamics of Salafism in Kuwait. The purists mainly focus on peaceful proselytism, obedience to the ruler (often backing autocratic Arab regimes) and daily religious practices, while the activists, or *haraki*, believe in broader political involvement and often see violence as an acceptable means to an end. Kuwaiti Salafis have an extensive worldwide influence, which has extended to backing a variety of Salafi armed groups in Syria. The activists gained ground after the 2011 'Arab Spring'. Pall considers that probably a purist majority within the RIHS has limited itself to sending humanitarian aid, especially for Syrian refugees in Lebanon, Turkey, Jordan and Syria itself, though this was also seen as an opportunity for proselytism. The activist faction, on the other hand, openly supported the armed opposition and, even after a clampdown by the Kuwait government in 2013, the flow of funds to Islamist opposition groups such as Jaish al-Islam (Army of Islam), supported by the Kuwaiti ruling family, has not ceased.

It is clear from Pall's lucid analysis that the regional and indeed worldwide impact of Kuwaiti Salafism has been underestimated. But the 'purist' current seems compatible with the norms of international charities (proselytism not being a monopoly of Islam) and it is open to the Kuwaiti authorities, as Pall suggests in his concluding recommendations, to encourage it further through regulation and monitoring.

Domestic Islamic charity in the United Kingdom

When Islamic charities constituted under English law began to grow in the 1980s, the Muslim diaspora was well acquainted with the living conditions of poor people in its various countries of origin, who had no government 'safety nets' to fall back on. These Muslim charity organizers saw their overwhelming priority as being to remit funds for the relief of poverty and suffering overseas. More recently, it was appreciated that there was plenty to do in Britain and the rapid growth of food banks all over the nation has made the extent of needs evident to all. Thus Muslim Aid diversified with its Warm Hearts Winter Campaign, reaching out to the elderly and homeless, its Prisoners Rehabilitation Project, and its Employment Training Project.

A rare exercise in the scholarly analysis of 'domestic' Muslim charity in Britain has been undertaken by Sufyan Abid in his research on Muslim business people and entrepreneurs of South Asian origin living in Birmingham. Common to their local and very public charitable giving is the conviction that by doing so they purify their profits and ensure their future commercial success; however, the choice of charitable organizations is determined by their particular religious affiliations: Barelvi, Deobandi or Salafi, with subdivisions within each group (Abid 2013). As well as remitting funds overseas, these Birmingham Muslims are committed to such local services as Muslim funerals, daycare centres, radio transmissions, vocational courses and anti-narcotics programmes, as well as assisting poor communities with access to state benefits.

One of the first Islamic charities concentrating on domestic British needs to be formally registered with the Charity Commission (in 2010) was the Al-Mizan Charitable Trust. This provides small grants and interest-free loans of up to £500. According to its 2013–14 Annual Report, most of its donors and volunteers are British Muslims, but 'over three-quarters of our beneficiaries subscribe to a faith other than Islam or no faith at all'.

In 2011, a new charity, the National Zakat Foundation (NZF), was launched in London under the inspiration of a charismatic Muslim leader, Sheikh Tawfique Chowdhury, of Bangladeshi origin, now resident in Australia after pursuing studies at the Islamic University of Medina. NZF was registered with the Charity Commission in 2013 and is part of an informal international network of charities that also includes the Mercy Mission. By 2015, NZF had already raised £2.7 million in zakat contributions. By way of compensating for the concentration by the first 'wave' of British Islamic charities on overseas operations, NZF emphasizes the origins of zakat as an essentially local initiative, which can now respond to serious needs in Muslim communities. It recommends that Muslim donors should distribute their zakat in a three-way split: one third to international relief, one third to friends and family, and one third to meet neighbourly needs. NZF's work has two main strands. The first enables individuals to apply for funding by filling in a form and some £60,000 per month has been distributed in this way. Cash is only given in emergencies; the norm is to provide food or clothing vouchers, or to pay rent to a landlord rather than directly to the applicant. The second strand is to supply shelters: one for ex-offenders and three for single Muslim women (catering for their cultural and religious as well as material needs). The headquarters is in Wembley, London, with a small paid staff of fifteen, including an immigration lawyer, complemented by volunteer case workers. The policy is to respond to local priority needs, which may be unemployment in an inner-city borough or a narcotics problem in a Home Counties town, and gradually to expand from the south-east to cities such as Birmingham and Bradford, building local links with mosques (but eschewing all proselytism).

With regard to the question of non-discrimination, NZF has outlined its policy as follows:

> Currently the majority of our work is focussed within the Muslim community. We have chosen to channel our initial efforts in this manner due to our limited resources as a young organisation, the particularly high level of poverty and deprivation within the UK Muslim community and our expertise in faith-sensitive provision. Our long-term ambition is for the National Zakat Foundation to be of benefit to all, regardless of colour or creed.[12]

The high rates of homelessness, drug addiction, juvenile incarceration and involuntary prostitution are specific to parts of Britain, but NZF's emphasis on working at the local level illustrates a wider principle which is a theme of this book: the malleability of zakat and the Qur'anic rules which are open to diverse interpretations and practical implementation.

A zakat movement?

Recognition of the practical potential of zakat as a resource for relief and development aid recently gathered momentum, especially in the light of the immense humanitarian needs in the Middle East and plans for the UN-sponsored Global Humanitarian Summit in Istanbul in 2016. 'Opportunity knocks: why non-Western donors enter humanitarianism and how to make the best of it' was the title – perhaps excessively candid – of an article published in the *International Review of the Red Cross* in 2011 (Binder and Meier 2011). The BRIC countries (Brazil, Russia, India and China) have not yet made a major contribution as 'new humanitarian donors', whereas Turkey has emerged as one of the most generous donor countries (though it is also major recipient of aid). Huge wealth in the Gulf states and the mandatory character of zakat acknowledged by practising Muslims everywhere offer much promise. Charity organizers in Britain have urged that zakat is a religious and moral principle that should not be reduced to a fundraising device. Traditionally it was centred around mosques and there is a risk of losing the 'spirit of zakat' that respects local communities and aims to strengthen their resilience.[13] 'There is evidence to suggest that once larger institutions become involved, including the state and international NGOs, the effectiveness of Zakat in terms of its capacity to empower the person receiving it is reduced' (Stirk 2015).

Prince Hassan of Jordan has been urging for some twenty years that an international zakat fund should be launched, but so far without success. There are strong arguments in favour of a revived 'zakat movement', not least the shortfalls in 'traditional' overseas aid budgets, but it will have to surmount stubborn political and regulatory obstacles.

It must be recognized too that zakat has always been a subject of controversy in the Islamic tradition. There can be no doubt that it began as a prescription to pay alms as a personal religious duty, but it soon became – perhaps even as early as under the Prophet Muhammad's rule in Medina – a legal obligation or tax collected by the Muslim authorities (Benthall and Bellion-Jourdan 2003: 10–11; Sijpesteijn 2013: 181–99; Kennedy 2014). However, this was always contested (Singer 2008: 46). I touch on this question in Chapter 9. Proponents of a zakat movement in the humanitarian cause will have to deal with the criticism that some influential commentators have interpreted the aims of zakat as embracing military activities in defence of Islam (Qaradawi n.d.: vol. 2). Charities such as Islamic Relief Worldwide and the Edhi Foundation, returning to the original Qur'anic injunction to care for the poor and disadvantaged, have had considerable success in dispelling these objections by setting a practical example of 'pure' humanitarianism.

Tools for a more comparative approach

This study assumes Christian, or secular post-Christian, charity as an implicit baseline for comparison. Further research will no doubt seek to free itself from this constraint. As yet, few studies have been published comparing Christian and Islamic charitable activities. Mirjam de Bruijn and Rijk van Dijk, however, have compared local Pentecostal Christian and Islamic charity in West Africa, arguing that Pentecostalism and Sahelian Islam tend to maintain insecurities as part of a natural order whereby the well off give to the poor and in exchange receive heavenly salvation (de Bruijn and van Dijk 2009). This is a familiar criticism made of charitable giving in all contexts and is specially applicable to some strains in conservative Salafi Islam. The obverse of spiritual merit is the curse uttered by those unjustly treated. Capital on earth is not only financial but has symbolic, informational and cultural forms, yet these are convertible into financial capital at varying exchange rates that are continuously being negotiated. Treasure in heaven may be accumulated as well, following the injunctions of both the Qur'an and the New Testament. As Fenella Cannell (2006: 21) writes, the believer's gift 'will, as it were, be converted from one economy to the other on the condition that he acts in the spirit of the heavenly economy while still on earth'.

I have suggested elsewhere how comparison might proceed, beginning with Marcel Mauss's dazzlingly innovative but enigmatic essay on reciprocity, *The Gift*, about which so much has been written (Mauss 1990; Benthall and Bellion-Jourdan 2003: 16–17; Benthall 2012c). In particular, a 'free' gift cannot admit that it has a dimension of reciprocity. This paradox is confronted in the teaching of all the world religions: alms are best given in secret. In Islam, intention (*nīyah*) is important: giving should come straight from the heart and its merit is negated by ulterior motives. It is in India that we find the most sophisticated working through of this paradox, suggesting that all the founders of great religions must – whatever privileged revelations may be ascribed to them – have also been accomplished anthropologists. Celibate Jain renouncers collect alms from families as they proceed from house to house, but are precluded in their spiritual quest from expressing gratitude or appreciation (Laidlaw 2000: 632). Erica Bornstein in her study of charity in India has shown how the beliefs and practices aggregated as modern 'Hinduism' interact with Buddhist, Islamic, Christian and secular traditions (Bornstein 2012).

At present, the study of Islamic charity is weighted towards the donor's side of the equation. Ethnographic skills are needed to gain access to the perspective of aid recipients as well as providers. Moreover, the need for security, both material and spiritual, is universal. It is catered for by a wide variety of risk-mitigating networks and caring institutions, some based on legal entitlements and others on customary obligation, but with increasing vulnerability in most regions because of the widespread withdrawal of the state from welfare commitments. An expanded concept of social security as 'the dimension of social organization dealing with the provision of security not considered to be an exclusive matter of responsibility', as defined by Franz and Keebet von Benda-Beckmann (Thelen et al. 2009: 2), may offer a framework for comparative analysis to supplement what anthropologists call 'emic' (insider) constructs such as 'charity', 'zakat', 'aid' and their lexical congeners, each of which is deeply embedded in an *idéologique*.

Part II, Chapters 10 to 17: Islamic humanism

From humanitarianism to humanism

The final third of this book stems from a long-standing interest in the anthropology of religion and specifically Islam, an immense and contentious field. Study of the

Islamic homologues of 'charity', a Latinate word with Christian and legal connotations, leads one inevitably to wider questions. Older interpretations of the rules of zakat (Qur'an 9: 60) – revised by some progressive Islamic authorities some two or three decades ago but far from defunct today – laid down in general that only Muslims could be beneficiaries; so what has been the general position of this traditional Islam with regard to non-Muslims? One category of permitted beneficiaries is those 'in the way of God', that is to say in jihad; so what does this key concept in Islamic theology mean? Another is 'those who are inclined to truth', which can authorize proselytism. Another is 'captives', which has been interpreted as including Muslims living under colonialism or in non-Muslim tyrannies. It is true that many of the Islamic charities discussed in Part I devote all or most of their efforts to the relief of poverty and suffering. However, the Qur'anic regulations on zakat may be seen as encapsulating concepts which go to the heart of current debates within Islam, and which are explored in Part II.

Since Chapters 11 to 17 consist of assessments of other people's work, no claim to a systematic approach is made. Some readers may object to the phrase 'Islamic humanism'. I have chosen this because other terms such as 'progressive', 'liberal', 'reformist' or 'modern' are all hard to use without seeming to assume a march of history in one direction only. But is not 'humanism' an imprecise term, and one that has been so eloquently deconstructed by Michel Foucault and others that it is no longer respectable?

I defend my usage because the Arabic language makes no distinction between 'humanity', 'humanism' and 'humanitarianism', having one word, *insānīya*, for all three. 'The use of *insānīya*', writes Jasmine Moussa in an erudite historical and legal paper,

> in a sense that reflects a transnational and universal empathy towards all members of the human race became widespread in the 1960s, particularly through the writings of scholars of 'humanism', who argued for the compatibility of Islamic principles with humanism's core values, such as justice, dignity and human rights. Most scholarly works from the region have not used the words *insānī/insānīya* in a specialised sense that is distinguishable from charity, philanthropy or other forms of social work or development. (Moussa 2014: 25)

Islamic morality insists that self-realization as a human being – *ibn Ādam* – is achieved not merely by piety but by practical generosity towards the less fortunate, and by reasoning and the search for knowledge. Islam insists on the dignity and responsibility of individuals as well as on communal solidarity. The most sympathetic and persuasive account that I know of by a non-Muslim of Islam as a great moral and political force is Marcel Boisard's *L'Humanisme de l'Islam* (*Humanism in Islam*), 1979.

However, I would include also under 'Islamic humanism' a respect for the human sciences as they have developed over the centuries, not excluding the work of Ibn Khaldun and other great Muslim scholars. These give insights into religion which allow for questioning and criticism that are absent from the writings of those who believe that Islam has the answer to all problems, and who consequently are restricted to an insider's view of their faith. The very term 'reform' is anathema to many conservative Muslims since it has the negative connotations of *bid'ah*, or 'heretical innovation'.

A crisis of authority

A starting point for these chapters is that there is a crisis of authority in Islam today. For instance, in so far as any one figure might be recognized by large numbers of Sunni Muslims as a supreme spokesman for the religion, it would be the Grand Imam of Al-Azhar based in Cairo, but the current incumbent, Sheikh Ahmed al-Tayeb, was appointed by President Mubarak and, though he is relatively conciliatory in his views, he is deeply implicated in Egyptian politics. No non-Muslim should presume to advise how the crisis of authority should be resolved, but it is possible that reflections by outsiders, inspired by the human sciences, may be found stimulating.

It has been objected that 'theologocentrism' distorts, in that it assumes a direct connection between Islamic theology and politics in the Arab and Muslim worlds. Indeed, many forms of anti-Muslim prejudice can be seen as examples of scapegoating, a social pathology that floats free from evidence, comparable to anti-Semitism and especially likely to become viral at times of economic stress. 'Islamophobia' – a problematic word in that it implies a passive, quasi-medical condition – is indeed rooted in white supremacism and in the colonial manoeuvre whereby Muslim societies were both eroticized and stigmatized, not to mention the recent increase in Western–Muslim tensions that came to a head in the attacks on the USA on 11 September 2001. Islamophobia is a real threat to civic harmony and much more than an accusation used by Muslims to deflect criticism. However, the attribution to Muslims of a choiceless victimhood needs to be questioned. There seems to be an increasing recognition among commentators that theology – taken in a broad sense to include all relevant sources of information about a religion (Renard 2011) – does matter. Muslims in the USA and Europe today, being minorities, present no threat to religious freedom. But Muslims belong to the global *umma* (community), and it is not irrational for those who accept Enlightenment values to be phobic about the laws against apostasy and blasphemy current in some major Islamic states. In the 1970s, Marcel Boisard set out to convey to non-Muslims an informed and positive view of what he saw as 'Islamic humanism', which indeed underpins the daily life of millions of Muslims today; however, today it would be negligent to avoid discussion of more awkward points. One of these is the popular habit of picking isolated verses from the Qur'an to validate arguments of different kinds, which more sophisticated commentators refrain from doing. It is clear that there are multiple reasons for the rise today of violent Islamist extremism and probably religion is not the most important reason, but, at the same time, one cannot understand this movement without including the religious factor.

The Somali-born writer and politician Ayaan Hirsi Ali deserves respect for her personal courage and integrity in calling for Muslims to embrace reformation, heresy and 'dissidence' (Hirsi Ali 2015). She has the right to express antipathy towards Islam in so far as the Islamic dimension in her own life has been mainly painful and distressing. Clive James memorably commented in her defence against a noted Islamic scholar who had upstaged her in reviewing her memoir, *Nomad*: 'She outranks him. She might know less than he does, but what she does know, she has felt on her skin' (Hirsi Ali 2010; James 2011). Militant atheists of all stripes tend to strongly approve of her writings. It is certain that ex-Muslim atheists will increasingly follow her example to 'come out' in criticizing fundamental doctrines such as the inerrancy of the Qur'an, whether retaining a sense of their Muslim cultural identity or rejecting it totally. I am interested here in reformist or progressive intellectuals who adhere to an Islamic framework, for their work has the potential to effect change from within the fold.

Perspectives on Islamic humanism

Chapter 10 compares and contrasts the histories of the Christian and the Islamic traditions of religious toleration, considering in particular the blurring of the distinction between 'People of the Book' and pagans or polytheists. It is argued that each tradition has strengths and weaknesses if we consider them both as contributions to a humanism acceptable to people today who subscribe to various religious beliefs or none. Chapter 11 evaluates the incidence of religious persecution and conflict in our own century as quantified and tabulated by two social scientists, Brian J. Grim and Roger Finke (2011), with special reference to the plight of Christians and other religious minorities in a number of Muslim-majority countries. Chapter 12 considers the argument put forward by the historian, Michael Cook, according to which Islam has a greater tendency towards politicization than other religions, alongside the views of the philosopher Akeel Bilgrami, who is more disposed to find fault with Western policies than with Islam but who underlines the need to listen to reformist voices from within Islam rather than the voices of outside critics. This leads the chapter into a brief consideration of the prospects for large-scale institutional reform instigated by Muslims themselves, as opposed to sporadic reformist initiatives that do not crystallize into organized movements.[14]

Four chapters then give sketches of the work of some leading personalities in contemporary Islam. Three are academics in Western institutions and in different ways
representative of progressive trends, in that all have a talent for self-reflection: Tariq
Ramadan (Chapter 13), Mona Siddiqui (Chapter 14) and Akbar Ahmed
(Chapter 15). Yusuf al-Qaradawi (Chapter 16) I see more as a brake on progress,
not so much for his political stances – widely shared in the Middle East, where he is
often seen as a moderate figure – which make him unacceptable to Western governments (though some of his statements are indeed indefensible), but for his authoritarian literary style which seems to appropriate the right to interpret.

Chapter 17 concludes the book with reflections on the alleged special association
between religion in general and violence, an association rebutted by both authors
under review: David Martin and Karen Armstrong. It goes on to consider briefly
the exorbitant reworking of Wahhabism that underpins the so-called 'Islamic State'
(ISIS), and finally the obstacles that beset all attempts to found non-violent movements. The hope must be that millions of ordinary Muslims will be so repelled by
the excesses of Al-Qaeda and ISIS that they will give a new impetus to the institutionalization of Islamic humanism from their own intellectual resources.

At the same time, Western countries must acknowledge that their foreign policies – in particular the occupation of Iraq in 2003, the pursuit of geopolitical interests at the expense of support for the 'Arab awakening', and the creeping extinction
of hopes for a Palestinian state – have unleashed political and religious emotions
that have a lethal backlash especially in the Muslim tribal periphery, as argued by
Akbar Ahmed, whose book *The Thistle and the Drone* is considered in Chapter 15.

We must look back further in history too. Over forty countries with Muslim
majorities were ruled in the past by European powers (including Russia), while a few
others such as Iran and Afghanistan belonged to what has been called an 'informal
empire'. It is possible to apply towards Islam the same kind of decentring, or depro-
vincialization, of the West that social anthropologists have used to apply towards
'indigenous' societies, except that the Islamic tradition has been as universalizing
and proselytizing as Christianity. Classical Islamic political thought had assumed
an expansion of Muslim rule (*dār al-islām*) rather than its contraction. For some
five to ten centuries an Islamic 'world system' was at the centre of world civilization and hegemony; now, as Abdelwahab Meddeb has written, Islam is 'unconsol-
able in its destitution'. Muslims responded to their domination by Europe in various
ways: through military resistance, through exodus or opting out of politics, and
through accommodation (Broucek 2014).

Institution building and its problems

The example of the most successful Islamic charities in Britain, Pakistan and
Indonesia, documented in Part I of this book, should inspire Muslims everywhere
not only how to think creatively about how to adapt their religious practices to

modern exigencies and specific regional contexts, but also how to crystallize their thinking in durable institutions – not merely in the field of charity and humanitarianism, but in education, social sciences, the media and political life.

Efforts are indeed being made by Muslims to encourage the growth of reformist institutions, but they are – no doubt inevitably – an ideological battleground. In 2015, the Gülen movement, mentioned above, had offended the Turkish regime so severely that it had applied for Fethullah Gülen's extradition from the United States. In 2014, two meetings of reformist Islamic scholars were held in the Middle East, evidently competing with each other. One meeting, in Istanbul, was for a group of over one hundred 'World Islamic Scholars for Peace, Moderation and Common Sense Initiative', convened by the senior Islamic cleric in Turkey, Sheikh Mehmet Görmez. He argued in his opening speech that, rather than pin all the blame for violence in the Muslim world on others, 'those who really have any sense of responsibility would care to look inside their own fold and make an analysis and come up with evaluations'.[15] A large Iranian delegation was attracted, for Görmez was able to draw on the Turkish traditions of Sunni and Shia coexistence by inviting Sufis from both sides, but neither Egypt nor Saudi Arabia was represented.[16] The second meeting was held in Abu Dhabi, with some 250 participants, under the heading of 'Forum for Promoting Peace in Muslim Societies', which led to the launch in July of the Muslim Council of Elders, associated with the Abu Dhabi-based Tabah Foundation and presided over by the Grand Imam of Al-Azhar in Egypt, Sheikh Ahmed al-Tayeb. This consortium was critical of both Wahhabism and the Muslim Brotherhood, favouring a neo-Sufism which has also been promoted by the Zaytuna College based in California, and which has elicited a sympathetic response from some American foreign policy experts.[17] It remains to be seen whether Sufism can be successfully adapted as a counter to Islamist extremism. 'In Western democracies … it represents a more palatable, socially acceptable Islam than the picture of tyranny and terrorism presented in the Western media' (Moad 2014: 455). As has been suggested by some commentators, international Sufism has become a kind of 'Buddhized' movement within Islam, but its adoption by the Egyptian military regime with a view to dissuading the public from organized political activity – including that of the execrated Muslim Brothers – places it in a different light. Those in Saudi Arabia who support an orderly movement towards reform within the Kingdom, while minimizing the risk of political chaos, regard both the Turkish and the Emirati initiatives as unnecessarily divisive, but they have yet to organize more unifying alternatives.[18]

Notes

1 Examples of these are discussed in Lacey and Benthall, 2014: 2 (Al-Wafa), and 199–225; 243–54 (Al-Haramain).

2 The reputation of Qatar's system of charity regulation, which underwent some changes since a new Authority for Charitable Activities was founded in 2005 (Mohamed 2014), has been

thrown into question by the designation by the UN Security Council (23 September 2014) of Professor Abdul Rahman Omeir Al Naimi as an alleged financier of Al-Qaeda. He was previously designated as a 'global terrorist' by the US Treasury on 18 December 2013. Al Naimi is said to have served as an adviser to government backed foundations in Qatar, including the Sheikh Eid bin Mohammad al-Thani Charitable Foundation; he was also a founding member and president of the Alkarama human rights NGO, based in Geneva. He has rejected the accusation as a political attack because of his opposition to US policies in the Arab world. A Yemeni national, Abd al-Wahhab al-Humayqani, was also designated. Al-Humayqani is also associated with Alkarama and is said to have been an adviser to the Qatari government on charitable giving (Warrick and Root 2013). Al-Humayqani robustly rejected the accusation and offered to face a court of law (Hauslohner 2014).

3 See Svoboda 2014; A. Rosen 2015a; 2015b.

4 Researchers like journalists who depend on an NGO for access to field operations run the risk of feeling an obligation to report favourably on what they observe, and have this in common with 'embedded' reporters in conflict zones.

5 See Price 2014; also Delmar-Morgan and Oborne 2014b.

6 A tabulation of these cases is given in Benthall 2011: 107.

7 For a denunciation by a British QC of what he calls the 'show trial' of the Holy Land Foundation see FitzGibbon 2015: 13–14; see also a letter, 5 February 2015, by Victoria Brittain deploring the conditions of incarceration in the Communications Management Unit in Illinois where the former chair, Ghassan Elashi, was serving his life sentence.

8 For a pioneering analysis of transnational Shia networks, see Corboz 2015. Sashiko Hosoya gives a sensitive ethnographic account of the work of religiously motivated female volunteers who assist impoverished elderly residents to bathe, in a charity care centre in Iran, the biggest welfare complex in the Middle East (Hosoya 2014). In the Eastern Province of Saudi Arabia, Shia institutions such as the Saihat Charity and the Qatif Charity are largely supported by private funds and are mobilized by 'identity entrepreneurs' vis-à-vis the state (Montagu 2010: 76, 79; Matthiesen 2015: 171).

9 Yilmaz 2011: 61–2. The same issue contains an article on the Muslims who make up some 5 per cent of the population of Nepal, including women converts whom IHH is specially interested in making contact with.

10 'Report of the Secretary-General's Panel of Inquiry on the 31 May 2010 Flotilla Incident'. The Israeli and Turkish representatives on the four-person panel registered their dissent on some important points. For a partisan defence of the flotilla, see Kor 2011.

11 Kimse Yok Mu, 2011 report.

12 FAQs, www.nzf.org (accessed 23 February 2015).

13 Meeting in London, 26 March 2015, for the launch of the briefing paper 'An Act of Faith' (Stirk 2015).

14 For a more extended discussion of this theme, see Benthall 2015. It should be added that rigorist schools of Islam, associated with Ibn Abd Al-Wahhab and others, have also seen themselves as advocating 'reform' (iṣlāḥ).

15 'World Islamic Scholars meet for peace', Presidency of Religious Affairs, Republic of Turkey, 17 July 2014.

16 'The scramble for religious authority', Islam Affairs online magazine, 9 October 2014 (accessed 31 March 2015; link later broken).

17 'Muslim Council of Elders', Islamopedia online, 5 September 2014, http://islamopediaonline .org/fatwa/muslim-council-elders (accessed 9 August 2015); 'Zaid Shakir: Identity, reason,

and political Sufism', *Islam Affairs* online magazine, 4 November 2014 (accessed 31 March 2015; link later broken); see also Baran 2004.

18 'Abu Dhabi's network of political Sufism and its implications on the security of Saudi Arabia', *Islam Affairs* online magazine, March 2015, http://islamaffairs.com/wp-content/uploads/2015/03/Islam_Affairs_Book_English.pdf (accessed 12 August 2015). This anonymous publication, strongly biased but very informative, gives biographies of a set of 'reformist' Muslim intellectuals whom the author sees as divisive. The question of Sufi support for the al-Sisi regime in Egypt is taken up hereunder in the prefatory note for Chapter 13.

Part I

Islamic charities

1

Islamic charities, Faith Based Organizations and the international aid system

This chapter originated in a conference held in May 2007 at the Center for Strategic and International Studies (CSIS) in Washington, DC. The CSIS is one of the world's leading think tanks and was rated in 2013 as the world's leading think tank specializing in defence and national security (Global Go To Think Tanks Report, University of Pennsylvania, 2014). My contribution appeared as the opening chapter in a volume published later that year, *Understanding Islamic Charities*, edited by Jon B. Alterman and Karin von Hippel.

It is an overview which I still stand by in 2015 despite all the geopolitical changes since 2007. A theme that occurs elsewhere in this book is the unsatisfactory state of academic interchange in studying the affiliations, real and imagined, between Islamic charities and terrorist finance. I expressed here reservations about Matthew Levitt's approach, which I was to expand on in later publications. As regards J. Millard Burr and Robert O. Collins's book *Alms for Jihad: Charity and terrorism in the Islamic world*, Cambridge University Press regrettably decided to pulp it after the threat of a libel suit. This threat was an outrage against the principle of free expression, although my academic objections to the book still stand. Despite the Press's decision, copies have continued to be available from online booksellers.

***

The conjunction of the words 'Islamic' and 'charities' has acquired a negative connotation in much of the non-Muslim world, even among the generally well informed. Certainly during the Afghan conflict of the 1980s and the Balkan conflict of the early 1990s, a number of Islamic charities, especially those deriving from the petrodollar states, engaged in activities that pursued a mixture of humanitarian, religious, political and sometimes military aims. It is less often noted that until 1989 the US government actively supported the mujahideen in Afghanistan and closed its eyes to at least some of the arms shipments to successors to the mujahideen in Bosnia until, in both cases, 'the honourable figure of the "combatant" was transformed into the blameworthy figure of the "terrorist"' (Benthall and Bellion-Jourdan 2003: 137; Kohlmann 2004: 46).

There is fairly strong evidence of support during the years before 11 September 2001 by some Islamic charity managers for the Chechen mujahideen, which the United States has never supported. Direct support for Al-Qaeda type activities by charities has been strongly suspected by the US authorities, but seldom if ever proved to the standard required by Western criminal courts ('Staff Monograph', 2004: 107–8). Since 9/11, evidence of the activities of controversial Islamic charities is equivocal as to mixed aims and always needs to be treated with caution because of the risk of observer bias.

No doubt the charity or non-profit or non-governmental organization (NGO) sector – terms that will be used here in a generic sense, irrespective of the divergences among different regulatory legal systems – has always been vulnerable to abuse. No doubt either that a significant proportion of Muslims involved with charity still subscribes to a seamless concept of jihad, according to which humanitarian, religious, political and even military aims are necessarily fused. Their argument – in which there is more than a grain of truth – is that the Western devotion to a pure domain of charitable altruism is hypocritical: the Western aid system is deeply connected to national foreign policies and security concerns; humanitarian action often provides a fig leaf for military intervention; Christian missions proselytize in many parts of the world; some unfortunate populations are reduced to exporting images of their misery through the Western-controlled media and thus become aid economies, and so on.

A strong tradition may also be identified within Islam that admires and enjoins selfless charitable giving for the benefit of the disadvantaged. Moreover, many Islamic charities increasingly accept that the charitable sector ought to obey strict disciplines in return for the privileges that it enjoys, which include tax exemptions and the relatively free mobility of both funds and employees. Yet politically sophisticated Muslims sometimes ask themselves whether the present administrations in the United States and Israel actually want to allow a healthy Islamic charitable sector to realize its potential.

The association of Islamic charities with transnational mujahideen will probably be looked back on as a short-lived historical episode. On a smaller, bilateral scale, an analogy could be made with Noraid, or Irish Northern Aid, the New York-based charity that, since 1969, has raised funds in the United States for Republican – that is to say, Catholic – charities in Northern Ireland, but that was regularly accused of spending some of the funds on weapons until the Irish Republican Army accepted the peace process in 1996.

Violent movements will continue to find ways to equip themselves with weapons, but the charity sector is under increasing scrutiny by watchdog organizations such as the Financial Action Task Force (FATF), by national regulators and by banking compliance officers. Many alternative channels exist whereby clandestine funds may be transferred: trade, tourism, labour migration, *hawala*,[1] cash couriers and bank remittances between individual account holders. The attack on Islamic charities since 9/11, which it will be contended here was an overreaction, has had the unintended consequence of driving money underground where regulators have no control over it.

The rise of Islamic NGOs is the result of a confluence of two historical movements, both of which date back to the 1970s. One was the rise of NGOs in general, which accelerated during this thirty-year period. The second was the Islamic resurgence, going back to the time of the Arab defeat by Israel in 1967. Although this resurgence has much older roots, it was only after 1967 that it began to succeed radical socialism and pan-Arabism as a political cause in the region, partly because Zionism was locally interpreted as an effective mobilization of religion to which pan-Islamism would provide a riposte. All Islamic charities share a family resemblance: for example, the way they draw on the potent religious idioms of zakat (mandatory alms) and *waqf* (the Islamic charitable foundation), in their references to the religious calendar and quotations from the Qur'an and hadiths, and in their special concern for orphans and refugees.

Two books on Islamic charities have been published recently by university presses in the genre of counter-terrorist studies (Burr and Collins 2006; Levitt 2006).[2] Studies of this kind follow the US government's policy of minimizing the distinction between an essentially nationalist opposition movement such as Hamas, supported or condoned by large numbers of Arabs, and international Islamist extremism of the Al-Qaeda type, which – although it is able to appeal with some effect to the loyalty of co-religionists – has attracted only a tiny minority of convinced adherents. But the method of enquiry is also debatable, for it depends to a great extent on building up webs of association through the analysis of meetings and communications by telephone, post, or e-mail, and on press reports and intelligence websites ('Staff Monograph' 2004: 9–10). This type of enquiry has its place in our dangerous world as an essential tool to help protect us all from terrorist outrages, but the association-building approach lacks the discipline of serious social science or history, which insist on contextualization, on triangulation of evidence and on taking account of the observer's own prejudices and of those of informants. Moreover, there is the risk of attributing guilt by association, whereas criminal law as we know it in the United States and Europe requires a higher standard of proof, normally including evidence as to intention, before determining guilt.[3]

It might be argued that amid the urgencies of the post-9/11 world, we can no longer afford such luxuries as scrupulous social research in the universities on the one hand and adherence to strict evidential rules in the courts on the other. However, Western academic institutions and law courts maintained their intellectual standards during the Cold War when the military threat to civilization was more immediate than it is now. It is generally recognized that McCarthyism was a mistake. Is it not by our adhering now to high academic and legal standards that the few genuinely implacable enemies of Western values will be isolated and defeated?

In a longer term view of Islamic charities – beyond the immediate concerns over terrorist finance – they can be considered part of the wider category of confessional or Faith Based Organizations (FBOs). Despite the mass of research on NGOs published over the past fifteen years, confessional NGOs have only recently attracted research attention but have now been the subject of a number of conferences.[4]

The Western tradition of charity derived directly from historic church sources, especially the schools, hospitals and orphanages founded since the Middle Ages. International NGOs began to be recognized as a growing force in the 1950s, but at that time they were almost exclusively Christian. Christian missions of the nineteenth century had developed the strategy of mobilizing mass subscriptions, using the publicity media of their day, such as newsletters and lantern slide lectures, and thus reducing dependence on rich patrons. The Christian missionary spirit might appear to have been supplanted during the last decades of the twentieth century by non-confessional NGOs such as Oxfam, CARE, Save the Children, and Médecins Sans Frontières. (Some of these, such as Oxfam with its early Quaker associations, we might characterize sociologically as faith-inspired, that is to say deriving from a loose commitment to Christian or post-Christian ethics and values, as opposed to confessional organizations that belong to particular religious groups.)

And yet the Christian agency World Vision recently overtook CARE International as the biggest US-based aid agency, and if the relief and development efforts of all the churches, Catholic and Protestant, were added together they would amount to an impressive bloc. The main reason for the past neglect of this fact would appear to be that in the dominant universalist paradigm of development, religion and modernization were regarded as antithetical.

Christian NGOs have tended to place less emphasis than their parent churches on an agenda of individual salvation and to concentrate on material aid and economic development, recalling the 'option for the poor' manifested in the Gospels. Agencies such as World Vision, the most thoroughly multinational of all aid NGOs and still somewhat evangelical in spirit, and the British-based Christian Aid, both pioneers in media campaigns, have owed much of their success to the breadth of their appeal to Christians of various denominations as well as to donors who may not be active Christians but who respect the Christian ethic. Christian groups have adapted the potential of the universality of their faith, previously expressed in missionary organizations, to energize international promotional strategies of a new kind. They have also negotiated new relationships with governmental and intergovernmental agencies.

The rise of the NGOs in general has been represented as a flowering of global citizenship in healthy counterbalance to the power of nation-states, and there is some truth in this. However, research over the past ten years has cast them in a harsher light, for example, through Alex de Waal's description of the 'humanitarian international' to which aid workers belong (de Waal 2002). Terje Tvedt has written of the international aid system as a relatively new phenomenon in history that dates back at the earliest to the foundation of the United Nations, but more precisely to the 1960s, when the US government asked other members of the Organisation for Economic Co-operation and Development (OECD) to follow its lead in funding private voluntary organizations.

Gradually, the role of the NGOs was enlarged. As a historian of irrigation, Tvedt aptly chose the metaphor of a river system in which the donor offices are reservoirs and the NGOs are diversion channels:

> Research has ... shown that personnel in public donor offices and NGO leaders share essentially the same ideas about NGO roles and NGO activities ... The system is socially integrated through continuous exchange of personnel. (Tvedt 2002: 367)

Tvedt's argument is that, whereas the international aid system as we know it is new and unprecedented, the world religions subsist in a *longue durée* and must be assumed on the face of it to be making use of the aid system for their own traditional purposes, that is, proselytism. Meanwhile, a host of newer organizations – such as the Brahma Kumaris Spiritual University or Soka Gakkai International (Japanese Buddhists) – have been granted consultative status with the United Nations Economic and Social Council; and others such as the Church of Scientology and the World Association of Non-Governmental Organizations, run by the Reverend Moon's Unification Church, are knocking on the door.

Intergovernmental organizations such as the World Bank and the UN Development Programme recently have shown a new interest in the power of religion to stir consciences to practical humanitarian action and in the privileged access that confessional NGOs can offer to vast civil society networks, a status that derives from their relative independence from both the market and the state and from their deep cultural roots.

There are attractions in the application of the idea of isomorphism to NGOs: 'a constraining process that forces one unit in a population to resemble other units that face the same set of environmental constraints' (Tvedt et al. 2006). This might be regarded as an example of Hotelling's law in economics, which holds that in many markets it is rational for suppliers to make their products as similar as possible. More debatable is Tvedt's contention that the world religions are unchanging or undergo change only very slowly. On the contrary, it is surely part of the genius of the world religions to be able to change quite rapidly as discursive systems while presenting a façade of changelessness.

This is clear from the history of major FBOs in Britain. Christian Aid was founded in 1956 (originally as part of Inter-Church Aid) as a practical expression of Christian values but eschewing all proselytism and pro-Christian discrimination. It was followed about thirty years later by the foundation of Muslim Aid and Islamic Relief Worldwide, both of which have followed a comparable path but with the substitution of Ramadan appeals for Christmas and Lent, zakat calculation forms instead of the 'Christian stewardship' scheme, and so forth. Christian Aid has adopted a campaigning and consciousness-raising role for which it is well known, whereas Muslim Aid and Islamic Relief have hitherto been largely concerned with crisis relief and have only more recently moved into programmes of long-term participatory development. They and several smaller British Muslim NGOs, such as Muslim Hands, certainly supply a model of practical integration for Muslims in a Christian (or post-Christian) country.[5] This has been made possible to a great extent by the benign supervision of the United Kingdom Charity Commission.

Islamic Relief is now the largest Islamic NGO in the world and is accepted both as a member of the Disasters Emergency Committee, which raises funds jointly for an elite of British NGOs after major world disasters, and as an operational partner with Oxfam and Catholic Agency for Overseas Development (CAFOD, the British branch of Caritas Internationalis). Field research undertaken by this author on the operations of British Muslim charities in two very different Muslim societies, Mali in West Africa and the province of Aceh in Indonesia, suggests that they are able to not only attain high effectiveness when assessed against professional norms, but also in some circumstances to benefit from privileged access to such societies, at both the official and the grass-roots levels, on account of the immediate trust made possible by a shared religion (Benthall 2006b; 2008c).[6]

Contributors to the present publication *[Understanding Islamic Charities]* have produced evidence to support the contention that in many Muslim regions – not only in the Middle East where we have documentation already – local and national Muslim networks can often provide effective relief and welfare services through their strength at the grass-roots. There is thus considerable potential for international Islamic agencies to expand their activities in Muslim countries on the same lines as the well-established aid programmes conducted by Christian aid agencies in majority Christian countries. Given the extent of need in the Muslim world, and the conspicuous wealth in some parts of it, a new flowering of Islamic charity could make a real difference.

There is at least one exception to the harmonious picture of Muslim charities in Britain presented here: an Islamic charity that the Charity Commission cleared of impropriety twice after investigations, but which it is now investigating a third time because it is blacklisted by the US government as an alleged supporter of Hamas and was also the subject of harsh criticism in a BBC television programme in July 2006. There is a sharp divergence between the picture that the US and Israeli governments paint of this charity, Interpal (Palestinian Relief and Development Fund), and its high reputation among many British Muslims and a representative body of British overseas aid agencies, BOND. Interpal officials, claiming that the organization has always acted within the law, have retained a leading firm of London solicitors to assist them in clearing its name, and its trustees have already sued the Board of Deputies of British Jews for defamation and successfully extracted a public apology and damages in December 2005. The eventual findings of the Charity Commission, whatever they are, will surely be dramatic.[7]

Whereas Islamic aid agencies were growing in the United States in the same way as British ones before 9/11, one result of that attack on the United States has been the disappearance of major US Islamic agencies in the course of the so-called 'war on terror'. Small mosque associations and the like survive, but apart from the British-based Islamic Relief Worldwide – whose US branch is allowed to raise funds and has indeed been awarded the maximum rating of four stars by Charity Navigator for four years running – the larger US Islamic agencies have had their funds frozen and in some cases their trustees and managers pursued by the law. To date, however, there does not appear to have been a successful prosecution of a major Muslim charity in the United States.[8] Yet, many US observers regret that the United States, having no equivalent to the UK Charity Commission, leaves regulation to the federal tax authorities, to the various state courts, and latterly to the draconian powers of the administration under new counter-terrorist measures that are perceived in some quarters as a form of martial law.

Meanwhile, parallel 'families' of Islamic aid organizations have grown up in other countries over the past thirty years. This consideration excludes the thirty-two Red Crescent national societies, which are formally non-denominational, as integral parts of the Red Cross and Red Crescent Movement, even though they sometimes take on an Islamic flavour. It also excludes a few one-offs. The Aga Khan Foundation, founded in Switzerland in 1967, is essentially a sophisticated Western-style development agency that happens to operate mainly in regions of East Africa and Asia where there are Ismaili minorities. By contrast, the Edhi Foundation in Pakistan was built up from nothing by a young refugee from India, Abdul Sattar Edhi, after Partition. Launched as a dispensary in Karachi in 1951, and funded largely by zakat and *sadaqa* (optional charity), it is now a prominent national and international agency specializing in emergency relief, medical care and refugee aid, and is supported by Pakistanis in all walks of life because it is seen as untainted by corruption.

One 'family' of Islamic charities is based mainly in the petrodollar states, and these have been until recently entirely ignored in the analysis of international aid flows despite their substantial scale of operations in the past. Some of these, such as the International Islamic Relief Organization and the World Assembly of Muslim Youth (WAMY), both based in Saudi Arabia, are still active but have been forced to downsize in recent years on account of government restrictions, apparently imposed in response to US pressure, and other less tangible clouds overhanging the sector since 9/11. Though until recently it appeared to outside observers that the Saudi private charities were spheres of patronage for individual princes, none of these charities is now permitted by the Saudi government to use the banking system to make transfers overseas.

Because some charities such as WAMY do still operate overseas, albeit on a reduced scale, it must be assumed that they are funded in some other way, such as the use of cash couriers, and thus completely outside the purview of international financial regulators. The Saudi government announced in December 2004 that it had set up a high commission to coordinate all private overseas aid ('Staff Monograph' 2004: 12), but there are as yet no signs of such a commission having been appointed. Morale in Saudi charities has consequently sagged. Islamic charities seem to operate with relatively little difficulty in the less politically charged environments of Qatar or the United Arab Emirates, but Kuwait forbade its charities to make bank transfers overseas beginning in March 2007 and also forbids cash collections in the street or in mosques.[9]

A snapshot of the damage to the interests of charities' beneficiaries that has arisen since 9/11 may be taken from the small, crisis-torn country of Chad. According to a presentation given in Qatar in February 2006,[10] eighteen Islamic NGOs were operating in Chad before 9/11. In 2006 there were only five, all of them funded from the Gulf. Three of these were threatened with closure. (Meanwhile, there were in 2006 some 300 active Western NGOs in Chad, including Christian missionary organizations.) One of the results was that nearly 500 orphans – some of them placed with families, some in residential orphanages – were abandoned by Islamic charities that had been supporting them. Many of these have probably become street children.

No systematic research appears to have been undertaken on the consequences, for Islamic charities and their beneficiaries, of the obstacles placed against them since 9/11, but it may be assumed that the case of Chad is quite typical and might be scaled up to give a negative picture of the humanitarian consequences of the clampdown on Islamic charities.

Another 'family' of Islamic charities is associated with opposition movements in the Middle East. In the Palestinian Territories, Egypt and Algeria, these derive from the ideology of the Muslim Brothers of Egypt; in Lebanon, Hizbullah represents the only successful export of Iranian Shia militancy. In common with Hizbullah, Hamas – the successor to the Muslim Brothers in Palestine – has secured its strong political base by means of extensive networks of hospitals, clinics, schools and other charitable activities with which it is seen as more or less loosely affiliated. Current US law considers all these activities – however indispensable to a population experiencing acute suffering and deprivation – as inseparable parts of Hamas, which the US and Israeli governments have designated as a terrorist entity. Yet, in Palestinian law, many of these programmes are registered as independent charities or zakat committees regulated by the Palestinian Authority, which has since its inception set out to exert tight control over the voluntary sector. The delicate question of what is meant by 'affiliation' in specific cases is likely to be a key point in some criminal and civil trials now pending (ICG 2003).

In the Middle East, charitable activities are usually associated in some way with party political interests of one kind or another, and we know that a large proportion of Palestinians are sympathetic to Hamas. But it does not follow that a personal political engagement on the part of individual zakat committee members or employees necessarily disables them from exercising their religious and moral duties as charity managers consistently with generally accepted charity law and with the specific provisions of international humanitarian law that apply in conflict zones.

Allegations relating to financial integrity and aiding terrorism are likely to be dispelled sooner or later by some accepted system of regulation and monitoring. Two international attempts have been launched to try to achieve this: the Montreux Initiative and the Humanitarian Forum, although the latter has recently been steering toward a broader objective of dialogue between differing humanitarian cultures.[11] It cannot be said that the short-term outlook is promising, because any such efforts are experiencing difficulties in the present increasingly complex political climate. Even when the immediate political problems are resolved, key issues relating to non-discrimination and cultural sensitivity are likely to remain contentious. These arise with all NGOs, not merely Islamic ones. One issue, that of gender, is likely to continue to be a source of tension between Muslim and non-Muslim NGOs. Again, we may note the imaginative step taken by Islamic Relief Worldwide in challenging significant forms of discrimination against women: it produced a notable video during the Bosnian war in support of women victims of military rape, seeking to dispel the popular prejudices that still often stigmatize victims of rape.

At present, owing to the difficulties outlined above, it is hard to see any Islamic charity other than Islamic Relief Worldwide soon becoming a genuinely transnational NGO. And, like many highly effective agencies such as the International Committee of the Red Cross (still essentially Swiss), Islamic Relief Worldwide is still mononational, that is to say under control from Britain, though with a markedly multi-ethnic staff. The transition to becoming fully transnational has been undertaken only recently by such world-class agencies as Oxfam, originally British, and Médecins Sans Frontières, originally French. It takes at least twenty years and probably more for an organization to acquire anything like the transnational and independent status of these two organizations, or of Amnesty, Friends of the Earth or Greenpeace. Yet this must be the reasonable aim of a major Islamic agency, given the claims of Islam to spread its reach over the whole world in the same way as Christianity, transcending all divisions of race and ethnicity. And transnational organizations of this stature will undoubtedly have great importance in the twenty-first century as a counterbalance to the power of national governments and multinational corporations.

It has been suggested by some French sociologists of religion that the Faith Based Organizations, with their relatively new and growing administrative bureaucracies, may be offering complementary alternatives to traditional religious hierarchies and thus subtly changing the balance of internal religious authority (Duriez et al. 2007; Liogier 2007). Much effort is being made by Western politicians to encourage the development of so-called 'moderate Islam' through sponsoring countless well-meaning seminars on the virtues of tolerance and dialogue and through intervening in the management of Muslim schools and the training of imams. Little harm is done by promoting dialogue, except when it disappoints the hopes of suffering people who are looking for effective action to reduce the misery of wars and disasters.

The attempt by some agencies such as the RAND Corporation to actively influence the theology of another religion may backfire by unintentionally alienating moderate Muslim intellectuals or stigmatizing them as tools of the West, and thus indirectly strengthening reactionary factions.[12] In contrast, when the representative of Islamic Relief Worldwide appeared on British television to launch the Disasters Emergency Committee joint appeal for the Kashmir earthquake in 2005, the appearance was on behalf of all the British aid agencies. Surely the appearance achieved something concrete and practical not only in tangible support for the earthquake victims but within the British context as well, at the expense of the fundamentalist Muslim factions.

This point – that high values and ideals are better expressed by actions than by fine words – has not yet been fully appreciated, or sympathetic steps would be taken to ease the way for bona fide Islamic charities. A significant opportunity to defuse the purported 'clash of civilizations' is thus being lost.

Notes

1 *Hawala* – a note of exchange – has become a widespread vehicle for financial transfers, sometimes used to bypass standard banking institutions.
2 This author cannot find a sentence in Levitt's *Hamas* recognizing that some, at least, of the volunteers who work for zakat committees and other Islamic charities in the Palestinian Territories might be motivated by altruism, although (p. 238) he does give a backhanded compliment to Hamas as being 'notoriously honest'. Burr and Collins in *Alms for Jihad* concede in their preface (p. xi) that 'there are thousands of Islamic charities … that have nothing to do with terrorism', but they name none of them.
3 See, by way of comparison 'Staff Monograph' 2004: 108.
4 See Simkhada and Warner 2006; Duriez et al. 2007. Note also the Religions and Development Research Programme, University of Birmingham, England.
5 Two examples of subtle changes in interpretation of Qur'anic rules, facilitating integration into the NGO mainstream, are (1) acceptance that the first-named of the eight categories of person eligible to benefit from zakat, 'the poor' (Qur'an 9: 60), means all the poor, whereas a widespread traditional reading reserved this benefit for poor Muslims, and (2) a 'humanitarian reading' of the key concept of jihad that zakat funds may also be used to support. See Benthall and Bellion-Jourdan 2003: 8–19.
6 *Reprinted in this book as Chapters 2 and 3.*
7 *Interpal was substantially cleared by the Charity Commission after its third investigation (Charity Commission 2009), March 2015.*
8 *The directors of the Holy Land Foundation were, however, found guilty in 2008 of having sent funds to alleged Hamas-affiliated charities in the Palestinian Territories. See Chapters 5 and 6.*
9 *For more up-to-date information on Qatar and Kuwait, see the Introduction to this book, p.22, note 2, and pp.13–14.*
10 Haqar Ahmad (presentation, Partners in Development conference, Doha, 21–2 February 2006); Dr Ahmad is director of WAMY's branch in Chad. The UK Disasters Emergency Committee Appeal estimated that in May 2007, 147,000 people were internally displaced in Chad and that 232,000 refugees had fled from Darfur to Chad since 2003.

11 *The Montreux Initiative is described in Chapter 5. The Humanitarian Forum was forced by financial constraints to downsize in 2014 and, in 2015, was concentrating on regional consultations, in particular on preparation for the World Humanitarian Summit in May 2016.*

12 See Mahmood 2006; and Benzine and Sebastiani 2006: 'The problem is that the West is too eager to recognize these voices, be they religious or political [the voices of Muslim intellectuals making use of modern scholarly methods of interpretation], in order to give them the responsibility of emancipating their people from ideological oppression of every kind. Now, when the West is the intermediary of their work or opens the spaces of freedom of expression that they lack, it can be a healthy thing. But that the West sees them as worthy disciples of "Western values" is something else, something quite harmful, because it separates them definitively from their compatriots [i.e. co-religionists], who at that point consider them to be followers of a derelict West. These moderate thinkers, instead, need first to convince their own compatriots in order to avoid breaking the dialogue with them'.

2

Islamic aid in a North Malian enclave

As noted in the Introduction, there is a small research literature on the question of 'cultural proximity'. My own attempts to explore it – based on field visits to Mali and Aceh – have partly confirmed the thesis that Islamic NGOs can, on occasion, benefit from a privileged relationship with beneficiaries in Muslim countries.

This article was published in *Anthropology Today* 22: 4, August 2006, shortly after a brief field visit. Though it included some caveats about the future, it presented a rather optimistic view of the Malian government's efforts to promote human development in the Timbuktu Region. I was in fact witnessing only an interval of peace in the 'Tuareg rebellions' which have persisted for four decades in Azawad (northern Mali). The collapse of the Qaddafi regime in Libya in 2011 contributed to the crisis in March 2012, when Mali's democratically elected president was deposed by junior military officers, partly as a result of his failure to suppress the latest Tuareg uprising. The Economic Community of West African States (Ecowas) immediately facilitated a return to constitutional order with an interim president. However, a 'State of Azawad' was declared in the north by the secularist National Movement for the Liberation of the Azawad (MNLA). Partly because of the presence of several armed Islamist groups, Gao and Timbuktu (the two cities nearest to Gourma Rharous, which I wrote about) became 'sites of pillaging and destruction, plunging their isolated civilian populations into a deep humanitarian crisis' (Yabi 2012). Timbuktu, after a period of occupation by rebels and implementation of a form of Sharia, was liberated in January 2013 by the French military in Operation Serval, but a peace deal negotiated in 2013 between the Malian government and Tuareg rebels proved to be precarious. In early 2015, French peacekeeping troops were still in the north. Many residents of Timbuktu had fled and were still living in refugee camps. Serious shortages of food security and drinking water were reported.

I understand that Islamic Relief's operations in their Gourma Rharous sub-office were not seriously impaired, despite a brief period of suspension, especially because the agency had gained acceptance both by the authorities and by communities in the region, and had become a reference point for external organizations including the United Nations.

Mayke Kaag has published an overview of Islamic charities in some other countries in West Africa, especially those funded from the Gulf (Kaag 2014).

***

The town of Gourma Rharous is the administrative centre of its *cercle* of 50,000 km² and 100,000 inhabitants in the Timbuktu Region of northern Mali. Yet it has no metalled road, running water, electricity or public transport, and only one telephone for public use. The nearest hospitals, internet facilities, banks, hotels and garages are in Timbuktu, 160 km to the west, or double that distance in Gao to the east. This is sometimes called the 'Tuareg enclave' because of the poor communications, though the population is a complicated mix of nomads, river people and traders with cross-cutting ethnic and linguistic divisions, and for many of them one of their most valuable resources is mobility. The *cercle's* struggling economy is mainly pastoral, but seasonal rains allow the cultivation of cereals, maize and rice.

Islamic Relief, founded by medical students in Birmingham in 1984 and now active worldwide, is the only NGO working in the town of Rharous at present,[1] whereas the historic towns of Timbuktu and Gao, once legendary for their prosperity (de Benoist 1998), have both become almost NGO settlements. Tourists sometimes drop in at Rharous, but the only building of note is the *maison du colon*, the commanding pink fortress-style residence of the French *préfet* until independence in 1960, now a roofless shell. For a time, Rharous was on the route of the controversial Paris–Dakar Rally. The death of the Rally's founder, Thierry Sabine, in 1986 when his helicopter crashed into a nearby sand dune, is commemorated by a small memorial, now collapsed, incorporating parts of the helicopter.

Today Rharous is tranquil, but it was caught up in the Tuareg Rebellion that began in 1990 (Oxby 1996).[2] Mali narrowly escaped all-out civil war between groups of the traditionally nomadic 'white' Tuareg and the sedentary 'blacks', with other ethnic groups also involved. It has been argued that the conflict may actually have been an unintended consequence of external development aid and that perhaps 'allocation and withdrawal of emergency aid has become the currency that regulates mobility, conflict and peace' (Giuffrida 2005b: 541). Many Tuareg fled to nearby countries such as Algeria and Burkina Faso. Those in the town of Rharous who stayed on sometimes had to take their families out to the bush at night for safety. Central government in Bamako stuck to the principle of a peaceful solution through negotiation, and undertook that education, health care and other services in the north would be improved. Refugees were repatriated in 1995 and a ceremonial burning of weapons, the *Flamme de la Paix*, took place in Timbuktu in 1996. A far-reaching democratization and decentralization policy was soon implemented. Various local and international agencies, including the International Committee of the Red Cross, were involved in the reconciliation process.

Islamic Relief's commitment began in 1997 when it contracted with the UN High Commissioner for Refugees to help facilitate the 'reinsertion' in Rharous of people who had fled. At that time there were no elected mayors – these were introduced as part of the decentralization process – and Islamic Relief enlisted the local imams and *chefs de village* as channels of communication, at meetings also attended by government officials, technical specialists and NGOs. The success of this programme gave Islamic Relief the opportunity to develop a range of aid programmes in the *cercle*, all in line with the new government policy, after an assessment of needs: food security, micro-credit schemes, drilling wells, a local radio station (co-funded by Britain's Department for International Development), a dairy, schooling in the 'national languages' Tamashek (Tuareg) and Songhay as well as French. They also provide meals to very poor villages for religious festival days. Islamic Relief's foothold in the north then enabled it to start a programme in the far more densely populated south of Mali, and to set up a national head office in the capital, Bamako.[3]

The main aim of my visit to Rharous last March was to investigate whether an Islamic charity has special advantages when operating in a Muslim country, northern Mali being almost 100 per cent Muslim.[4] Though I could not undertake a comparison with the work of a secular NGO such as the deeply experienced Oxfam, which operates in the adjoining Gao Region with a mainly African staff, there is no doubt that Islamic Relief has achieved an extraordinary degree of entrenchment in the social life of Gourma Rharous. All its staff are from the Timbuktu Region, except one who comes from southern Mali. Office hours and appointments with secretaries count for nothing here. Islamic Relief's Tamashek coordinator, Azarock Ag Inabrochad, compactly built with gimlet eyes, makes himself available to the high and the low of Rharous at any time. His front yard, lit by an electrical generator, is a centre where men drop in every evening to discuss problems, make plans, drink tea and, at the appointed times, pray together. Islamic Relief never preaches, but slips easily into the daily life of a country where religion and popular culture are closely intertwined. Azarock's small fleet of 4x4s and motorbikes, communicating by radio, is deployed to maximum advantage, for here even the mayors of the nine communes in the *cercle* have to hitch lifts in order to cover the long distances, and night-long journeys are made along the Niger in fragile *pirogues*. One morning when we were having breakfast, a man passed by to show Azarock a cut on his shin. He and some friends had been crossing the river, whose south bank is a hundred yards away from the house, when their *pirogue* was nearly capsized by a hippopotamus protecting her young.

Until recently, the most prominent NGO in the wider area, since its arrival in 1984, was Norwegian Church Aid. They invested generously during the difficult years of the war, played a major role in the peace negotiations (Lode 1997) and turned Gossi, a village near Gao (but in the Gourma Rharous *cercle*), into a bustling market town after a metalled road was built. They are remembered with personal esteem, but criticized by some for having distributed supplies such as petrol and grain without much control, thus encouraging dependency. They have now with-drawn, leaving behind in Gossi a large walled compound complete with offices, air-conditioned cottages and a tennis court for over thirty staff – built at a time when the agency's staff were subjected to attacks – but now defunct and empty.

There is no way here for an NGO to work outside the structures of the govern-ment *préfet*, the mayors and their councillors, the *chefs de village*, the deputies and other elected politicians. The big challenge for Islamic Relief is the challenge for all aid programmes: how to help the very poor and the socially excluded, especially, in this area, the Bella, who have historically been subservient.[5] However, the govern-ment has promoted such a wide variety of associational life – which is well known to be one of Mali's most auspicious assets[6] – that potential chinks in the power of trad-itional relationships of patronage and dependence have been disclosed, chinks that can be opened up through discussion and persuasion. Moreover, there is a broadly shared determination that the decentralization policy must be made to succeed, to lift the country out of the poverty generated successively by colonial exploitation, then state socialism allied to Eastern Europe and China, then military dictatorship, then the rebellion – to which must be added, in the north, problems of drought and food security. Islamic Relief's staff are committed both to cooperating fully with government policy and to trying to reach the worst off.

One example of this is their support for women's associations. In Arbechi, a vil-lage 45 km west of Rharous that is fortunate in its unusually dynamic mayor, the women have converted their tradition of making mats from palm leaves – mainly for roofing material given between women as wedding gifts – into a marketable craft. They are also learning how to cut out intermediaries and about foreign tourists' preference for natural rather than artificial dyes. Before the introduction of these associations, women in such a village had no source of independent revenue, and in this village they show huge enthusiasm for the project. However, in another village I visited, inhabited by mainly sedentarized Tuareg, it was clear that women's role is still behind the scenes.

Mali's welfare services now depend heavily on international NGOs, which are generally improving their standards of evaluating the implementation of their pro-jects, as well as on a burgeoning domestic NGO sector. Ideally, an NGO should aim to make itself redundant. Yet in northern Mali, at least, it seems to be long-term commitment that really counts. I came across a new village school built by a small French NGO, but left with cracked walls and a caved-in roof owing to bad workman-ship.[7] Another NGO has made a practice of installing closed wells with mechanical pumps, rather than simple wells with buckets, which is fine until they go wrong and no one has been trained to repair them. Unsurprisingly, NGOs as a class can come to be seen as fickle friends to be milked while the going is good.[8]

This is a region where true wealth is traditionally seen as residing in richness in human relationships, rather than an abundance of material goods. Christian agen-cies in Christian Africa have long been able to build relationships between poor people and the various Churches of the entire world. Islam is now beginning to do the same through the rise of professional Islamic NGOs, drawing on much older practices of Muslim philanthropy (Benthall and Bellion-Jourdan 2003; Benthall 2006a). Islamic Relief's highly practical way of interpreting and articulating these Islamic values, analogous to that of Britain's Christian Aid, seems well in tune both with Mali's religious traditions and with official economic and humanitarian priorities.

Over the last half-century, it seems that a determined effort has been made, mainly from Saudi Arabia, to steer Islam in Mali in a rigorist 'Wahhabi' direction, especially through privately funded Muslim schools (Brenner 2000[9]). It also seems that the effort failed. This is partly because the petrodollar donors are less interested than before, and their Malian partners more commercially than doctrinally minded, and partly because of Mali's long association with Sufism – always at odds with Wahhabi rigour – even though the number of Malians consciously practising Sufism is tiny, and partly because for centuries her different ethnic groups have been learning to live together with tolerance and moderation. These qualities were manifested in the surprisingly rapid reconciliation that was achieved at the end of the Tuareg Rebellion. Moreover, the Islamist radicalism deriving from the Muslim Brothers of Egypt and similar movements seems so far to be very marginal in Mali, though if this were to break through in Algeria to the north, Mali would be vulnerable.[10] Patriotism is strongly promoted by the state – in every school, the national flag is ceremonially raised and lowered at the beginning and end of the day, while the national anthem is sung – and the nation's most conspicuous financial backers apart from France are the unlikely duo of the United States and Libya, both seeing Mali as a bulwark against Islamic extremism.[11] If, as is rumoured, marketable oil reserves are now being discovered in the northern desert by Australian prospectors, this is likely to reignite conflict, because the northerners are unlikely to accept that 'the cow in the north is milked for the cream to be drunk in the south'.

Very few Islamic charities funded from the Middle East operate in Mali, and consequently the country's aid flows have been little affected by the difficulties facing many bona fide Islamic charities elsewhere since 9/11, including the freezing of bank accounts and blocking of financial transfers. Islamic Relief itself has barely been touched by these difficulties: it is now the largest Islamic aid charity in the world and its reputation is intact even in the United States,[12] whose government has imposed draconian sanctions on a number of other Islamic charities, without realistic rights of defence and appeal.

For all the mass of research on the aid system carried out over the last fifteen years, Islamic relief and development agencies have been almost completely ignored hitherto in the analysis of aid flows. But, quite suddenly, Faith Based Organizations have been discovered, given their acronym (FBOs), and become the subject of a number of conferences. I came to Gourma Rharous to find out what happens downstream, as it were, on a bend in the Niger, in a Muslim society where the global future of Islam is not a matter of daily debate.[13] The vexed issues of proselytism and 're-Islamization' have no relevance here (though Islamic Relief is totally committed to non-discrimination when it works in mixed religious areas). There is a problem with mosques near Rharous, since many of them – the most modest places of worship imaginable – are in serious need of repair and refurbishing. Unlike many other Islamic charities, especially those based in the Gulf, Islamic Relief's rules do not allow it to build or repair mosques, since it wants to avoid any hint of proselytism and some of its funding partners, such as the British government's Department for International Development, insist on this too. However, these mosques are precious cultural assets in the lives of people who generally bear their tribulations with quiet dignity; they are also places of face-to-face communication where vital practical messages may be conveyed by the imam, for instance in the recent past about avoiding cholera and possibly in the future about stopping avian flu. This is an example of the kind of discussion about values and priorities that goes on within Islamic Relief.

A road through the town of Gourma Rharous is promised soon. If it comes, it will cause rapid expansion into a market. Other NGOs will move in with their roadside signs. But Islamic Relief will, I think, continue to have a high reputation in the Timbuktu Region because it came in at such a critical time, sharing the difficulties with the people it set out to help in order to gradually build confidence, and so far it has stayed the course. While some aid agencies – classically, Médecins Sans Frontières, which was once in Rharous – set great store on their mobility, there are virtues also in sedentarization.

Acknowledgements

Thanks are due especially to the staff of Islamic Relief – in Birmingham, Bamako and Gourma Rharous – for their cooperation and hospitality; also for advice and information from Souweidi Adiawyakoye, Bouya Baba, Louis Brenner, Ousmane Diallo, Violet Diallo, Alessandra Giuffrida, Mohamed ag Mahmoud, Salem Ould Elhadj (a historian resident in Timbuktu, strongly recommended to visitors) and Sara Randall, and staff of the International Red Cross and Red Crescent Movement, among many others, and to three anonymous *Anthropology Today* referees. Since this was my first visit to West Africa, no doubt deficiencies remain in the article. The visit was funded by the Nuffield Foundation and facilitated by the Royal Anthropological Institute.

Notes

1 GTZ (Deutsche Gesellschaft für Technische Zusammenarbeit), a development arm of the German government, is active in providing technical assistance in the Timbuktu Region, and still has a presence in Rharous. It has invested heavily in sedentarization programmes (Giuffrida 2005b), building for instance an impressive covered space for meetings in the village of Hamzacoma, whose nomadic population is 80 per cent sedentarized.

2 Since my visit, a Tuareg insurgency re-erupted in May 2006 in the desert town of Kidal, 350 km north of Gao, and the government has deployed the army.

3 A further article comparing Islamic Relief's work in southern Mali with that of another Islamic charity, funded mainly by Saudis, is currently in preparation [Benthall 2008b].

4 Generalizations such as the following, by a major authority on the Tuareg, writing of a neighbouring group in Niger – 'Kel Ewey Tuareg society is characterized by nominal adherence to Islam combined with pre-Islamic beliefs and rituals' (Rasmussen 1992: 107) – now seem to assume too essentialist a view of Islam.

5 For a historical analysis of dependence and stratification in the neighbouring *cercle* of Goundam, to the west of Timbuktu, see Giuffrida 2005a. This is no doubt a key to understanding the region.

6 It is true that an 'associational ideology' is actively promoted by the government in Mali today (Brenner 2000: 300), but it seems to be based on a historical reality. Some commentators argue that the traditional *ton* (rural association with both economic and ludic aspects) is a Bambara concept that does not exist in the north, but according to some of my informants it is merely a Bambara *word* that has northern equivalents in Songhay, Fulfulde (Peul) and Tamashek. Vernacular associations for young men, old men, hunters, fishermen, etc. are also widespread, apart from the many associations recently encouraged by the government, e.g. for school parents.

7 An 'ex-rebel and local leader' is quoted by Giuffrida as saying that 'sedentary settlements are "ghost factories" or "traps" aimed at accessing aid. After aid resources are exhausted, people start moving again' (Giuffrida 2005b: 541). This view must be given weight, but we may set against it the widespread local support for the introduction of village schools, for instance in the semi-sedentarized village of Hamzacoma (see n. 1 above). Here Islamic Relief was planning to install canteens for the two village schools, providing breakfasts as an incentive to school attendance for children who otherwise have often had to study all day without food.

8 Long-term commitment in Mali is not of course confined to fellow Muslims. Sister Anne-Marie Saloman, a Catholic missionary, has run a local dispensary on the edge of Gossi since 1992, when it was originally founded to care for Tuareg nomads displaced during the war.

9 This is a masterly study of the politics of education in Mali under and after French colonial rule. Malian Wahhabism – its adherents prefer to call themselves 'Sunni', implicitly denying that Sufis are proper Sunnis – has a history of confrontation with the state dating back to the 1930s (Brenner 2000). See also Sanankoua and Brenner 1991.

10 Some 1,000 people demonstrated peacefully in Bamako on 5 February 2006 to protest against the Danish cartoons depicting the Prophet Muhammad. One informant told me in March that there was a presence of radical Islam in Kidal to the north of Gao, which is where the insurgency was to break out in May (see n. 2 above).

11 [*The reference to aid from France was omitted in error in the original text.*] The intricate relations between various schools of Islam and the Malian state and society today are well analyzed in Soares 2006, with special reference to development policies. One cannot exclude the possibility that economic development in Mali is a case of 'extraversion', the mobilization of external resources to reinforce internal positions of power (Jean-François Bayart cited in Brenner 2000), while the policy of decentralization has clearly been designed to legitimize the present government (Giuffrida 2005b). But in the present geopolitical climate it is difficult to suggest realistic alternatives to current government policy, except the need for tighter regulation of NGOs and monitoring of their performance.

12 Though not in Israel, whose government detained Islamic Relief's representative in Gaza for twenty-one days in May 2006 and deported him, on no convincing evidence of misconduct (McGreal 2006).

13 For a very different take on politics in the wider area, see Gutelius 2006. He sees the Pentagon's Pan-Sahel Initiative – part of the 'war on terror' – as potentially stirring up unnecessary violence by outsourcing intelligence gathering in the Sahara to African allies including the Malian government.

3

Have Islamic aid agencies a privileged relationship in majority Muslim areas? The case of post-tsunami reconstruction in Aceh

The city of Banda Aceh, in northern Sumatra, had by 2015 recovered an appearance of normality, ten years after the Indian Ocean tsunami which ravaged it, though with marked social consequences such as ownership of land by orphans, huge discrepancies in housing quality, and an increase in individualism at the expense of mutual aid (Lamb 2014). The Sharia-based criminal code was extended in September 2014, amid sharp controversy.

The main motivation for the article (first published in the online *Journal of Humanitarian Assistance*), based on a visit in 2007, was to explore what special contributions Islamic charities can make in majority Muslim countries. As in the case of Mali, the finding was guardedly positive.

An incidental theme was the tendency of the international aid system to emphasize its own efforts and overlook the importance of local organizations in responding to disasters, and seismic disasters in particular. The experience of the Indian Ocean tsunami and the major earthquake in Haiti in 2010 suggest that not much has changed since the conclusion reached in 1990 by John Seaman, then Save the Children UK's senior medical officer: 'The assumption, sometimes implicit in appeals for assistance for disaster afflicted populations, that these are passively dependent upon outside relief and, in poorer countries, without material resources, is false. A consistent theme of the disaster literature is the speed and coherence of local response' (Seaman 1990: 7).

The Indian Ocean tsunami attracted an unprecedented amount of international funding – reportedly a total of US$7,000 on average for each person affected, by contrast with only $3 per person after floods in Bangladesh or Mozambique. Unlike most other agencies dependent on fundraising, Oxfam deserves credit for publishing a candid evaluation of its own response to the tsunami, including an admission that 'in common with much of the humanitarian sector, Oxfam had little experience of building permanent houses prior to the tsunami disaster … Given the challenges that Oxfam and its partners faced in permanent shelter construction, as well as its limited experience, many people questioned the wisdom of engaging in permanent shelter construction' (Oxfam International 2009: 20–1). It may be that Islamic Relief's success in constructing houses and schools was partly due to its having operated on a relatively small scale, though its achievements were more extensive than those described in my article, including water and sanitation projects, and the construction and staffing of health centres.

Islamic Relief later moved its regional head office from the centre of Banda Aceh to nearby Neusu. In 2015, it had shifted focus in the province of Aceh from recovery to sustainable development and disaster risk reduction, working especially through schools. Islamic Relief was also formulating an integrated three-year sustainable development programme in another province, West Nusa Tenggara in eastern Indonesia.

Muslim Aid retained its national field office in Banda Aceh and continued its commitment to diverse nationwide programmes including emergency response to floods, disaster risk reduction, mangrove planting, handicraft training, and so on.

A comprehensive retrospective study of physical rebuilding in Aceh, 'Lessons from Aceh', was published by the Disasters Emergency Committee and Arup in 2010 (da Silva 2010).

In a perceptive article, Ismet Fanany and Rebecca Fanany argue that the Acehnese gave a strongly religious interpretation to the tsunami disaster: 'In practice', in such circumstances, 'it may be difficult to determine in advance what specific elements of assistance are seen locally as being of first priority and, conversely, which are seen as expendable or have not even been thought of. The desire of the public in Aceh to have mosques rebuilt or repaired first is an example of the former, while the perceived lack of need for counseling services is an example of the latter' (Fanany and Fanany 2014).

Katherine Marshall has speculated that maybe international NGOs acted as magnets attracting trained and moderate Muslims in the area to work with them, leaving more fundamentalist groups to gain some ascendance in the wider population of Aceh (Marshall 2011a: 197).

***

Most research to date on Islamic charities has given special attention to political aspects, which inevitably come to the fore in conflict zones and in areas of mixed religious affiliations (Ghandour 2002; Benthall and Bellion-Jourdan 2003; Soares and Otayek 2007). Whereas we should not exclude the political dimension from analysis of any humanitarian aid, of whatever ideological provenance, it would be unjustified to lay so much stress on it in the Muslim case that the question of efficacity was sidelined. There is an increasing recognition of the importance of Faith Based Organizations and their role in the international aid system (Duriez et al. 2007; Rakodi 2007; Clarke and Jennings 2008). Few would question that Christian NGOs such as CAFOD and Christian Aid are often able to make advantageous use of their confessional networks in majority Christian areas such as southern Africa and Latin America.

Islamic charities in general – apart from a few UK-based ones – have experienced considerable difficulties since 9/11 owing to suspicions on the part of some Western governments that they have been used as fronts for terrorist activities. Steps are being taken, for instance by the Swiss government, to try to have obstacles from bona fide Islamic charities removed. No research as far as I am aware has been undertaken to evaluate, let alone quantify, the damage that this campaign against Islamic charities has done to the interests of their beneficiaries – such as the many thousands of orphans that they have sponsored – and potential beneficiaries. It must also remain a matter for speculation how powerful a force in the humanitarian movement the Islamic charities might become if they were encouraged to develop their potential as a vehicle for redistribution of resources and disaster response and preparedness in the Muslim world. However, I have undertaken a modest research project myself to see whether it can be shown that an Islamic charity has special advantages or legitimacy when operating in a Muslim society.

The reason for choosing two virtually all-Muslim societies was in order to exclude the complicating factor that arises when an Islamic charity engages in – or is thought to engage in – a programme of proselytism or 're-Islamization' as an adjunct to its humanitarian goals. The two societies I chose were ones in which Islam is so strongly entrenched that the issue arises only marginally, if at all. The first of two case studies was in Mali, where I found two British-based Islamic charities, Islamic Relief Worldwide and Al-Muntada al-Islami, both functioning impressively – though in very different ways – as development agencies in a country poor in economic resources but rich in associative networks, with a moderate form of Islam deeply embedded in the national cultural landscape (Benthall 2006b [Chapter 2]; 2008b).

The second case study was of reconstruction in Aceh, the westernmost province of Indonesia, after the 2004 tsunami. I visited two of the most hard-hit coastal towns, Banda Aceh and Meulaboh, in April 2007, and conducted numerous interviews. Acehnese Muslims have in common with the Malians that most people in both countries have no interest in religious militancy. However, the situation of NGOs and their relationship to the people they set out to help is much more complicated than in Mali. This article resulting from my visit cannot be other than a provisional exercise. For my field experience is in the Middle East and, while I have a general knowledge of aid organizations, I have no technical knowledge of rehousing programmes, which turned out to be a key issue in Aceh. My comments on the relative successes of various agencies' rehousing programmes are entirely second-hand, though cross-checked from a number of different sources. My visit lasted for just under two weeks only and I was able neither to randomize my interviewees nor to have any but the most superficial contacts with aid beneficiaries.

About 170,000 people in Aceh lost their lives as result of the tsunami on 26 December 2004, 500,000 were made homeless and 800,000 lost their source of livelihood. Banda Aceh lost about one third of its population and Meulaboh about half, and large areas of both towns were completely destroyed by waves up to twenty metres high which came in up to five or more kilometres from the shore. The highly publicized tragedy of the tsunami had the indirect effect of encouraging reconciliation between the Indonesian government and the Aceh independence movement – brokered by Finnish mediators and overseen by European Commission monitors – after a long-running civil conflict. Aceh now has democratic elections, a provincial governor who was formerly a member of the Free Aceh Movement (GAM) and greater autonomy than before. The recent introduction of Sharia (*syariah*) is extremely controversial and does not seem to enjoy majority support. It has been aptly described by an observer as 'tropical Sharia', in that, unlike its counterparts in hard-line Islamic states, it does not, for example, discourage people from talking to strangers or a man and a woman who are not married from riding on the same motorcycle. But religion is most important for the Acehnese; witness the impressive gleaming mosques in all but the smallest villages.

The devastation caused by the tsunami was comprehensively covered by the world's media, both because so much television footage was available and because many international tourists were victims – though in Aceh there were no tourists, for foreigners were banned from visiting the province at the time. Whereas normally relief agencies have to use sophisticated marketing tactics to wrench funds from donors after a disaster (Benthall 1993), the tsunami provoked a vast outpouring of compassionate charity from all over the world. The consequences of this in Sri Lanka have been well documented: competition among the NGOs to spend funds quickly, and acute difficulties in local coordination (Stirrat 2006). But the scale of the disaster in Aceh was even larger, as it was nearer the epicentre. Some 8 billion US dollars were pledged by governments and NGOs to rebuild Aceh, and an estimated 4 billion had been spent already by April 2007: a huge injection of funds into a previously isolated province. The number of registered international NGOs in Banda Aceh rose to about 180 in June 2005, with some 430 local NGOs also registered (Telford and Cosgrave 2007: 21, fig. 7). The result has been a bubble economy with high local inflation, substantial levels of fraud and corruption, and a high turnover of staff in NGOs. Programmes such as 'cash for work' – continued by certain NGOs too long after the initial crisis – have encouraged some degree of dependency, and the departure of most of the NGOs in 2008 will probably be a factor putting Aceh's new political stability under strain.[1]

My study has focused on the role of international NGOs, including Muslim ones, and on the medium-term reconstruction effort. A study by John Ratcliffe complements this by paying attention to the more immediate response by Indonesian Muslim organizations, which was extensive but relatively spontaneous and fluid. As has happened time and again in disaster zones, the contribution of local relief workers was seriously underrated by the international aid agencies. This neglect was unintentionally symbolized by their often conducting coordination meetings in English without interpreters, and is further reproduced in the copious published evaluations of post-tsunami aid which pay little attention to this aspect. A particular feature of

the relief effort in Aceh was the role played by the Muhammadiyah, a reformist
Muslim social organization with 30 million members all over Indonesia. It acted as
an ad hoc national network for communication, despite having no normal connection with the disaster response system.

> As international groups became more active, they tended to displace local actors.
> Muhammadiyah, for example, drew up elaborate reconstruction plans but faced
> extreme difficulty in obtaining funding to implement them. This represents a failure
> to engage moderate groups, illustrated by the fact that no Muslim organization was
> awarded a prime USAID contract for post-tsunami relief work in Indonesia, despite
> recent U.S. government efforts to reach out to religious actors. (Ratcliffe 2007: 53–4)

For fifteen years or so, critics of NGOs have been calling for more accountability
to beneficiaries. Perhaps it was the scale of the humanitarian response in Aceh, as
well as the disappointing performance of some international NGOs and the government agency BRR (Badan Rehabilitasi dan Rekonstruksi, for Aceh and Nias)
that has stimulated a high degree of local criticism. Some of the best-known names
in humanitarianism did not deliver to the standard that might be expected, partly
because of the large scale of their commitment: one of them was managing a thousand staff for a short time, including some 300 expatriates. Lack of 'surge capacity'
in the international aid system has been identified as a general problem (Telford
and Cosgrave 2007: 22). But an experienced aid worker in Aceh told me (on condition of anonymity) that he had never experienced in other places such high levels
of aggression and threats among the communities he was working with. This may
be partly due to tensions arising from unsatisfactory post-conflict integration. 'The
Acehnese have been betrayed and lied to for centuries, and they have lost faith in the
value of dialogue', generalized this aid worker.

But also the Acehnese are no doubt aware of the huge aid budget available and
the patchy performance. Some Banda Aceh journalists have been particularly
assiduous in exposing poor service delivery. Defenders of the NGOs point out
that the scale of the disaster and in particular acute difficulties of transport made
their work unusually difficult in the early stages. To some extent they may have
been scapegoated: for instance, the blame tends to fall on them exclusively for
being defrauded by dishonest building contractors, rather than on the building
industry itself as well. However, some of the messages coming through to the head
offices of international NGOs must have been disturbing. There is no shortage of
evaluation reports, but the bland idiom chosen in what is released for publication
seldom applies a comparative method, which would be the only means of achieving a truly convincing level of accountability. We do not read of the X National
Red Cross Society having been obliged to leave Aceh because it was seen as failing to deliver promised houses after eighteen months. Nor, by contrast, do we
read much about the work done by military forces during the early stages after

the tsunami, though one NGO manager told me, 'The German army did really well and were escorted all the way to their ships when they left: they did the dirty job of clearing up, day and night, and they left their bulldozers'. In general, military humanitarian aid after natural disasters – as opposed to its controversial role in conflict zones – seems to be neglected in the otherwise burgeoning field of research on humanitarianism.

I have set out to ask a specific question about what has been called 'cultural proximity'. Islamic Relief has major commitments to livelihood programmes, education, health care, and water and sanitation, Muslim Aid to skills enhancement and a long-term flood mitigation programme funded by the European Commission. But I focus on the issue of rehousing, which was soon identified by the Indonesian authorities as a priority, though there have been many delays and, according to the BRR, there was still a target of some 42,000 new houses to be built in 2007, in addition to 57,000 built and 22,000 under way at the end of 2006 (*Jakarta Post* 2007). In addition to material, transport and organizational difficulties, one of the reasons for delay has been legal problems over the ownership of land when land registries were destroyed by the tsunami.

Any hankering for reconstruction efforts to be less politically motivated, or at least to disguise their political motivation, is dealt a blow by the operations of the Turkish Red Crescent Society (TRCS) in and around Banda Aceh. Aceh prides itself as the 'verandah of Mecca' (*Serambi Mekkah*), a channel to the heartland of Islam, and its sultanate, in its increasingly desperate efforts to find allies against the Dutch, engaged up to the nineteenth century in a 'long love affair with the Ottoman Turks' (Reid 2006: 14). The Acehnese separatist flag is the same as the Turkish flag, white crescent and star on a red ground, except that it is sandwiched between horizontal black and white lines. The country director of the TRCS told me that they did not come to Aceh for political reasons, but only because of the disaster, and that they also built 400 houses in Sri Lanka, where Muslims are in the minority, and rebuilt a Buddhist temple. He also explained that very few people in Turkey apart from a few scholars had been aware of the historical links between the Ottoman Empire and Aceh. Despite what he says about TRCS's original motivation, the reputation of Turkey now rides high in Banda Aceh after the construction of a splendid community centre in a prime site – specializing in psycho-social trauma counselling, sport and vocational activities – four schools and over a thousand houses. I visited two housing estates built by the TRCS in suburbs of Banda Aceh: one in Bitai, where Ottoman soldiers who settled there are said to be buried in a graveyard, and one in Lampuuk, where the TRCS has also restored a large mosque. The Turkish houses, each marked with the red crescent and star, are more attractive than most of those built by other agencies, and about twice as expensive: Islamic Relief's houses cost 50 million rupiah each, or about £3,000, while the TRCS's cost about 100 million rupiah and are now being sold on by some of their owners for 150 million – one of the unintended consequences of the Turkish people's generosity. The TRCS drew on its long experience of reconstruction after earthquakes in Turkey and also decided to work with local construction firms and architects.

The TRCS, while asserting that it values its membership of the International Federation of Red Cross and Red Crescent Societies, raised its own funds from Turkish donors with a big appeal and declined to join in the Federation's coordination plans, as it also did in Sri Lanka (Stirrat 2006). It also refrained from attending coordination meetings of the NGOs in Aceh. The quality of these coordination meetings has been criticized in the international evaluation report on coordination as ' "rudderless" and ultimately unproductive' (Bennett 2006: 18).[2]

Although Turkey is a secular state and the International Red Cross and Red Crescent Movement is strictly non-confessional, it seems likely that a common religious, or religio-political, heritage did make access easier for the TRCS with its focused, high-profile intervention. However, competing with the Turks for the most desirable houses are those built by a French agency, Atlas Logistique, which is strictly secular and practical. They adapted a local technique for minimizing earthquake damage in small houses, the 'chicken-leg', a reinforced concrete footing that will shake under stress, but enlarged the size of the bar. Atlas Logistique, funded by ECHO and some other donors, completed 240 houses as well as providing other kinds of practical support, and then withdrew from the scene. Thus to make any claim for the merits of 'cultural proximity' as overriding those of technical proficiency would clearly be a mistake.

In my interviews with authority figures – the Mayor of Banda Aceh, the leader of the local Muhammadiyah branch and chief of the Sharia Law Enforcement Department,[3] and the President of the Ulema Council – I was repeatedly told that help in the reconstruction effort was welcomed from all sources, including Christian NGOs. However, there has been keen sensitivity in Aceh with regard to any perceived threat by outsiders to change Acehnese culture, especially its religious traditions. Soon after the disaster, a scandal erupted because WorldHelp, an evangelical charity from Virginia, USA, was rumoured to have taken possession of 300 Acehnese orphans for placing in a Christian orphanage. It turned out that this was untrue, though the management had indeed toyed with the idea of educating the children as a foothold for conversion of the Acehnese (Sipress 2005: A16). Some Catholic as well as Protestant NGOs have been criticized, rightly or wrongly, on similar grounds.

However, Catholic Relief Services (CRS), the United States arm of Caritas Internationalis, has a good record in rebuilding houses and town markets. At one time, too, its local director reportedly offered to rebuild a mosque, but the community objected that for a mosque to be funded by Christians was *haram* (forbidden). A solution was found: a local personality lent the money and was later reimbursed by CRS. Meanwhile, the British counterpart to CRS, CAFOD, has subcontracted to Islamic Relief Worldwide the building of schools and houses for which it received a share of funding from the Disasters Emergency Committee (the British coordinating body that pools the fundraising campaigns of leading aid agencies after a major disaster). Perhaps more surprisingly, the Mormon humanitarian agency, Latter Day Saints Humanitarian Services, in its first major disaster relief programme, has sub-contracted to Islamic Relief Worldwide the building of ten schools and three health clinics in Aceh. Its spokesman is reported as saying that in Indonesia, 'the predominately Muslim community members receiving assistance understand the law of the fast … It resonates with these people when we explain the principles behind the contributions that allow us to be in their village doing this good. I am very grateful for this and other principles that Islam and the restored gospel share in common, allowing us to bless one another's lives' (Weaver 2006). The fact that such cooperation is now being practised routinely between Muslim and non-Muslim NGOs is surely an example of practical integration which ought to be given more consideration by those who emphasize the recalcitrance of some other elements in the Muslim world.

It remains to look briefly at how the two British-based Islamic NGOs that I focused on made their initial entry to Aceh and how they fared.[4] Islamic Relief Worldwide, founded in 1984, and Muslim Aid, founded in 1985, are fully integrated with the international development community. Both, for instance, are signatories to the Red Cross/Red Crescent code of conduct for NGOs, which bans both proselytism and discrimination in favour of co-religionists. It is ironic that the secular Turkish Red Crescent Society allows itself to build mosques, whereas Islamic Relief's policy is not to do so, though it is explicitly a confessional NGO, in order to avoid any infiltration of religion into its relief and development goals. Both Islamic Relief and Muslim Aid are regulated by the UK Charity Commission and essentially directed from Britain. Islamic Relief is considerably larger – indeed, now the world's largest Islamic NGO – with fundraising branches in a dozen countries. Muslim Aid has one fundraising branch, in Australia. (The Gulf States, whose charities have been very prominent in other disaster zones, made some contribution to rehousing in Aceh but seem to have concentrated largely on rebuilding or repairing mosques; see Ratcliffe 2007.)

Islamic Relief had conducted a needs assessment in Indonesia in 1999, concluding that economic growth had not greatly benefited rural populations, and it had opened an office in Jakarta in 2003. Its consistent policy is to work with the poorest. At the time of the tsunami, it was attempting with the encouragement of some UN organizations to get access to Aceh, which was closed to NGOs on account of the long-running civil conflict. Helped by some political connections, it embarked on a joint assessment with the Muhammadiyah and the government was giving out positive signals before the tsunami. It had been agreed that Islamic Relief could work through partners, but not send in expatriates. This enabled it to send national staff in very early, so that its first response was within two to three days. Connections with the Nahdatul Ulama (NU), a more conservative counterpart to the reformist Muhammadiyah, were also useful. Islamic Relief's logo – uniting the motifs of a mosque with twin minarets and the globe – is especially popular.

At the time, Islamic Relief Worldwide was not yet a member of the Disasters Emergency Committee, but it was given £6 million by CAFOD (to whom it reciprocally channels some funds for work in Latin America). It set up an office in Banda Aceh reporting directly to the headquarters in Birmingham, with a sub-office in Meulaboh.

In many ways Islamic Relief is similar to a score of international agencies working in Aceh: with its fleet of 4x4s, its reporting officer, accounts department, gender officer and so forth. Praying is not compulsory: some of the staff are indeed non-Muslims. But a space is set aside in the foyer of the office for prayer; and, on Friday afternoon, loudly amplified recitations from the Qur'an make the building feel an integral part of the wider society's piety.

Though directed from Britain, Islamic Relief's expatriate staff are remarkably varied in their ethnic backgrounds. Of the twelve, I met only one ethnic European (a Macedonian Christian) and only one British citizen (a British Pakistani); among the rest were two Bangladeshis, a Sudanese, a Kenyan (Christian), a Lebanese and an Egyptian. In addition there are some 150 national staff. Like other international NGOs in Aceh, Islamic Relief has had some management difficulties in scaling up and ensuring continuity. It would be naive to assume that because a Bangladeshi and an Acehnese are both Muslim, the cultural differences between them will somehow dissolve. The religious aspect to its work is rather subtler and I record the testimony of two Islamic Relief expatriate staff.

One of them, an experienced manager, has to confront the serious problem of dishonest contractors. A Christian himself, he says that it is his practice everywhere to look for entry points into the local culture. In Aceh, he does not accuse contractors of corruption, but asks them what their religion tells them to do. So for a healthcare project, he says: 'anyone who takes money from the fund is causing someone to be killed and is worse than the tsunami, as someone's blood is on your hands. The same is true of finishing late'. Another informant told me that the egalitarian values of Islam made a specially good impression. 'It is good to see Islamic Relief's expats praying and fasting with the people – and the brotherhood spirit during Ramadan. People stand shoulder to shoulder to pray, and the driver may be the prayer leader, with the head of mission behind him.'

It is clear in any case that Islamic Relief's record of construction is good. At the time of my visit, it had completed about 560 houses and was to build 300 more, as well as thirteen new health clinics and seventeen new schools, all in close consultation with local committees and learning from the example of the most technically successful agencies such as Atlas Logistique. While I was in Banda Aceh, a newspaper article appeared in an influential newspaper *Surambi* alleging that the standard of houses built by BRR was a national scandal, already requiring extra funds for them to be put in order, and comparing them unfavourably as regards both cost and quality with Islamic Relief's.

The Muslim Aid operation in Banda Aceh has a very different style. Its country director, Fadlullah Wilmot, is probably, of all international NGO managers in Aceh, the most experienced and the best informed about the culture. British by origin, he migrated to Australia as a child and converted to Islam as a student. Trained as a psychologist, he taught English in Aceh in the 1970s and kept in close touch with the province ever since. Muslim Aid was able to get access a few days after the tsunami, working with Global Peace Malaysia, a Muslim agency. At one time they had a thousand volunteers, some Malaysian but mostly locals. After deciding that housing was the priority, they embarked on a successful construction programme and will shortly have completed 1,450 houses. Banda Aceh is now to become the South East Asian headquarters of Muslim Aid, and there are plans to launch new programmes in the Philippines and Cambodia as well as in other parts of Indonesia. It seems clear that Wilmot is given considerable autonomy by the Muslim Aid head office, providing an unusual personal link between the international aid system and Aceh. He is also raising funds from sympathetic Muslim foundations in the Gulf area.

While there are some local advantages, according to Wilmot, to be derived from the Islamic label, both among elites and among the population at large, it can actually be a disadvantage in relations with international aid organizations, and 'you have to work doubly hard … What is important is whether you can deliver what you promise, and the quality of the delivery'. Public opinion would be no less severe on a Muslim than on a non-Muslim NGO if it failed to deliver.

My conclusion, therefore, based on admittedly incomplete data, is that the 'cultural proximity' between Muslim aid agencies and the people of Aceh has been a factor in making access possible and, to some extent, in smoothing the way for good working relationships. There is undoubtedly considerable potential for such agencies to make specially valuable contributions in future when Muslim countries are afflicted with disasters of any kind; and also for non-Muslim agencies to form productive partnerships with Islamic agencies that can show a good track record.[5] But if any Muslim agency were tempted to rely on its cultural proximity to such populations as an excuse for neglecting all the other factors that make for successful aid delivery, that would be a mistake. The cultural differences that divide Muslims from one another also work against the theoretical solidarity of the Muslim *umma*.

In conclusion, the evidence suggests that Islamic agencies are capable of doing at least as well as secular or Christian agencies. Their actual and potential efficacy needs to be set in the balance against suspicions, almost certainly much exaggerated, that the privileges of some Islamic charities are being abused for nefarious purposes (Benthall 2007a; 2007b). It should not be necessary to demonstrate that they do better than secular or Christian agencies. It is surely enough that they can do as well.

The issue of 'cultural proximity' or 'communitarian aid' is clearly sensitive: especially in conflict zones, it can call in question the Dunantian principles of humanitarian action: neutrality, impartiality and universality. Significantly, some secular agencies such as Médecins Sans Frontières and CARE are now making tentative moves towards collaboration with Islamic NGOs in Muslim regions where they have serious difficulty in working. Some academic attention is now being given to the issue of cultural proximity (De Cordier 2007; 2009a), but there is a lack so far of sustained field research which would provide a solid evidential base for debate in the humanitarian community.

Acknowledgements

I am grateful to the Nuffield Foundation for a travel grant, and to the Royal Anthropological Institute for facilitating it; also to Islamic Relief for logistic support and hospitality. Thanks are also due to many people in Aceh associated with governmental and non-governmental organizations for giving time to me, and to C. W. Watson and Jonathan Zilberg for background information.

Ethical guidelines agreed with the Royal Anthropological Institute have been observed in reporting the views of informants.

Notes

1 The impact of this change will be softened by the implementation by aid agencies of medium-term infrastructure, economic recovery and sustainable livelihoods programmes, and by the inflow of increased funds to Aceh from the central government budget as a result of the new political settlement.
2 However, the authors of international evaluation reports have themselves been locally criticized for making judgements based on short visits. I noticed an 'evaluation fatigue' which made my own research project harder to carry out in Aceh than in Mali.
3 Colloquially known as the Sharia police, though they do not in fact have police powers.
4 My singling out of these two UK-based NGOs was due to contacts I had with them already in Britain, where I am based, and to that extent reflects an observer bias. However, it is also true that Islamic NGOs are particularly well established and active in Britain, partly owing to the sympathetic policies of the UK Charity Commission. A third, smaller, UK-based agency, Muslim Hands, has also undertaken field operations in Aceh.
5 In June 2007, the US-based United Methodist Committee on Relief (UMCOR) signed a partnership agreement in London with Muslim Aid, intended to result in a flow of about $15 million to relief in disaster and conflict zones, including Indonesia. The question of collaboration between Muslim and Christian NGOs is raised by Benedetti (2006).

4

The Palestinian zakat committees 1993–2007 and their contested interpretations

This chapter was originally drafted for a sociology journal's special issue that was not eventually published. Then the Graduate Institute for International and Development Studies agreed to publish the text as an Occasional Paper in 2008 in a section of the Institute then known as the Program for the Study of International Organization(s) (PSIO), with the support of the Swiss Federal Department of Foreign Affairs, Political Division IV.

The adverse interpretation of the zakat committees during this period, that they were simply fronts for Hamas, is held up to the light, and a more benign alternative interpretation is proposed. Throughout the text is faithful to the principle of open enquiry: that further evidence could necessitate a change of view. (This could be characterized as a Popperian-falsificationist approach to social research.)

I subsequently assisted Emanuel Schaeublin in his further research on West Bank zakat committees, which resulted in his Working Paper, also published by the Graduate Institute (Schaeublin 2009). He later published a matching study on the zakat committees in Gaza (Schaeublin 2012).

A more precise title of this chapter would have emphasized that my study was restricted to the West Bank, with no data on Gaza.

***

Foreword

The Graduate Institute of International [and Development] Studies created the PSIO in 1994 to facilitate collaboration between the international and academic communities in Geneva and worldwide. It is both a research programme and a forum to stimulate discussions between academics and policy makers within the environment of the Graduate Institute in Geneva.

For ten years, the PSIO has been steadily expanding and diversifying its activities. In September 2005, it launched, with the Swiss Federal Department of Foreign Affairs, Political Division IV (DFA-PD IV), the project 'Religion and

Politics: Initiatives and Applied Research', aimed at making an effective contribution to transforming conflicts in which religious and political factors are deeply interconnected and developing a platform of knowledge and expertise in this field. Since then, the project is being implemented through both operational and research activities, touching upon a variety of topics and situations worldwide.

Within the activities of the project, the initiative 'Towards cooperation in removing unjustified obstacles for Islamic charities' (also known as the Montreux Initiative) was launched in 2005. The objectives of the initiative are to build confidence between governments, Islamic charities, and support NGOs in order to give Islamic charities better tools for the post 9–11 context by means of capacity-building, and to improve the general atmosphere in the charity field which has suffered as a consequence of the 'war against terror'.

The Montreux Initiative has given attention to the Islamic charities set up to help Palestinians, and in particular the Palestinian zakat committees, which have attracted much controversy. This Occasional Paper reviews the argument that these committees have been engaged in abuse of the privileges of charities, and it concludes that the argument is, on the balance of evidence available, faulty. Though the author is one of the advisers to the Montreux Initiative, this Paper is published as an exercise in social research that represents the views of its author only.

Dr Daniel Warner, Executive Director, PSIO

Introduction

The nature of the Palestinian Islamic charities, known as zakat committees, has proved an extremely contentious issue, especially in Israel, the United States and some European countries. We shall contrast the current official position of the US government, that they are subsidiaries of a seamless and conspiratorial terrorist organization, with an alternative approach that contextualizes their religious and humanitarian aspects rather than limiting itself to a purely political and counter-terrorist analysis. Such is the heat of political conflict in Israel–Palestine that ostensibly innocuous humanitarian actions – the gift of beehives to support a destitute family or the management of a clinic to treat gallstones – can acquire a nefarious reputation.

This article will argue that, difficult as it may be to arrive at complete certainty in such a fluid and contentious environment, the balance of evidence is against the conspiratorial theory. The article will draw on personal observations, commissioned information gathering and published research, to argue in favour of a more benign interpretation, without falling into the error of denying that charity in any social context can be analytically divorced from politics. It will be suggested that the zakat committees are, among other things, an example of grass-roots, community-based local Faith Based Organizations that were a meeting point for politically inspired Islamists and the devout middle class. They were beginning to tap successfully into the international aid system, and would have continued to develop in this direction if they had been encouraged to, and if they had not become the victims of a campaign since the end of 2007 to reorganize them under central control.

Zakat or almsgiving is one of the five pillars of Islam, closely associated with prayer – which without the observance of zakat is considered of no avail. It is the religious obligation for Muslims to give annually one-fortieth of the value of their assets, over and above basic property such as their home and working tools, to charity. Eight eligible categories of beneficiary are listed in the Qur'an, beginning with 'the poor'. Though the principle of zakat is deeply entrenched in Islamic law, teaching and historical practice, there is no country in which it functions as it ought to do in an ideal Islamic society: that is to say, automatically redistributing surplus wealth to those in need and thus purging private capital of its undesirable features. In some Muslim countries such as Pakistan it has been absorbed into the national tax system; in others, such as Oman, it is considered an entirely private matter. New-style Western Islamic aid agencies, such as Islamic Relief Worldwide, have adapted the teaching on zakat as an opportunity for professional fundraising on an impressive scale, relying on modern readings of the Qur'anic prescriptions that enable zakat funds to be disbursed for the benefit of those most in need, regardless of whether or not they are Muslims (Benthall and Bellion-Jourdan 2003: 7–28). In the Palestinian Territories a rather complex situation has arisen, reflecting tensions that have radiated transnationally into courtrooms, universities and polemical websites.

The basic facts are clear enough.[1] The extent of deprivation and need in the Palestinian Territories has become more serious over the last thirty years, as a result of the failure of a succession of initiatives to try to resolve the Israel–Palestine conflict. In several major towns in the West Bank, some ninety zakat committees, as well as numerous Islamic charitable associations, have been gradually expanding their activities in providing services to local communities: hospitals and clinics, food distribution, income-generating projects, orphan sponsorship, schools, bursaries for students, summer camps, and the like. The largest such organization in the West Bank, at Hebron (Al-Khalil),[2] had in 2006 an annual expenditure of some $7 million; the medium-size ones less than $1 million; and there are many considerably smaller ones – much less than the support given by the United Nations and other international agencies to alleviate poverty and distress in the Territories, but still a substantial contribution.

We shall here confine our discussion to the West Bank. The legal status of zakat committees in Gaza is similar, in that, though Gaza was administered by Egypt between 1948 and 1967, Jordanian law was applied in this respect since 1967 (as explained below) over all the Palestinian Territories. Nearly all our evidence antedates the takeover of Gaza by Hamas in June 2007, which resulted in a new political convulsion in both Gaza and the West Bank, fast moving and outside the scope of our present research. In particular, the Fatah-dominated Palestinian Authority based in Ramallah decided in December 2007 to radically reorganize the West Bank zakat committees under central control.[3] We have used the present tense, but in most cases the past tense would be more accurate.

The 'pyramid' model

The view of the West Bank zakat committees advanced by the US government is simple. It is influenced by the publications of Matthew Levitt, the counter-terrorism expert (Levitt 2006). The organization of Hamas is likened to a pyramid, with a political section at the top, which rests on a military section, which in turn rests on a broad social welfare section.[4] This social welfare section is supposedly sometimes referred to as 'the Dawa'.[5]

It is common ground that *da'wa* in Arabic means the call to Islam, missionary activity, and sometimes, by extension, the provision of religious education and social services with a view to reviving the faith of a community. Though the details of its structure are not made public, there is little doubt that Hamas is indeed hierarchically organized, with a representative council (the Shura) at the apex, a military command structure (the Al-Qassam Brigades), and various committees. These no doubt include specialist committees dealing with charitable and welfare matters as well as finance, public relations, religion, women's issues and the like (Hroub 2006: 118), and were certainly set up with a view to facilitating wide consultation. There is no evidence to my knowledge to support the contention that there is a social welfare section called 'the Dawa'. It is true that Hamas does operate some relief and welfare services directly – that is to say, under its own control without any independent charity structures – and it would be reasonable to regard these as subsidiaries; but this does not apply to the independently constituted committees and societies. *Da'wa* is a principle, a set of values, not the name of a department. Levitt's is in sociological terms an 'etic'[6] or outsider's interpretation, but presented as if it were an 'emic' description using insider categories, that is to say an organization chart. This might seem a pedantic point to make, except that the outcomes of some major current court hearings relating to Islamic charities depend partly on what judges and jury members may make of such nuances, and the justification by the Palestinian Authority in Ramallah of its recent reorganization of the zakat committees depends on whether the zakat committees actually deserved to be radically reformed or, on the contrary, were operating legally and effectively as grass-roots charities.

As an 'etic' construct, the pyramid model is contentious. It omits two foundation stones that have underpinned Hamas's popularity: first, religious conviction as a social determinant in itself, expressed with particular vigour in the idea of the *umma*, or brotherhood in Islam; and, second, opposition to the Israeli military occupation which is by common consent responsible for much hardship. Another 'etic' interpretation of Hamas's motivation, advanced for instance by the French researcher Jean-François Legrain, contends that its military and political functions are subordinate to an overriding priority which has been to promote a moral and spiritual reawakening based on a particular reading of the Qur'an: the principle of *da'wa* as a primary objective, not as a means to a merely political end (Legrain 2006). However, the pyramid model is used by the United States and Israeli governments to argue that all Palestinian charitable organizations having, or deemed to have, an affiliation with Hamas, are in effect its subsidiaries. Hence any support given to these organizations is 'material support for terrorism', which is under US law tantamount to terrorism itself and in particular to the suicide attacks on unarmed civilians that Hamas has at various times organized. Allegations of material support for terrorism have led to designation (blacklisting) of individuals and institutions under US law, to freezing of assets, and to criminal prosecutions.

It seems likely that the criminalization of material support for the zakat committees has in fact had the result of driving money underground, where it is outside the purview of banking regulators, because there are many ways of remitting funds other than through banking remittances between registered charities. If this is correct, 'designation' has the reverse effect to that intended. However, we are mainly concerned here with the validity of the process whereby designation has been decided as a policy, rather than with the practical consequences of the policy that have ensued.

An alternative 'emic' model in three phases

I propose instead an 'emic' description of the West Bank zakat committees that confines itself to categories recognized by all the participants and that also provides some time-depth. We will take as a case study the heritage town of Nablus, a commercial centre with a population of some 135,000. It is especially notable for a site sacred to Jews ('Joseph's tomb'[7]) and for a history of political opposition dating back to the British Mandate before World War II. The history of its zakat committee may be divided into three phases.

Phase 1, till 1967

During the first phase, before the Six-Day War of 1967 and Israeli occupation of the Palestinian Territories in 1968, when the West Bank was still under Jordanian control, the Nablus zakat committee was based in a historic mosque in the Old City. Funding came largely from well-to-do Muslims in the vicinity, in compliance with their zakat obligations, but also from income derived from some *waqf* real estate – assets donated for the inalienable benefit of the zakat committee.[8] Alms were distributed to the poor and needy of the city, following the traditional practice of zakat committees all over the Muslim world. The main responsibility lay with the imam of the mosque, governed by Islamic law but also under the supervision of the Jordanian government's Ministry of Awqaf (the Arabic plural of *waqf*), which had charge of religious affairs[9] and holy sites.

Phase 2, 1968–94

The second phase, of twenty-six years, was a transitional period between Israel's victory in the Six-Day War and the foundation of the Palestinian National Authority (PNA) in 1994. The big change was Israeli military occupation of the Palestinian Territories. However, oversight of the Palestinian zakat committees, including Nablus, was still retained by the Jordanian Ministry of Awqaf even after 1988, when King Hussein of Jordan decided to disengage from territorial claims to the West Bank. The Nablus committee was first registered under Jordanian law in 1977. During this second phase, the committee developed its activities: undertaking various charitable and community projects, beginning to secure external funds from bodies such as the French government and the World Bank, and investing its own funds for the future.

Phase 3, 1994–present

The third phase lasted from the foundation of the PNA in 1994 until the time of writing. The overall Israeli military occupation continued during this period, but the PNA acquired control of many aspects of the day-to-day administration of the Palestinian Territories. During the second phase, non-governmental organizations (NGOs) had acquired considerable influence in the Territories on account of the vacuum in government and welfare services (Brown 2003). After 1994, the PNA exerted much political effort (against considerable opposition) to establishing control over the NGOs, passing new legislation with this in mind and insisting on rigorous registration and monitoring procedures. The zakat committees were treated as a special category and came under the control of the PNA, but now through the Palestinian Ministry of Awqaf.[10] Each zakat committee was required to register with this ministry, as well as with other specialist ministries if it was working in the fields of social affairs, health, education or agriculture, and to submit to regular inspections. The Ministry of Awqaf is required to approve the election of each of the members of a given zakat committee, between seven and thirteen in number, none related by close kinship ties, and they are not allowed to accept any payment for their services (unlike their employees). In effect, the zakat committees have operated under a combination of Jordanian zakat law and the new Palestinian regulations that lay down reporting and external auditing requirements for all voluntary associations.[11]

Since 1994, the Nablus zakat committee has expanded its activities considerably. Its many projects include an orphan programme, an eye hospital, a day clinic and a dairy. A large part of its funds are still generated locally as before: from zakat dues, income from real estate, and stock market investments. However, there has also been a considerable expansion in international funding. International donors have included the World Food Programme, the UN Development Programme and well-known American, German, Japanese and French agencies. But, as might be expected, much of the external funding has come from Arab and Muslim individuals and institutions, in many countries, that are sympathetic to the plight of the Palestinians.[12] In neighbouring Jordan, some zakat committees have specialized in sending the product of their local fundraising to help Palestinians in need. But it is the action of European and American Islamic charities in sending funds to Palestine that has made them such a subject of bitter controversy, for according to the pyramid model this is equivalent to the financing of suicide bombing.

Allegations against the zakat committees

Perhaps the strongest charge against the zakat committees is the allegation that they directly support paramilitary activities, including the offer of a kind of advance insurance policy for Hamas suicide bombers, providing benefits for their families. One reason why this charge has gained credibility is that the suicide bombers are often called 'martyrs' (*shahīd*, plural *shuhadā'*), and it is true that funds have sometimes been disbursed to support explicitly the families of 'martyrs'. However, the committees' defence is, first, that in the Arab world a *shahīd* is anyone who dies in a just cause or as a result, direct or indirect, of injustice (including anyone killed under Israeli fire, or even the victim of an electrical fire due to defective wiring in a deprived neighbourhood, or a woman who dies in childbirth when the ambulance transporting her is detained at a checkpoint);[13] and, second, that they carry out a needs assessment before helping bereaved families, so that the aid they give is based on need, irrespective of how the deceased met their deaths.[14] Evidence to substantiate the strong charge is scarce, based on sources such as Israeli intelligence reports that are not only selective and heavily biased,[15] but also sometimes compromised by semantic discrepancies, such as the ambiguity of *shahīd*, due to translation problems between Arabic, Hebrew and English. In some cases, alleged confessions appear to have been elicited under duress.

An equally strong charge, but strong in a different way because it is so sweeping, is advanced. This is that the zakat committees are engaged in 'social engineering' on behalf of Hamas, 'critical to winning the hearts and minds of the Palestinian people and to creating a military and operational pool for Hamas'.[16] The implicit effect of the pyramid model is to seek to persuade that Hamas is like a narcotics mafia, a corporate body whose ostensibly charitable aid to local communities is actually nothing but an instrument to further criminal activities, and which enforces obedience to its dictates. The allegation could be definitely verified or falsified only by the adducing of field-based sociological evidence, which is extremely hard to obtain in a zone of conflict and military occupation where a large proportion of the Palestinian people are already radicalized, irrespective of any actions that Hamas may take. However, evidence (summarized below) as to the high degree of public trust that the zakat committees have earned, by contrast with all political parties and movements in the Territories, suggests that the pyramid model is deficient.[17]

A less strong charge is also put forward by Matthew Levitt that the zakat committees' work creates a sense of indebtedness. 'If a person is a taxi driver and they are asked to deliver a package somewhere they don't ask. They do it. If they are asked to shelter someone in their house overnight, they do it. It creates a sense of indebtedness that Hamas is able to call upon.'[18] This charge is anecdotal and somewhat inchoate. It is possible that a taxi driver may occasionally deliver a dubious package, but equally possible that he may convey an injured child to a clinic at risk to himself because of crossfire. I can find no sentence in Levitt's book on Hamas which acknowledges that the Islamic charities in Palestine may be even partly motivated by altruism, though with regard to Hamas he does refer to its 'notorious honesty' (Levitt 2006: 238).

The weakest charge – but maybe that on which the campaign against the zakat committees ultimately depends – is that, even if it is conceded that such a charity provides genuine health and welfare services, financial support for the charity is nonetheless a support for terrorism, on the grounds that it is relieving Hamas from costs and hence frees up funds for paramilitary operations.[19] This has been called the doctrine of 'asset substitution', founded on the fact that money is 'fungible'. The implications of this argument have not perhaps been fully thought through. No one denies the extent of health and welfare needs in the Palestinian Territories, yet US prosecutors contend that it is a criminal offence for external funds to be sent for a poor man to be given a cow to milk, or for a patient with eye disease to be given medical treatment, on the grounds that, without those external funds, the money for buying explosives and training suicide bombers would be tied up with charitable services, and so a terrorist attack would not take place.

One can appreciate the conscientious motivation of prosecutors who seek to deter financial transfers that, according to their theory, are facilitating acts designed to cause terrible carnage and suffering. Nonetheless, such an argument seems to be at variance with International Humanitarian Law as applied to zones of conflict, which gives priority to relieving the suffering of non-combatants. The logical consequence would be to prohibit funding of the International Red Cross and Red Crescent Movement, because some of their funds go to support Red Cross and Red Crescent National Societies in countries that are definite military threats to the West, and because the work of these National Societies includes the provision of military ambulances and hospitals.

Moreover, the argument suggests that the greater the professional integrity shown by the zakat committees – in delivering their services effectively to those most in need – and hence the greater the trust they earn from the communities they serve, the more successful they are likely to be in winning 'hearts and minds', and therefore the more culpable they are in allegedly sustaining Hamas. According to the argument, even if the charity managers, medics and others concerned were to succeed in satisfying a neutral adjudicator that they are committed to acting in a totally professional manner, this would not clear them of the charge of spreading an atmosphere of opinion supportive of Hamas. Such an argument places the zakat committees in a 'no win' double bind.

Some field evidence from 1996

My own fieldwork on Islamic charities in Palestine dates back to February 1996 and gave some attention to a Jordanian zakat committee in Amman that collected funds for Palestinian zakat committees: the Islamic Zakat Supporting Committee for the Palestinian People. My field notes of an interview with the general manager of this Amman committee (Mr Murad al-Adayileh)[20] read in part as follows:

[On their orphan programmes:] Birth cert., family background, death cert. of father. Children's files. Reports. School certificate. [...] Follow also health, medical checkups. [...] Regularly get harassed by Israeli authorities. [...] Tightening up by authorities after the creation of the PA but so far is still operating. Due to Western misrepresentations of Islam, local authorities in Arab world have to tighten control of Islamic associations. [But] programme not politicized. Members of the [Amman] committee are all independent – no party or affiliation. Humanitarian aid and Islam know no boundaries. All agree a poor man is a poor man. In assisting these children, the fathers could have been martyrs or sons and daughters of informers. Don't distinguish between son of hero and villain. [...]

'Caravans of charity': offer special first aid or medical care on a temporary basis [...] organized from local medical centres to isolated or distant villages or communities. Provide free medical checkups for poor families and advocate health and hygiene. [...]

Familial solidarity and rehabilitation: aim is to try to stop these families from being dependent on charity. Five points: 1. income generation (e.g. beehive – family becomes a productive unit and therefore charity stops); 2. cows; 3. sheep; 4. reuse of land; 5. textile clothing or knitting. 1 to 4 aimed at rural areas, 5 at cities. [...]

Sponsorship of university students: [...] stipend of 50 Jordanian dinars [about 50 British pounds] per month, linked to achievement; priority given to those doing well. Any subject: medicine, agriculture, Sharia – twenty students per year, West Bank or Gazan institutions only. Conditions: students must be living in the Occupied Territories; good moral background; registered in further education institution; evidence of need for support; not a beneficiary of another grant; must return to Occupied Territories after study; committee's approval needed. [...]

Donors give specifically to programmes and get feedback and follow-up. [...]

When 400 Palestinians expelled from Palestine into Lebanon, the committee sponsored their families, also visited in Lebanon. [...]

Type of relief is when Israelis destroy houses in Gaza, massacre in the [Hebron] mosque. Gave out 30,000 dinars for families of victims, distributed food and helped those who were injured. [...]

Don't refuse help – don't distinguish between poor. [...]

[On attempts by the Jordanian government to centralize the collection of zakat and restrict local fundraising:] Government attempt to please Israelis. [...] a critical issue since the peace treaty [between Israel and Jordan] – now restricted to Amman, charity fleamarkets, etc., banned. But humanitarian aid must not be politicized. Zakat is one thing, a spiritual venture, nothing to do with tax. Question of trust is very important – a local charity more popular. [...]

Two or three days ago, celebrated 1,000th sponsorship of an orphan. Had *iftar* [Ramadan breakfast meal] with seven children from Palestine. Children spoke, people cried. [...]

Government zakat funds try to imitate local funds and revive trust. Entrepreneurs shift paying to government funds to get popular with government, rather than to local ones. Wants to emphasize trust. [...]

Not allowed to have volunteers working for them – one strategy to limit them. But has not affected level of donations. Only eight staff, Ramadan work is twenty-four hours on twenty-four. [...]

Budget is 500–600,000 dinars per year. [...] PNA authorities are cautious as to how to deal with these organizations.

It could be argued that Mr al-Adayileh was lying through his teeth and that I was deceived by him. This is the problem with individual fieldwork. I can only add that he made a favourable personal impression as a young man with modern fundraising skills, pragmatic but committed to Islamic ideals (he also said that it was difficult to persuade secular people to contribute), and, as far as I could judge, sincere. His committee certainly had some kind of affiliation with the Jordanian Muslim Brothers, and had problems with the Jordanian government (as summarized above), but if he was merely a member of a conspiracy to further the interests of Hamas then the conspiracy was one so deep that I failed at the time to see through it, and still today fail to see through it, because what I have seen and heard of the Palestinian zakat committees since 1996 is consistent with the picture given me by Mr al-Adayileh.[21]

The functioning of the zakat committees and their reputation

A key question is to what extent the zakat committees are 'affiliated' with Hamas. As we have seen, the Israeli and US governments' position is that they are so closely affiliated as to be, in effect, subsidiaries. The position of the committees themselves is that they are entirely independent charitable associations. The most serious, first-hand, unbiased data publicly available to date is contained in an International Crisis Group report (ICG 2003).[22] This suggests that some organizations in the Territories such as the Islamic Association (Al-Mujamma' al-Islami) in Gaza are strongholds of Hamas, but that otherwise the concept of affiliation is problematic and a matter of degree. Some zakat committees are popularly seen as loosely affiliated politically with Hamas, some with Fatah, some are independent; but loose affiliation is not the same as the control that Hamas is accused of exercising.

My own investigations into the zakat committee in Nablus have concluded as follows. In the early summer of 1997 there were twelve committee members. The breakdown of its annual expenditure of US$1 million was reported approximately as follows:

40%   sponsorship of needy families through monthly payments
30%   sponsored orphans
7%   educational support for needy students
8%   medical support
10%   monthly staff salaries
5%   other[23]

The committee also manages the Islamic Medical Compound and a dairy, Al-Safa, on a cost recovery basis. Decisions are taken by majority vote and are confirmed by the Ministry of Awqaf.

The Chairman, Dr Abdel-Rahim Hanbali, is a member of an ancient religious family associated with the Hanbali mosque in Nablus: his father was imam of the mosque and was the first chairman of the zakat committee. The deputy chairman, Sheikh Hamid Bitawi, is a well-known religious authority and a member of parliament, and clearly a preacher of militant, even inflammatory anti-Israeli views. Though he might justifiably be seen as a sympathizer with Hamas, he declares that he has no political affiliation, and aspires to be more a national and Islamic icon than a party politician. According to my information (some of which, though not all, I have been able to confirm from independent sources), none of the other six members of committee whom the Israeli government labels as 'Hamas' are members of Hamas.

Two of them are affluent businessmen. One of these, the honorary treasurer, Hajj Adli Yaish was elected Mayor of Nablus in municipal elections in 2005, on the 'Change and Reform' ticket, which was a coalition group including Hamas and other parties and individuals (including a number of Christians) and widely regarded as the Hamas party. At the time of going to press with this article, he was detained in an Israeli prison after his arrest in May 2007. I met with Mr Yaish in 1996 and was favourably impressed by him. I was not at the time aware of his political involvement: he seemed typical of the kind of practical businessman who is appointed as honorary treasurer for charities all over the world. Impartial media reports confirm this impression:

A reputation for clean hands and caring about the people is why Islamist politicians like Mr Yaish, in alliance with Hamas, won 74% of the municipal election vote in Nablus. (Dan Damon, BBC News website, report from Nablus, 30 December 2005)
   [Mr Yaish] is devout, but wealthy from auto parts and a Mercedes agency. He studied mechanical engineering in England from 1970 to 1975 and speaks English fluently; he speaks the modern language of efficiency and budget oversight; he keeps a picture of Yasir Arafat in his office and not Sheik Ahmed Yassin, the Hamas leader killed by Israel in March 2004.

'This is a government office,' Mr. Yaish said. 'President Abbas said to leave the photos of Arafat in offices, so we left it. Sheik Yassin was not elected, and this is not my house.'[24]

Mr. Yaish agrees that some people will vote differently on national and local issues, and he expects Hamas to get nowhere close to the 73 per cent of the local vote it received a month ago. 'We want partnership with Fatah,' he said. 'Democracy is competition and makes us stronger.'

Hamas in the legislature will monitor government work, especially finances and accounts, to prevent corruption, he said, and to improve tax collection. 'The same party as judge and jury is not good,' he said. 'If there is no oversight, even a good man can be tempted.'

Hamas opposes negotiations with Israel, but Mr. Yaish thinks its presence in the legislature will stiffen the Palestinian Authority's back in dealings with Israel. 'I don't like the Palestinian Authority to negotiate from a weak position,' Mr. Yaish said, pragmatically. 'We're occupied, and I want my government to talk harder to Israel.' (Steven Erlanger, *New York Times*, 23 January 2006)

Since 1994, Hamas's popular approval rating among Palestinians, as manifested either in opinion polls or in municipal and parliamentary elections, has varied between 25 and 50 or even 60 per cent.[25] It is to be expected statistically that in a Palestinian committee of seven to thirteen members, up to a half of them will probably sympathize with Hamas as individuals. It does not however follow that they are unable to carry out their duties as committee members in a manner consistent with the local laws and with generally accepted principles of charity management.

As far as I know, no solid impartial research has yet been conducted into the detailed operations of the zakat committees in the Territories, which would be particularly difficult to undertake, on account of the highly charged political context.[26] However, a public opinion poll was conducted on two occasions in recent years by Birzeit University in Ramallah, to ascertain the degree of popular confidence in various civil institutions. This university has one of the best academic reputations in the Palestinian Territories. The results, though somewhat crude as sociological data, are highly suggestive:[27]

Universities	70.9%
Zakat committees	62.5%
NGOs and charitable societies	50.0%
Local press	46.0%
Formal judicial system	43.5%
Trade unions	37.5%
Palestinian opposition	34.2%
Political movements/ parties	27.8%

It seems clear enough that during the period 2002–4 popular confidence in the opposition and political parties, presumably including Hamas, was very low. Second only to the universities, the zakat committees enjoyed a high level of confidence, higher than that of other types of NGO. This supports the conclusion of Nathan Brown, an American political scientist who has studied the Palestinian voluntary sector and conducted extensive fieldwork in the Territories, that 'Zakat committees enjoy a tremendous amount of legitimacy. Even secular leftists admire their authenticity and ability to operate without reliance on Western funding' (Brown 2003: 14). It may be speculated that part of this legitimacy has been gained by responding spontaneously to obvious local needs, rather than trying to satisfy the agenda of the Western donor community.

A corroborating opinion is given by Professor As'ad Abdul Rahman, a senior independent Palestinian political scientist without party allegiances: 'In the past [that is, before the so-called reforms introduced by the PNA in Ramallah in 2007–8] zakat committees were formed in a free electoral or consensual mode'. He foresees damaging consequences arising from the current move to bring them under government control: 'This major and dangerous decision had major and dangerous reasons and consequences'. And he describes the zakat committee system as a protection against terrorism rather than a fomenter of terrorism:

> [a] popular, credible and democratic structure [...] that had helped in fighting poverty and bridging the internal Palestinian social gaps and consequently leading to creating such atmospheres that are neither tense nor extremist nor terrorist.[28]

If we look to a wider Middle Eastern context, including Egypt (Sullivan 1992; ben Néfissa 1995) and the Arab villages in Israel (Israeli 1993), convincing evidence is available that the Islamic voluntary sector is often able to provide effective welfare and relief services to populations that the state is unable or unwilling to cater for. Similarly in Algeria, a team of British consultants concluded as a result of a commissioned survey in 2000 that Islamic charitable associations throughout the country, though markedly out of favour with the Algerian military government, were 'almost without doubt the strongest NGOs in Algeria', especially in the poorest rural areas.[29] Zakat committees are exactly the kind of grass-roots, community-based, voluntary institution that many international donors now look to as an alternative to the waste and corruption that often accompany aid flows through large bureaucratic institutions.

An alternative 'etic' model

There is no reason to question the good faith of counter-terrorism experts, and indeed citizens everywhere have reason to be grateful to the police and intelligence services that track down and forestall terrorist attacks. However, the methods of enquiry used for this purpose depend critically on the construction of patterns of association through analysis of communications and meetings between individuals.[30] There is thus a grave risk of attributing guilt by association. This risk is compounded by the citation of highly biased press reports and intelligence websites, and sometimes by reliance on statements extracted from detainees under coercive interrogation. It is further compounded by the insistence of the US government on minimizing the distinction between transnational terrorism of the Al-Qaeda type – which appeals positively to only a tiny minority of Muslims, despite its ability to call on the loyalty of co-religionists – and a movement such as Hamas which has a limited territorial motivation, the desire to displace an occupying power.[31] Counter-terrorism has validity as a practical response to crisis, but it is not an intellectual discipline like political science or cultural anthropology that insists on scrupulous examination of sources, cross-checking of evidence from different viewpoints, and correction for observer bias.

An alternative 'etic' explanation may be proposed to the pyramid model. The Palestinian zakat committee is an instance of a deeply embedded 'civil society institution' that had been operating unobtrusively for centuries across the Muslim world. The principle of zakat is one on whose importance all Islamic apologists of whatever political complexion have agreed. Hamas was founded in 1987–8 as a successor to the Muslim Brotherhood's Palestinian branch, which was founded in Jerusalem in 1946, two years before the establishment of the State of Israel. The Muslim Brotherhood itself, the matrix of Sunni political Islam in the Middle East, had been founded in Egypt in 1928 and has splintered into numerous national movements varying greatly in their degree of radicalism, degree of nationalism and degree of commitment to violence – contrary to the view of some American counter-terrorist groups that it is an integrated Islamist International. In Jordan, which has close ties with Palestine, the Muslim Brothers constitute a kind of 'loyal opposition' to the Hashemite monarchy. The rise of the Muslim Brotherhood must be seen historically as part of a wider Islamic resurgence with counterparts in the Indian subcontinent, parts of South East Asia and elsewhere.

Hamas viewed the defeat of the Arabs at the hands of the Israeli army in 1967 as a punishment for bad Muslims. The success of the Israeli state in imposing its will was seen by Hamas as an achievement of the Jewish faith (whereas in historical fact Zionism was more of a secular–ethnic than a religious movement and Israeli politics in the 1950s and 1960s were much less influenced by the religious parties than today). Hamas's response to the Zionist claim to biblical lands was a new claim, that the whole of Palestine was *waqf*, inalienable till the end of days. 'Since Palestine can only be recovered as an Islamic state by Muslims who have returned to their religion', wrote the political scientist Beverley Milton-Edwards in 1996, analyzing the Hamas view, 'the secular-nationalist approach is doomed to failure. Hamas, then, is concerned with individuals, re-educating them, encouraging them back to

Islam and using the individual as a starting-point for the re-Islamisation of society'
(Milton-Edwards 1996: 184).

This re-Islamization included attracting people back to the mosques, the encouragement of Islamic dress and morals and praying and fasting, the banning of cin-
emas. Hamas has worked particularly hard to re-Islamize the youth of Palestine. But
the programme also included almsgiving and here it was possible for those who
sympathized with re-Islamization to engage with established institutions – such
as the Nablus zakat committee, registered in 1977, or the older Hebron Charitable
Association – and with new committees founded since 1988. It is possible for a
Palestinian 'Islamist' to support re-Islamization as a religious principle without being
a member of Hamas or supporting its paramilitary activities. Re-Islamization has
also harmonized with the practice and motivation of traditional observant Muslims
uninterested in politics, a coalescence documented in the wider Middle East context
by Gilles Kepel (Kepel 2002).

It would thus appear that the zakat committees provided a meeting point
between the new-style Islamism and the old-style Muslim piety. Hence it was not
necessary, to achieve its objective of stimulating a vigorous Islamic welfare sector,
for Hamas to establish control over the zakat committees. The re-Islamization policy has led to the translation of Islamic principles and values into effective charitable
relief and welfare.[32] As we have seen, the evidence suggests that the zakat committees have operated strictly according to Palestinian law, and have earned considerable popular trust. The Palestinian Authority (dominated by Hamas's rival party,
Fatah, and widely considered to be corrupt, at least before 2005–7) and the Israeli
state have both viewed these committees with suspicion, sometimes detaining committee members, confiscating documents or closing offices; but, on the whole, the
committees were until 2007 allowed to operate and to receive and disburse funds,
even though Israel has complete control over financial flows into the Palestinian
Territories through the banking system. Only relatively recently, in 2002, did the
Israeli state declare the Nablus zakat committee and some thirty others to be illegal,
but inward funds continued to flow.[33] All actions taken against the zakat committees
by the Israeli authorities have apparently been authorized by administrative military
order, not through the Israeli courts – presumably because these courts, being independent, would require more solid evidence of irregularities before condemning the
committees.

No doubt the aspect of Hamas's activities that has made it so hated in Israel
and the United States is the policy of organizing suicide-bomb attacks ('martyrdom operations'). Most commentators in the West regard these as inexcusable and
are particularly shocked by Hamas's unashamed deployment of religious symbolism to glorify indiscriminate killing. However, several opinion polls conducted in
the Palestinian Territories between 2002 and 2005 show that the proportion of
Palestinians endorsing suicide attacks against Israeli civilians has varied between 61
and 81 per cent (Tamimi 2007: 161–5) and even if this were to be scaled down very

substantially to allow for bias or error[34] it would still amount to a disturbing proportion.[35] The Israeli and US governments have set out to characterize Hamas as a
conspiracy to radicalize the Palestinian population, a conspiracy to be unveiled and
opposed as part of the 'global war on terror'. It is surely more historically objective to
see Hamas as one party in a bitter, long-running territorial conflict where no side has
a monopoly of righteousness.[36] The leader of one of the main Christian denominations in Jerusalem, Monsignor Michel Sabbagh, recognized this when he called in
2006 for Israel and the West to resume negotiations with Hamas (*Le Monde* 2006),
as have many commentators and political figures since then, including ex-president
Jimmy Carter.

It would be surprising if examples of clientelism and patronage were not to be
identified in the operations of the zakat committees, because these are survival
mechanisms in a society such as Palestine where the state is so weak as to be practically non-existent. As Emanuel Schaeublin has observed, '[t]he Islamists have been
successful in creating a solid and widespread base of support because they were able
both to enlarge the notion of the patronage system – the uniting factor being Islam
and a political ideology.'[37] One reason why Islamism has gained support among professionals such as lawyers, doctors and engineers in the Middle East is that they see
it as offering alternatives to kin-based social structures. A further strand in political
support for Islamism is the adherence of former communists and socialists, since
these secular political theories have found little resonance with the Arab populace.

The 'pyramid' model strips Palestinian Islamic institutions both of their geopolitical context – a military occupation widely considered to be illegal – and of their
religio-political context, the resurgence of Islamist movements in many parts of the
world that gathered force over the past thirty years. Our alternative etic model allows
the Palestinian zakat committees to be seen in a different light, as local instances
of a worldwide trend, the growth of Islamic NGOs, which are themselves a special
case of Faith Based Organizations – but within the unique historical context of the
Israel–Palestine conflict.

Zakat committees as Faith Based Organizations

Beginning towards the end of what we have called the second phase of development of the Palestinian zakat committees (1968–94), and continuing during the
third phase (1994 to the present day), they began to tap into the international aid
system.[38]

The Nablus zakat committee, to take our case study again, adapted its procedures to enter into substantial contracts to supply long-life milk from its dairy to
American Near East Refugee Aid and the World Food Programme, for distribution to Palestinians in need. The zakat committees also received donations from the
international Islamic aid agencies that began to be founded from the 1980s onwards
and are now established in most countries where there are either Muslim donors or

Muslim beneficiaries or both. In Britain particularly, thanks to a sympathetic environment for Muslim charities fostered by the UK Charity Commission, some major NGOs such as Islamic Relief Worldwide and Muslim Aid have emerged.[39] These have followed in the footsteps of Christian agencies such as Christian Aid and the Catholic Fund for Overseas Development (CAFOD, the English branch of Caritas Internationalis) by renouncing all proselytism[40] and embracing international codes of conduct such as the commitment to non-discrimination and transparency. They are beginning to project a public image of Islam that contradicts widely held negative stereotypes, even to offer implicitly in their new bureaucracies an alternative focus of authority for Muslims to traditional religious hierarchies based on the mosque.

The process of integration of Islamic charities into the international aid system has been intermittent rather than following a uniform path. Some large Saudi-based charities may be thought of as constituting a kind of parallel aid system that has relatively few connections with their Western counterparts, and reliable information about their programmes is hard to obtain. However, in Europe and particularly in Britain the process is unmistakeable. With so many humanitarian crises afflicting Muslims in many countries, fundraising is energetically pursued by European Islamic charities, and the sufferings of the Palestinian people inevitably become a priority because of the consistently high media profile of the Israeli–Palestinian conflict.

The impasse for Palestinian Islamic charities in its geopolitical context

The development of Islamic aid agencies in the USA, by contrast, came to a halt after 11 September 2001, when they immediately became major suspects in the 'global war on terror'. Though there were almost certainly some real abuses in the past of the privileges of Islamic charities[41] – in which respect they are not unique, for the whole charitable sector is always vulnerable to abuse, resting as it does on the principle of trust – political pressures have in my view resulted in a serious overreaction against these charities (Benthall 2007a; 2007b). The Palestinian zakat committees were beginning to benefit from the encouragement given everywhere by international aid agencies since the 1990s to 'civil society institutions' and grass-roots organizations. Further evidence of their credibility as charities is the fact that a number of them were successful in securing financial support from major international agencies – such as USAID (the US governmental aid agency) and the large aid organization CARE – that impose demanding procedures for access to funds and evaluation of performance. In 2003, FAO (the Food and Agriculture Organization of the UN) reported that 'the Islamic social welfare organizations (including Zakat committees) were collectively the largest food donor in the occupied Palestinian territories after UNRWA [the UN Relief and Works Association]'.[42] At about the same time, the International Crisis Group estimated that the Islamic organizations were providing, directly or indirectly, emergency cash/food assistance and medical and psycho-logical care to at least one out of six Palestinians (ICG 2003: ii).

Since 2001, the zakat committees and their Muslim donors in the USA and some other countries have been exposed to considerable obstacles, for reasons we have examined. Muslim donors to these Palestinian charities have been prosecuted. And yet, in 2002, memoranda from the US Embassy in Tel Aviv to USAID stated that it held 'no derogatory information' about the zakat committees in Jenin and Tulkarem,[43] whereas for a Muslim donor to have sent funds to these West Bank com-mittees is now held by US government prosecutors to be a serious criminal offence.

We may note in passing that the Jewish National Fund, describing itself as 'the caretaker of the land of Israel, on behalf of its owners – Jewish people everywhere', encounters no legal obstacle in the USA when it raises tax-exempt funds for improve-ments to military installations in Israel.[44] The Palestinian zakat committees, by con-trast, have never been accused of overtly spending funds on military projects, yet its American donors are charged with giving material support to terrorism when they remit funds that are demonstrably applied to support clinics, food aid and the like.

This is not the place for a general discussion of the Israel–Palestine conflict. I share the widespread view that it is a tragedy in the strict Hegelian sense, that is to say a collision of two rights. But some thoughts on how aid and charitable giving fit into the conflictual relations may be permitted.

The Palestinian resistance too readily equates Zionists, Israelis and Jews as if they all meant the same: hence the notoriously anti-Jewish passages in the Hamas char-ter.[45] Whereas Israel is supported by the global Jewish diaspora, the Palestinians are to some extent supported by the Muslim *umma*, or community of believers. However, so deep are the political and sectarian divisions within the Muslim world that the *umma* has hitherto been more a rhetorical trope than a practical resource for resolving the Palestinians' dilemma.

Hamas's philosophy is that on the long time scale of Islamic history it can afford to ride out short-term setbacks. Some leaders of Palestinian civil society advocate the non-violent or Gandhian option, which might have a valid future if it were adopted as a mass movement, but which has so far attracted scant support from poli-ticians. Religion is one of their few remaining trump cards. This includes both the Hamas claim that the whole of Palestine is *waqf*, and a devout hope that justice for Palestinians will eventually be granted. But the religious commitment also includes zakat, which, if it were seriously implemented on a large scale, could not only give new impetus to desperately needed humanitarian relief aid, but also help regenerate the Palestinian economy. It offers a practical contribution towards reconstruction in Palestine, which must be a prerequisite for a lasting peace with Israel. Indeed, as one of the cornerstones of Islam, the principle of zakat has a reach that extends far beyond the specifics of Israeli–Palestinian politics, having the potential to effect a significant redistribution of resources within the entire Muslim world.

The campaign mounted by the Israeli and United States governments against Palestinian zakat committees and their donors resident in the West has the defensible aim of preventing terrorism, but it is a campaign that can be criticized as both conceptually questionable and practically ineffective. Such criticism should not be directed at these governments as unitary entities, for divergent views are no doubt expressed and ventilated among government officials. Nor should we necessarily infer any lack of sincerity or integrity on the part of those individuals who conduct the campaign. However, from an outside point of view it can seem like an attempt to neutralize the potential of zakat. In the eyes of many thoughtful Muslims, the campaign gives an impression, accurately or not, that these governments want to monopolize humanitarian action as a political tool to serve their own interests. The US government proclaims its wish to enter dialogue with and to encourage moderate, modernizing influences within the Islamic world, but when it is faced with a practical, internally generated modernizing movement – the development of a transnational Islamic charity sector in harmony with international humanitarian norms – the response seems to be an unfortunate one, with implications that are probably not fully intended: a decision to block and criminalize. Yet if we analyze the evolution of zakat committees as a special case of Faith Based Organizations, it may be possible to identify a substantial ongoing change that will affect the entire Muslim world. It is, after all, part of the genius of all the great religions that they are capable of quite rapid change, while maintaining the appearance of immobility.

Notes

1 I visited Jerusalem, the West Bank (including Nablus) and Gaza personally in 1996, and Jerusalem in 1999. As well as published sources, I have also used in this article information gathered in the course of giving advice on Islamic charities to the Swiss Federal Department of Foreign Affairs, Bern, since 2005 – on the 'Montreux Initiative' – and to a number of legal teams, in the USA and Europe, since 2006. This has included participation in meetings of experts in Britain, Switzerland, Belgium and Qatar. I am grateful to all the members of the Montreux Initiative core team; also specially to Mr Waleed al-Salhi, an experienced Palestinian NGO manager originally from Nablus and now resident in London, for valuable information on the history of the Palestinian zakat committees since 1967 that he has collected and to Sheila Carapico, Emanuel Schaeublin, Natalie Schweizer and Haim Malka for helpful comments on drafts.
2 Technically, the Hebron Charitable Association is not a zakat committee, but a society formed in 1962 under an Ottoman law of 1909. There are a number of similar Islamic charitable associations in the West Bank which are regulated by the Palestinian Authority, but not (unlike the zakat committees) under the Ministry of Awqaf. Except for this technical difference in regulation and monitoring, the issues raised by the charitable associations are similar to those raised by the zakat committees. They are treated as one broad category in this article.
3 At the time of writing, the Palestinian Authority had had to surrender control of Gaza to rule by Hamas.

4 The 'pyramid model' is a descriptive name chosen for the present article, not a term used by Matthew Levitt himself.

5 Transcript of Trial, US District Court, Northern District of Texas, Dallas Division, *USA* v. *Holy Land Foundation et al.* (no. 3: 04-24-G), 25 July 2007, evidence of Matthew Levitt, 09:49.

6 The neologisms 'emic' and 'etic' derive from an analogy with the terms 'phonemic' and 'phonetic'. The emic perspective focuses on the intrinsic cultural distinctions that are meaningful to the members of a given society, in the same way as phonemic analysis focuses on the intrinsic phonological distinctions that are meaningful to speakers of a given language (e.g. whether the 'glottal stop' is recognized as an alphabetical letter). The etic perspective relies on extrinsic concepts and categories that have meaning for analytic observers, in the same way as phonetic analysis relies on the extrinsic concepts and categories that are meaningful to linguistic analysts (e.g. dental fricatives). ' "Emic knowledge is essential for an intuitive and empathic understanding of a culture, and is essential for conducting effective ethnographic fieldwork … Etic knowledge, on the other hand, is essential for cross-cultural comparison.' (Letts 1996: 383).

7 The site was evacuated and subsequently vandalized in 2000.

8 The institution of *waqf*, though not Qur'anic, dates back to the foundation of Islam and became widespread over most of the Islamic world. Setting aside some legal technicalities, it is similar to the European charitable trust. On *waqf*, see Benthall and Bellion-Jourdan 2003: 29–37.

9 Christian as well as Muslim.

10 This does not apply in East Jerusalem, where the Ministry of Awqaf, including control of the holy sites, is still under Jordanian control.

11 Jordanian law on zakat, *Zakat Fund Law and the Administrative Financial Instructions Issued According Thereto*, 1988; PNA, Office of the President, *Regulation No. (1) for the Year 2000 Regarding Charitable Societies and National Institutions*.

12 Documents show that, in 2004, Caritas, the international Roman Catholic aid agency, accepted food aid for kindergarten schools in Jericho, supplied by the Nablus zakat committee's dairy company, Al-Safa, with funds provided by the German government. In 2005, the Saint Nicolas Home for the Elderly (Orthodox) in the Bethlehem area cooperated in the Palestine with Milk project launched by Al-Safa; likewise the SOS Children's Village, Bethlehem, the Arab Evangelical Home and School, Hebron, and the Crèche de la Sainte Famille, Bethlehem. Funds for the 2005 project appear to have been provided by the Islamic Bank in Jeddah.

13 A related word, *istishhādī*, is used specifically for suicide bombers. [*Or, perhaps more precisely, at least in Palestinian usage, for any fighter who carries out an operation regardless of his or her safety. March 2015.*]

14 It is true that the families of suicide bombers and other deceased militants have a special status in Palestinian society. But, according to my information, Hamas has its own funds, mainly based on subscriptions from members, to help support the families of suicide bombers – not through charities. In addition, the Shahid Fund was set up by the PNA in 1994. Apparently, Arafat agreed to this fund being used to support the families of suicide bombers, even when the latter were Hamas members. There has hence, it would seem, been no need for the zakat charities to give special support to these families.

15 This is the author's opinion. It is based on: 1. an evaluation of Israeli intelligence websites such as www.terrorism-info.org.il (e.g. Special Information Bulletin, Intelligence and Terrorism Information Center, Center for Special Studies, January 2005). It is significant that despite being able to draw on Israeli intelligence findings of this kind, the Board of Deputies of British Jews was unable to defend the defamation case brought against it in 2005 by the British charity Interpal (see n. 41 below);2. some of the 'raw material' for these websites, in the form of Israeli

intelligence officers' reports, made available to me on a confidential basis in legal proceedings. There is no pretence made in these documents of assessing the available evidence in an equitable manner. Much of it is based on alleged personal associations.

16 *USA* v. *Holy Land Foundation* (see n. 2 above), Superseding Indictment, para. 3.

17 This is not to support the naive view that charitable activities inhabit a political vacuum. For comments on the political dimension of all humanitarian aid, with special reference to tensions between Islam and the West, see Benthall and Bellion-Jourdan 2003: 153–6.

18 *USA* v. *Holy Land Foundation*, Evidence of Matthew Levitt, 4: 51.

19 *USA* v. *Holy Land Foundation*, Superseding Indictment, para. 4. This argument was legally weakened by the decision of a Federal Appeal Court in the 'David Boim case' (*Stanley Boim et al.* v. *Holy Land Foundation et al.*, US Court of Appeals for the Seventh Circuit, decision of 28 December 2007). However, according to recent reports, the Seventh Circuit Court of Appeals has decided to overturn the appeal verdict and rehear the whole case en banc, that is to say with all eleven active judges sitting. *[See Chapter 6 for the result of the en banc hearing.]*

20 The interview was conducted in Arabic with the help of Mr Riyad Mustafa as translator and research assistant. [...] here indicates omissions from the original field notes.

21 It is logically impossible to completely disprove any conspiratorial theory, because its adherents are able to argue that all evidence against it is mendacious or otherwise flawed. One can only set out to advance an alternative theory, accepting that if new, clinching evidence in favour of the conspiratorial theory were to come to light, one would change one's mind.

22 The International Crisis Group's reputation and authority are in general very high. In particular we may note here the thoroughness of its field research.

23 Information supplied by the committee.

24 It should be noted here that the late Sheikh Yassin is considered a national Palestinian figure as well as the Hamas spiritual leader, and his photograph is to be found in many houses, shops, etc., not necessarily owned by Hamas supporters. Over 100,000 people attended his funeral in Gaza ('Israel vows to hit Hamas again', BBC News, 23 March 2004).

25 The CPRS, an independent research institution, estimated the mean level of support among the Palestinian public for Hamas during 1993 to 1997 as 18 per cent, which Hamas said was too low. Hamas has claimed up to 50 or 60 per cent. Khaled Hroub gave a personal estimate of 30 per cent in 2000 (Hroub 2000: 231–2). At the time of writing, June 2008, Fatah was leading Hamas in a public opinion poll in the Territories as a whole, after declaring that it wanted to reopen negotiations with Hamas (52 per cent for Abbas [Fatah], 40 per cent for Haniyeh [Hamas], in the event that a presidential election was called – compared to 47 per cent for Haniyeh and 46 per cent for Abbas in March – 'Abbas overtakes Haniyeh in Palestinian survey', Reuters US edition, 9 June 2008. According to a number of reports, Hamas was still more popular than Fatah in Gaza.)

26 Two recently published articles relating to Hamas and social welfare are consistent with the argument presented here. Haim Malka argues that social welfare has been a vital component in Hamas's overall strategy, offering a favourable ratio of reward to risk, and he does not explicitly criticize the Matthew Levitt model (Malka 2007). He writes however: 'Ideological affinity plays a more crucial role in mobilizing Hamas's network than does formal political affiliation' (p. 105). 'Although these institutions [the zakat committees and similar charities] may not be officially linked, Islamic charities work towards the same goal within a similar religious and political context. [...] Although Hamas does not have any visible centralized organizing body for charity organizations affiliated with the movement, these numerous educational institutions, *zakat* committees, and clinics share the same worldview and identify

with Hamas's broad concept of creating a religiously observant and strong Muslim society' (p. 107). 'Whether Hamas extends aid as a quid pro quo for political support is debatable. *Zakat* committees in general claim to distribute aid in a non-partisan fashion based on specific criteria. Beneficiaries are generally required to fill out forms and a questionnaire and accept a home visit to determine eligibility. Yet it is difficult to imagine a totally fair method of distribution in a system where family and clan loyalties are so important and religious-political divisions so deep' (p. 109). (We may note that this last is a problem faced by 'Western' NGOs as well, and many NGOs appear to have close informal links with Fatah politicians.) Malka's article has the merit of being even-handed in intent, but is not explicit on its sources of oral or unpublished information. I understand, however, that his article is based on many years' field experience as a reporter and researcher in Jerusalem and the Palestinian Territories (personal communication). Lars Gunnar Lundblad has made five field visits to the West Bank between 1999 and 2007 (Lundblad 2008) and interviewed a wide variety of informants. Though he does not discount the possibility that some of the allegations of political favouritism made against the zakat committees are justified, he is impressed by the level of legitimacy and trust achieved by them and concludes 'The stereotypical image of Islamic activism as a cover for terrorism needs to be redressed' (p. 198). Lundblad makes an original contribution in noting how these zakat committees have only limited relations with the extensive NGO networks in the Palestinian Territories. [*See also Lundblad 2011.*]

27 Birzeit University Development Studies Program 2004, pp. 104–5 (http://birzeit.edu/cds). I have here consolidated and averaged the percentage findings of two polls, no. 1 (August to September 2000) and no. 17 (June 2004). Allowance has been made for obvious misprints in the published tables. Confidence in the zakat committees was apparently rather higher in Gaza than in the West Bank but the difference is not great enough to affect the ordering. An analysis of the raw data may be found on the same website under 'Opinion Polls'. They are based on a sample size of 1,256 in 2000, 1,197 in 2004, and seventy sample locations in 2000, seventy-five in 2004. Eighty-five researchers were engaged for the 2004 poll. A margin of error of +/– 3% is suggested. [*I subsequently discovered an earlier report as to the degree of confidence felt in various types of institution in the Palestinian Territories, published by the Human Development Programme, Birzeit University, in April 2000, in association with the UN Development Programme and the Palestinian Ministry of Planning and International Cooperation's Department of Human Development and Institution Building. Whereas the Palestinian universities scored the highest confidence rating (67 per cent), zakat committees scored 57 per cent, well above 34 per cent for professional and trade unions and 24 per cent for the political opposition (Palestine Human Development Project, 1998–9). These findings are roughly in line with those of the two later surveys.*]

28 Abdul Rahman 2008a; 2008b. Professor Abdul Rahman is executive chairman of the Palestine International Institute, based in Amman and Ramallah.

29 Confidential report from a British consultancy team. For further comments on Algerian civil society, see Benthall and Bellion-Jourdan 2003: 92–8.

30 See the official US government report *Monograph on Terrorist Financing: Staff Report to the National Commission on Terrorist Attacks upon the United States* ('Staff Monograph' 2004: 9–10).

31 This view is not uncontested (e.g. 'Chapter 8: Will Hamas Target the West?', Levitt 2006: 203–28). However, Hamas has consistently disavowed any intention to spread its cause beyond the boundaries of Palestine. There is certainly a danger of 'al-qaidization' of the conflict if the political situation deteriorates further.

32 This point is well made by Malka 2007.

33 At the time of writing, it is reported that President Mahmoud Abbas has decided to clamp down on charitable associations in the West Bank seen as Hamas-affiliated (Barthe 2007). The Hebron Islamic Charitable Association has been closed down and its assets confiscated by the Israeli military (Levy 2008). A number of external donors have withheld funds, pending clarification of the new legal and administrative arrangements.

34 The polls referred to were conducted by the Norwegian organization Fafo, the (Israeli) *Jerusalem Post*, and the Palestinian Authority's State Information Service.

35 Defenders of these attacks argue that they began in revenge for the massacre of worshippers in February 1994 by Baruch Goldstein in the Al-Haram Al-Ibrahimi mosque, Hebron; and that the 'martyrs' deserve respect for their sacrifice, whereas Israelis who kill Palestinians do so at little risk to themselves owing to their advanced military technology. Islamic scholars are divided as to the admissibility of suicide attacks in Palestine, but perhaps the most prominent and influential of them in the Middle East, Sheikh Yusuf al-Qaradawi, has defended them. *[See Chapter 16.]* For further analysis of the Hamas position, see Tamimi 2007: 180–6.

36 For an overview of the historical context of different forms of 'terrorism', see Chaliand and Blin 2004.

37 Personal communication, January 2008.

38 To look further back in history, both Jewish and Christian Arab communities in Palestine have been receiving external aid for hundreds of years.

39 The cause célèbre of Interpal is more complex. This British Islamic charity, founded in 1994 to help Palestinians and widely supported by British Muslims, has been designated by the US government as an alleged terrorist entity. The UK Charity Commission has cleared it twice of malpractice, but after a BBC television programme screened in the summer of 2006 it decided to investigate it for a third time, an investigation which has not been concluded as this paper is completed in July 2008. In 2005, Interpal's trustees obtained a public apology and financial compensation from the Board of Deputies of British Jews, which had accused it of sponsoring terrorism. *[For more recent details of Interpal's position, see pp. 7 and 94.]* Much has been made, in the criticism of Interpal, of its links with the Union of Good (I'tilaf al-Khair), an umbrella organization of some fifty Islamic charities, based both in the Middle East and in Europe, committed to aiding Palestinians in need, particularly through the zakat committees. The Union of Good's use of a map of an undivided Palestine in its publicity, and the leadership exercised within it by the controversial Sheikh al-Qaradawi (see n. 35 above), are among the reasons for its being accused of being a front for Hamas. However, it appears to operate openly, rather than conspiratorially, and to confine itself to humanitarian aid (Source: twenty-page report in Arabic for 2004–5, with list of members). Recently, it has extended its work from merely fundraising to training and institutional capacity building. In July 2008, the Israeli government declared that all members of the Union of Good are prohibited in Israel (Weiss 2008). The Union of Good has an Arabic-language website: www.101days.org. Leaving aside the heated rhetoric on both sides of the dispute, the key question remains the one addressed in the present paper: whether or not the zakat committees are legitimate charities implementing policies based on needs.

40 This is not necessarily the case for many of the Islamic charities based in the petrodollar states, which combine religious and humanitarian aims (as do many important Christian NGOs).

41 For instance, the use of charities to send arms to the mujahideen in Afghanistan during the 1980s. It has also been alleged that some Islamic charities were made use of to remit funds to make possible the 11 September 2001 attack on the United States, though this has never been proved.

42 FAO Report of the Food Security Assessment, West Bank and Gaza Strip, Rome 2003 (USAID document 002483). UNRWA is mandated to assist only registered Palestinian refugees.

43 Interoffice memoranda on 'trace requests', 24 June 2002 (relating to Jenin) and 19 November 2002 (relating to Jenin).

44 The aim is to improve living conditions for young military recruits. Source: www.jnf.org, 9 September 2007.

45 The Hamas charter and other key documents are reproduced in full in English translation in Hroub 2000. Apologists for Hamas argue that the charter has little practical relevance today and that the movement is opposed to the Jewish state, not to Jews as such. Yet it is clear that traditional Middle Eastern anti-Jewish sentiment has combined with European anti-Jewish sentiment and anti-Zionist politics to form a new, toxic mixture.

5

The Islamic Charities Project (formerly Montreux Initiative)

This personal account of the Swiss government funded mediation or conflict resolution project (2005–13) was first published in *Gulf Charities* and *Islamic Philanthropy in the 'Age of Terror' and Beyond,* edited by Robert Lacey and myself (Gerlach Press, 2014).

Special attention is given here to the Gulf-based charities. One of the reasons why the effort to persuade them to submit to Western-style transparency and regulation proved so difficult to follow through is that, according to Islamic tradition, charitable alms are best given discreetly. Moreover, the idea of transparency is somewhat alien to these cultures. But, in any case, it turned out that there was no willing interlocutor with whom conflict resolution could take place.

In the event that renewed efforts are made in future – as they surely will be – to reach a better understanding between Islamic humanitarianism and the international aid system, it could be recalled that the doctrine of *hisbah* or accountability is well established in Islamic tradition.

***

The proposal arose in the framework of a decision by the Swiss Federal Department of Foreign Affairs (FDFA), Political Division IV (PD IV) in 2004 to 'make "religio-political conflicts" a new sector of activity of its peace promotion activities; in other words conflicts where the mix of religious and political factors is a determining factor. In this sphere of activity there is a special, albeit not exclusive, emphasis on Islam and the Middle East'. FDFA/PD IV's overall mission is promoting peace and security. Already in 2003–4 it was engaged in various confidence-building endeavours. An important aspect of this approach was to foster communication not only with Muslims already sympathetic to Western values and institutions, but also with those less favourably disposed.

At about this time, the President of Islamic Relief Worldwide, based in Birmingham, England, Dr Hany El-Banna, was circulating an open letter. This drew attention to the serious difficulties being experienced by bona fide Islamic charities since 9/11, especially the apparently draconian blacklisting of charities by the US government and other authorities, without realistic rights of defence or appeal. The overreaction against Islamic charities had, he argued, a number of adverse effects: blockages in the flow of aid to beneficiaries; a reduction in donations; recourse by donors to transactions outside the purview of banking regulators; suspicions directed against bona fide charities; aggravated pressure on the resources of the few Islamic charities still able to operate normally; and disruption to local economies, resulting in scapegoating of local staff. The solution, he wrote, was effective regulation and monitoring.

Feasibility study

In January 2005, FDFA commissioned me to write an external feasibility study for a new initiative, which was circulated. The study, 'Towards cooperation in removing unjustified obstacles from Islamic charities', envisaged a pilot process of confidence building, in addition to the specific objective aimed at. The study began by distinguishing the various types of contemporary Islamic charities, and went on to argue that the immemorial Islamic tradition of charitable giving was having difficulty in expressing itself amid a growing climate of mistrust between Islam and the so-called West. Among the many institutions and individuals working to alleviate these tensions were Islamic charities, which, in addition to their concrete help to victims of disaster and the disadvantaged, had a vital contribution to make in reinforcing civil society in the Muslim world. Their relations with the non-Muslim world had already been problematic well before 9/11 (and there had also been tensions between Islamic charities of different persuasions and national origins), but the difficulties thereafter became much more severe, particularly with the freezing of the accounts of some large US Muslim charities and the blacklisting of many others. It was undeniable that in the past there had been some abuse of the privileges of charities. The study outlined some of the steps taken by the US government, the UN Security Council, and the Financial Action Task Force (FATF) to counter such abuses. A number of observers were coming to see these steps as a damaging overreaction.

In Britain, the Charity Commission had taken effective action against some radical mosques, but in no case had it discovered any other major abuses of Islamic charities. The feasibility study included as an annex some detailed information on the case of Interpal, a medium-sized British Islamic charity set up to help Palestinians, that had been blacklisted by the US Treasury as an alleged financial support for Hamas, but twice cleared of any wrongdoing by the UK Charity Commission.

Concern about the negative effects of counter-terrorism measures on bona fide charities was shared by some of the non-Muslim mainstream charities and their consortium groups. However, tensions between the 'West' and the Muslim world were particularly strained. It was recalled that freedom 'to establish and maintain appropriate charitable or humanitarian institutions' is acknowledged as part of the 'right to freedom of thought, conscience, religion or belief' recognized by the UN General Assembly in 1981 (Declaration on the Elimination of All Forms of Intolerance and Discrimination Based on Religion or Belief, Article 6).

The study went on to outline the various kinds of regulatory and monitoring systems that obtain in different jurisdictions (there being no international harmonization of charity law), and argued that the Charity Commission of England and Wales was generally considered to be one of the most effective. In particular, their policy in dealing with a difficult case was not to close down a charity except as a last resort, but rather to identify trustees who were committed to using its resources properly and then to have objectionable trustees removed: the guiding consideration was to ensure that charitable assets were used for the purposes for which they had been donated.

The issue was not, the study argued, one purely of adherence to the minimum of charity law. Standards of international aid had been emerging – articulated in such texts as the 'Code of Conduct for The International Red Cross and Red Crescent Movement and NGOs in Disaster Relief' – which insisted in particular on principles of non-discrimination and there were increasing demands for transparency, accountability, and good governance, to which the international NGO community as a whole was responding positively. These principles had been adopted by some Islamic charities, though not yet by all, and there did seem to be a trend in that direction. Though Islamic charities were often seen from the 'West' as unhealthily politicized, Western NGOs were reciprocally criticized in the Muslim world for allegedly representing the interests of powerful states.

It was then argued that, in the light of various other initiatives in recent years, an intervention by the Swiss government would be timely and appreciated, and would not duplicate any other programmes. Furthermore, in view of the controversial nature of the theme – aggravated by the US government's refusal to make a distinction between international Al-Qaeda style extremism and nationalist opposition movements in the Middle East – publicity would be best avoided, at least for the time being. The Swiss government, with its long tradition of neutrality and support for humanitarianism, was as well suited as any government to initiate such a programme.

There followed a section on the choice of prospective participants in such an initiative. A two track approach was proposed: (1) public, involving 'opinion formers', and (2) low key and private, with a view to feeding into the public track. 'If it turns out that the "private" track fails owing to intransigence on the part of some organizations, the "public" track would still have validity.' The main upshot of preliminary meetings (held in May 2005 in Lausanne and Geneva) was that the objective should not be merely more dialogue, but a practical proposal for removing the obstacles. At all times the principle was observed that this would be a joint project with equal participation from Muslim and non-Muslim experts, even though the facilitation and secretariat were Swiss.

Concepts and implementation

The output of these deliberations was a concept paper, which provided an agenda for the first meeting of the 'core group'. This outlined the context of the project, referring back to the Feasibility Study, and formulated the Aims as follows:

> The immediate aims of the project, devised in consultation with a wide range of interested parties, are:
>
> 1. to articulate criteria for the delisting or admissibility of *bona fide* Islamic relief and development charities in order to enable them to operate normally in a way that has often not been possible because of the blacklisting or 'designation' of many Islamic charities by the UN Sanctions Committee and by the United States Government as a reaction to the 9/11 attacks; and
> 2. to articulate policy recommendations to governmental regulatory authorities with regard to Islamic and other faith-based charities;
> 3. to circulate the above with a view to achieving a practical impact.
>
> It is *not* the aim of the project to secure the delisting of any specific existing organization, but rather to articulate criteria and principles for the future.
>
> A consequent longer-term aim for follow-up initiatives, if the above aims are realized, is:
>
> 4. to build confidence with a view to facilitating exchange and cooperation focused on 'good practice', capacity building and the potential for partnership arrangements.

A two-day residential workshop was held in Switzerland in June 2005. The immediate aim of the workshop was to make recommendations that could then be referred back for confirmation to the various organizations and constituencies involved. 'Chatham House rules' were observed. The focus was, for the time being, on the Arab–Muslim world. The guiding topics proposed were:

1. Suggested criteria for the *delisting or admissibility of a given charitable organization*, adoption of *explicit charitable objectives*; observing the principle of *public benefit* with no element of personal profit, except for the employment of paid staff where necessary; *accountability*; *transparency, non-discrimination*, i.e. allocating help to beneficiaries in a given territory on grounds of need rather than of religious or other identity.
2. Suggestions for government regulatory authorities with regard to Islamic and other faith-based charities.
3. Possible options for development of mechanisms for positive accreditation of Islamic charities that meet all the desired criteria: i.e. systematic procedures for admissibility rather than merely ad hoc de-listing.

It was expected that participants would agree on joint practical recommendations within the framework of the aforesaid aims. They would be asked after the workshop to go back to their constituencies and confirm their support for the conclusions reached. Further 'technical discussions' might be organized. Governments and intergovernmental organizations could then be approached and informed about the findings of the workshop. Further steps for confidence building and implementation would then be considered by the Department of Foreign Affairs, possibly in cooperation with other sponsors, if the initial results of the workshop were promising.

The Concept Paper ended with an Appendix on the principle of non-discrimination, which set out to explain, in essence, that this principle – namely, non-discrimination between beneficiaries in a given territorial area – is not breached either by a charity that concentrates its activities on regions inhabited by a large majority of co-religionists or by a charity that has mixed religious and humanitarian aims. It was, however, argued that 'there is a trend in the West, and increasingly elsewhere, for a distinction to be made between charities that further religious aims and charities engaged in relief and development'.

The project was named after the Swiss lakeside town where the first meeting was held. A decision was made to try to persuade Islamic charities that faced obstacles or potential obstacles to embark on a process of self-regulation, with a view to endorsement by an independent validating institution staffed by a small secretariat and headed by a group of eminent, internationally accepted personalities as trustees; and thus to provide evidence that these charities were compliant with international codes of accountability, transparency, and good governance. At the same time, recommendations were formulated to governments as to how Islamic charities should be treated fairly, on a par with all other charities. It was agreed that the Montreux Initiative should proceed on a low-key basis without media exposure. A core group was formed consisting of representatives of the FDFA and a number of experts with knowledge of humanitarian institutions, both Muslim and non-Muslim.

The group considered and rejected the option of merely agreeing to a general statement of internationally accepted codes of practice for NGOs, to be followed by lobbying, capacity building, and other activities. A decision was made that, if the new initiative were to succeed, especially in view of the need for short-term results, it must set a high bar of good practice for charities to reach. Otherwise there would be no chance of the processes being taken seriously by the US and other governments. The group agreed in draft to some detailed recommendations on 'international good practice and code of conduct' for charities, borrowed from existing US Treasury and FATF guidelines, with some minor changes.

At the end of 2005, some seventeen Islamic charities – from Europe, but also from the Gulf and other Middle Eastern countries – agreed in principle to the 'Montreux conclusions' at a meeting in Istanbul:

> Suggestions for governments with regard to charities, with special reference to Islamic charities

1. In the minority of cases where misuse is suspected, the emphasis in regulation of the non-profit sector should be on identifying individuals who are abusing the privileges of charities. It was noted that the UK Charity Commission: (i) emphasizes each charity as a resource fund and has powers to replace trustees and freeze accounts in order to preserve the integrity of the charitable fund, and (ii) regulates charities with a proportionate approach based on issues such as the size of the charity. This approach may have some advantages even under different jurisdictions.
2. The standard of proof against individuals or organizations suspected of malpractice should be as high as that required in a criminal trial.
3. When legal measures are taken to blacklist individuals or organizations, their rights of defence and appeal should be observed. Procedures should be accessible and timely. However, States must reserve the right to close down through legal process any organizations that are demonstrably engaged in serious malpractice.
4. In the event that a charity is closed in accordance with the last sentence of paragraph 3 above, its accounts should be transferred in a public and timely way to an organization with similar objectives.
5. The participants in the workshop emphasize the importance of national regulatory systems, which should be given due weight by international bodies and other governments.
6. Governments should allow charities to make use of the formal banking system. (There are examples of charities being refused access to the formal banking system even though they have not been blacklisted.)
7. Governments should influence intergovernmental organizations such as FATF along the lines suggested above.

General criteria for endorsement by Islamic charities – which should be treated no differently from other charities – to demonstrate to all interested parties their membership of the international community:

1. Compliance with local national definitions of charity;
2. Adherence to the principle of non-discrimination between beneficiaries, and a commitment to acting for the benefit of all humanity and to recognizing the dignity of all individuals;
3. A commitment to act lawfully in all aspects of their operations;
4. A commitment to transparency, accountability and other aspects of international good practice … The workshop reviewed a number of existing standard recommendations for 'good practice' and agreed that it is possible for Islamic charities to comply with the most exacting requirements for good practice. However, during the implementation of these codes of conduct by individual charities, there must be due recognition of cultural sensitivities and of pressures on organizational resources and capabilities;
5. A commitment to distinguish charitable activities from non-charitable activities.

International good practice, code of conduct and other recommendations for Islamic charities

The code proposes standards additional to local national legal standards. In the unlikely event of a conflict, the local legal requirement will take precedence.

There follow six pages of detailed prescriptions categorized as follows:

Governance: Governing instruments; Board of directors (or trustees);
Disclosure/transparency in governance and finances: Board of directors; Key
    employees;
Financial transparency: Budgets; Financial practice/accountability; Receipt
    and disbursement of funds; Reports; Bank accounts; Foreign recipients;
    Solicitations; Oversight and programme verification; Administration.

Among meetings attended over the next few months of 2005 was a major conference in London, organized by Islamic Relief with funding from the UK Foreign
and Commonwealth Office (FCO), with the title 'Humanitarian Forum: Building
Partnerships between Muslim NGOs and the International Community'. The
Montreux Initiative was explained to officials of the FCO (which at that time had
launched a programme called 'Engaging with the Islamic World'). It was subsequently agreed in principle that the FCO would co-sponsor the Montreux Initiative
until further notice.

During the summer, members of the core group made contact with Islamic charities in the Middle East including the Gulf in order to assess their willingness to
cooperate. A questionnaire form had been designed and circulated, and the results
were generally favourable.

A threefold structure for the inclusion of charities was proposed:

1. capacity building;
2. compliance with the Code of Conduct measured by an external assessment;
3. a supervisory board, consisting of eminent persons with access to technical
   experts on regulation and monitoring of charities, the whole to be coordinated
   by a secretary general.

Steps were taken to investigate the difficulties experienced by Saudi charities, in
particular, as a result of political pressures since 9/11. These included restrictions
on sending funds abroad and on fundraising, and some freezing of certain funds.
The Saudi government had announced in 2004 their intention to form a national
commission to oversee Saudi charities working abroad, but this commission had
not yet been formed (and has not been convened at the time of going to press
with this book [*Gulf Charities* and *Islamic Philanthropy in the 'Age of Terror' and
Beyond*]).

Priority themes for capacity building were suggested, as follows:

1. governance and accountability;
2. international NGO law and codes of practice;

3. transparency;
4. management techniques including new technology;
5. fundraising, consistent both with Montreux criteria and with local culture;
6. the full cycle of project management.

A process was established whereby a given charity might be granted Montreux certification:

1. setting up an internal structure within the organization;
2. review by consultants of existing work practices;
3. agreement of action plan;
4. establishing programme and action teams;
5. defining new work practices and implementing them;
6. awareness and training programmes;
7. internal audits on the new work practices;
8. pre-assessment by an independent monitoring group;
9. implementation of the changes if necessary;
10. a clear separation of formal assessment from the capacity building process;
11. certification awarded;
12. continuous assessment and follow-up.

A Technical Workshop was held in November 2005 in Istanbul. The participants, in addition to members of the core group, were representatives of the FDFA, the UK FCO, the UK Charity Commission, the INTRAC[1] consultancy team, and seventeen Islamic charities.

Members of the core group invited participants to review and ratify the Montreux Conclusions, so that the 'implementation phase' could proceed, since it appeared that the chances of removing the 'unjustified obstacles' facing Islamic charities by simple persuasion were poor. The best chance was to accept a rigorous discipline of compliance and self-regulation, followed at a later stage by lobbying and media coverage. There would be some inconvenience to smaller and informally managed charities, but there would be overall benefits to the sector as a whole at a time of crisis.

It was emphasized that all conclusions had been arrived at jointly and that the aim was to defend Islamic charities against unjustified attacks. The goals were tightly defined to maximize the chances of success. It was felt that a possible eventual outcome might be the facilitation of future cooperative partnerships, but this was not assumed as a condition for taking part.

The following pilot project was proposed:

Stage 1 – Design in the UK and Switzerland of a compliance self-assessment method and tool.

Stage 2 – Compliance self-assessment visit to four to six or more Islamic NGOs
   in three or more Middle East countries.
Stage 3 – Design of Capacity Building Training Programme, UK based.
Stage 4 – Training process – Middle East based, with five-day training periods.
Stage 5 – NGO implementation of the new procedures and governance changes.
Stage 6 – Self-assessment of success for each NGO by external consultants.
Stage 7 – Self-evaluation of overall process.

A supervisory board of trustees was proposed, consisting of eight to ten eminent persons, balanced between the relevant constituencies (that is, Islamic charities and their sponsors, and governments and inter-governmental organizations). Their task would be defined as confidence building, defending and promoting the Montreux Initiative, and supervising the Montreux process. The organization that they headed would employ a chief executive officer (CEO) and secretariat, whose responsibilities would be twofold: (1) a *capacity building unit* (based on the principles described above) and (2) an *assessment unit*.

It was proposed that the core group would be entrusted with the selection of the trustees, after consultations with all the charities present at Istanbul, and that the trustees would each be appointed for an initial three-year period. They would be unpaid, but their travel expenses would be reimbursed.

The external consultants would be required to have an appropriate mix of skills and experience – not merely knowledge of charities, but also knowledge of, for example, techniques of investigative enquiry. The funding for all elements was estimated at US$300,000 to US$600,000 per year. It was envisaged that this would be shared between Middle Eastern governments, Western governments and financial institutions (including Islamic and private Arab banks). The charities themselves should not pay for the assessment process.

It was stressed that the assessment process would be both *voluntary* and *confidential*. At the same time, it must be *objective*.[2] Assessors would have to be rigorously chosen for their professional competence and mindset. There would be a channel for complaints to be made to the CEO and trustees. The entire Montreux process itself would be evaluated annually by an external organization in order to satisfy the stakeholders that the assessment of charities was credible and objective.

A number of difficulties arose during the meeting, which may be summarized as follows:

1. Objections that Islamic charities were being singled out for special treatment, with the implication that they were deficient administratively and/or suspect as to their intentions. Members of the core group set out to explain that the only reason for singling out Islamic charities was that they were being exposed to unfair discrimination.

2. Suspicion that there was a 'hidden agenda' behind Montreux, i.e. a desire to extract information for purposes of control or intelligence gathering.
3. Scepticism as to the value of commitment to a process that, even if completed, did not offer any promise that it would mollify the US government. A strong argument in favour of this viewpoint was the case of Interpal (see above).The core group's response was that, if a charity passed the assessment process and was still blacklisted, a process of lobbying would be undertaken and this would be spearheaded by the trustees of the supervisory body.
4. At the more technical level, reluctance to accept some of the detailed provisions in the Montreux Conclusions. For instance, it was argued that the procedures for vetting 'foreign recipient charities' were too demanding. Regulation by the national government of a 'foreign recipient charity' should be enough, since a typical international charity had to deal with a large number of foreign organizations.
5. The possibility of ex-police investigators assessing charities did not appeal, despite the argument that this would strengthen the Montreux Initiative's credibility with the US and other authorities (again bearing in mind the need for an emergency response).
6. Confusion between Montreux and the Humanitarian Forum, which was a separate project which the Swiss government was also interested in supporting.

Despite these difficulties, the meeting eventually endorsed the proposals in principle, and encouraged the Core Group to proceed to the next stage, which would include setting up a legal structure for the Montreux Initiative, raising funds, and eventually appointing a CEO and trustees. Individual charities were invited to express their willingness to participate in the pilot phase and also to suggest possible trustees.

Subsequently, an aide-memoire was prepared for financial institutions that might be willing to be partners in the Montreux Initiative, for instance through co-sponsorship of meetings, publications, training courses and the like, through co-sponsorship of the Secretariat, or through secondment of individual experts to the project on a pro bono basis, especially those familiar with local conditions in the Arab–Islamic world.

Preliminary steps were taken to set up the new supervisory body on a reduced 'pilot' scale to begin with, and a 'compliance manual' was prepared for future use.

Political turbulence

After an intervening meeting in Doha, the Core Group, including a UK FCO representative, met in Montreux in May 2006. A frank exchange of views took place about the impediments to a confidence building process.

From the viewpoint of some of the Islamic charities, especially those in the Gulf, it seemed to them that they were being asked to make concessions, whereas in fact they were the victims. Western governments were making no concessions. Suspicions about a possible 'hidden agenda' were reiterated and fears that the objective might not be achievable. Perhaps the most telling reservation expressed by the Islamic charities was motivated by the Interpal case, the outcome of which is described below.

It was stated that what the Islamic charities really wanted was: (1) lifting of financial restraints; (2) lifting of restraints on travel; (3) removal of unjustified intelligence and security allegations; (4) a legal route rather than a political one. However, their representatives also pointed out that there were objections to the idea of an external, international assessment agency (the proposed new organization) intervening in matters that were properly the concern of domestic regulators and auditors. The problem was that it was precisely the element of external assessment that made the Montreux Initiative interesting to some Western governments (which had been approached by the FDFA with regard to possible participation). Western intelligence agencies and some Western governments were suspicious that some Islamic charities might be funding terrorism, and even that by approaching the Montreux Initiative some such charities might be seeing some form of 'cover'. Though terrorist operations were 'cheap' in themselves, their preparation was long term and required 'cover'. Two books alleging close links between some Islamic charities and terrorism had recently been published by leading university presses and were bound to be influencing public opinion, whatever adverse criticisms of these books might be deserved (Burr and Collins 2006; Levitt 2006). It was reported that US Treasury officials were just as interested in the risk of charities increasing the legitimacy of undesirable movements as in what precisely they finance, and this concern was hard to deal with.

In an attempt to resolve the impasse, it was suggested that auditing by locally registered independent firms, including local branches of international firms, might be acceptable to Gulf charities.

It was suggested that the Montreux principles should be applied in the first instance to Palestine, where the scale of need was evidently serious, in particular after the elections. It was agreed this would be a good starting point which, if successful, would encourage other Islamic charities. (There was a hope at this time that international aid could be channelled through local community-based Islamic charities in the Palestinian Territories. Further political developments made this for the most part impracticable, at least for the time being.)

Beginning at about this time, the Montreux Initiative encountered political turbulence and it became clear that it was not possible to achieve the objectives as originally proposed. The UK FCO withdrew at about the same time as its 'Engaging with the Islamic World' programme was wound up – in official terms, merged with the government's counter-terrorist programme. The difficulties could be summarized as follows:

From the Gulf – suspicions about alleged foreign interference or even the involvement of intelligence services, coupled with fear of displeasing the US government.

From the United States government – a hardening of the position of the US government towards Palestinian charities after the 2006 elections. (However, the US government was not a homogeneous organization and some branches of it could be more sympathetic.)

From the UK – the FCO was under pressure since June on the question of contacts with Islamists and was currently undergoing a policy review that would be finished by the end of November. A BBC TV *Panorama* attack on Interpal screened on 30 July added to the pressure.

The Montreux Initiative as such did not recover from these setbacks and there was a pause until a resumption of activity in the latter part of 2009, when the director of the Charity and Security Network (CSN) in Washington, DC, was co-opted into the Core Group. (CSN was sponsored by OMB Watch, a consortium of American charities.) President Obama's Cairo speech on 4 June 2009 – with its explicit reference to the need for Muslims to be able to fulfil their zakat obligations, and more generally its opening out to the Muslim world – seemed to suggest new opportunities to influence US government policy, which under the Bush administration was responsible for the most serious of the 'unjustified obstacles' facing Islamic charities. The specific contribution that the Montreux Initiative could make was in a context of participatory conflict resolution, which should be distinguished from advocacy. It was noted that this aim was compatible with that of the CSN. Some representatives of US Muslims were also co-opted into the core group.

The US Treasury was particularly concerned about 'dual use', where a charity could be providing valid services to those in need but still serving a political objective. The Montreux Initiative should aim at changing the conversation, with more emphasis on the 'receiving end', namely, how charitable funds actually reach their beneficiaries – especially, whether on a basis of assessed need (as prescribed by international codes of conduct for NGOs) or in accordance with other criteria such as political, religious, or kinship affiliation which could compromise a charitable organization's integrity. Some recent legal decisions in the USA appeared to be in contradiction with traditional humanitarian principles, which needed to be upheld.

It was agreed that contacts with the US Treasury should be resumed and that other constituencies in the USA, such as Christian organizations, should be invited to become involved in the Montreux Initiative. The aim should be to determine exactly where the 'unjustified obstacles' were located in the US administrative system and how they could be removed to the satisfaction of all parties. It was agreed that the new project proposal submitted by the Graduate Institute to FDFA would be entitled the 'Islamic Charities Project' (ICP).

A comprehensive historical review of the Montreux Initiative was prepared for internal use, including an analysis both of the extent to which its objectives were achieved and of a number of problems, some of them extremely sensitive, which remained largely unresolved in 2010 on the fifth anniversary of its inception.

However, it could be stated in very general terms that a political initiative of this kind – involving interlocutors from different institutions, countries and cultures – had to contend with fluctuating factors, in this case:

1. extreme turbulence in the international political environment;
2. changing participation (the UK FCO entering and then exiting);
3. changes in regional focus, as particular countries became more or less rewarding, in political and/or humanitarian terms, as objects for the allocation of attention and resources;
4. changes in thematic focus, as an emphasis on internal management had changed into an emphasis on the 'receiving end' of charity.

Nonetheless, the Montreux Initiative made an appreciable indirect impact. Its focus on capacity building was by 2010 no longer necessary, since numerous 'Support NGOs' in the Arab-Muslim world had become committed to this type of work. The recommendations with regard to compliance, self-regulation and governmental policies remained highly relevant, as a European Centre for Not-for-Profit Law report recognized.[3]

In two specific ways, too, progress was made. First, three working papers were published by the Graduate Institute relating to the Palestinian zakat committees, questioning the adverse view of their role (before the West Bank/Gaza split in 2007) that was dominant in Israeli and US government and judicial circles (Benthall 2008a *[Chapter 4]*; Schaeublin 2009; 2012; see also Benthall 2010–11 *[Chapter 6]*; 2011) – and still was in mid-2013. Consideration has also been given by the FDFA to the possibility of assisting the Palestinians in a programme to depoliticize the zakat committees, representing as they do such an important part of the Islamic religious and humanitarian tradition.

Second, steps were taken to try to change the conversation in Washington, DC, complementing the work of groups such as the CSN, which has strongly argued that misplaced efforts to counter terrorism may actually foment more terrorism, and that security and humanitarian considerations are not necessarily in conflict. In 2005, the mainstream non-Muslim NGOs in the USA had tended, with some exceptions, to stand aside as mere observers of the process of stigmatization and criminalization of Islamic NGOs, without realizing that the evolution of American law and administrative decisions actually had adverse implications for the whole humanitarian and

aid sector. That by 2012 was no longer the case and the centre of gravity for the
ventilation of these issues had moved from Europe to Washington, New York, and
Harvard.[4]

In succession to the Graduate Institute, a new Swiss host institution was appointed
by the FDFA in 2012 for continuation of the Islamic Charities Project: the Centre
for Security Studies, ETH Zurich. Meanwhile, part of the Montreux Initiative's role
was being well carried out by the Humanitarian Forum, based in London and a
more broadly based organization founded by Hany El-Banna at about the same time
in 2005, and there was no need to duplicate it.[5]

Gulf charities and the Montreux Initiative

Considerable effort was put by the Core Group into discussions with representatives
of Gulf-based charities and here some particular problems arose. By way of background, we must recall the history of the Afghan war of the 1980s, when Western
and Gulf-based organizations were united in supporting the mujahideen in order to
bring down the Soviet empire.[6] US regulation of its overseas aid charities at that time
was lax and did not set a rigorous example (Benthall 2011).

Without breaching any confidences, I suggest that the difficulties in the relationship were two-way. For instance, the Gulf charities were suspicious of the proposal
that they should provide accounting and other information to an external institution, and argued that validation by this independent body would probably not
solve their problems, because some European Islamic charities that satisfied all the
requirements of their national charity regulators were nonetheless still designated
by the US Treasury as 'terrorist groups'. Interpal was eventually cleared three times
after investigations by the UK Charity Commission (Charity Commission 2009),
but was still in mid-2013 designated as a terrorist group by the US government,
and the same was true of a number of other European Islamic charities specially
concerned with Palestinians.[7] The crux of the disagreement was whether the US
and Israeli governments were justified in regarding the Palestinian zakat committees and other Palestinian Islamic charities, pre-2007, as fronts for Hamas – the
same issue that the Holy Land Foundation criminal case in Dallas, Texas, hinged
on. [...]

The Gulf charities argued that they would have little to gain from submitting
to the rigorous external assessment and monitoring proposed by the Montreux
Initiative if the exculpation of Interpal by the UK Charity Commission, with its
access to intelligence and police information, had no effect in convincing the US
government that it was a genuine humanitarian charity. They were also hoping for
a more positive reaction from Western governments than the Swiss initiative was
able to elicit. On the other hand, a number of US and European experts felt that the
tradition of discretion and secrecy, especially in Saudi Arabia, was still very strong

and at odds with the requirement for transparency. Moreover, while many Christian charities combine religious with humanitarian objectives, those Gulf charities with a similar dual role were criticized in the West for having promoted a particularly rigid interpretation of Islam.

In keeping with the original intention of the FDFA to seek to mediate 'religio-political conflicts', moral support for the Islamic Charities Project was sought in the USA from Christian leaders committed to the principle that all religions have the right to organize humanitarian activities. The question of comparability between Christian and Islamic charities with 'mixed' religious and humanitarian aims has not yet been given detailed examination in the research literature, but was extensively discussed at meetings of the Montreux Initiative Core Group. As a vehicle of the Hanbali school of Sunni Islam, the World Assembly of Muslim Youth (WAMY), perhaps the most important Saudi-based Islamic charity, has set itself up to compete with laxist, Christian and secular influences, as well as with the Shia denomination of Islam which happens to be dominant in several petroleum-producing regions of the Middle East.

A loose analogy may be drawn between WAMY and, say, the US-based evangelical charity Samaritan's Purse, which declares its aims as follows: 'We are an effective means of reaching hurting people in countries around the world with food, medicine, and other assistance in the Name of Jesus Christ. This, in turn, earns us a hearing for the Gospel, the Good News of eternal life through Jesus Christ'.[8] The difference is that Samaritan's Purse, as well as the much larger and rather less overtly evangelical charity World Vision, have negotiated a relationship of symbiosis with governmental and intergovernmental donor agencies so that the missionary role is downplayed, at least officially, while the Catholic family of international charities, known as Caritas Internationalis, has renounced it completely.[9] Some Gulf-based charities of an Islamic hue, such as WAMY, subscribe characteristically to the view that Islam is a 'comprehensive way of life', a seamless whole (*shumūlīyyat al-islām*); therefore, material assistance and *da'wa* (the call to Islam) are indissoluble. Such a holistic vision of religion in society is now marginal in the West, with the important exception of parts of the United States, but it is still mainstream in the Gulf (as documented by Juul Petersen 2014). The current worldwide trend is surely towards the disallowing of the promotion of religion by humanitarian charities. Some Saudi organizations such as IIROSA (a signatory to the Red Cross/Crescent code of conduct mentioned above) are moving in that direction, so that maybe any successor to the Montreux Initiative will have a rather easier task.

A further factor inhibiting the potential of Islamic charity as a vehicle for modern development aid is the role that some conservative Islamic teaching ascribes to the poor, as being necessary to the spiritual well-being of the wealthy through their charitable deeds – a doctrine that gives only a limited incentive to eliminate poverty.

This attitude to social poverty has had analogues in other religious traditions, including some branches of Christianity, as well as conservative Islam. Islamic charities today are likely to move in the direction clearly established by leading agencies such as Islamic Relief Worldwide, which is to work together with governments and non-Muslim agencies with the aim of alleviating poverty through practical means, seeing poverty as a scandal that should be rectified.

The Palestinian issue as such is excluded on geographical grounds from the present publication [*Gulf Charities and Islamic Philanthropy in the 'Age of Terror' and Beyond*]. However, it is also to some extent paradigmatic of the dilemmas that face Islamic charities more generally. Palestinians have been recipients of very substantial aid flows from Gulf states, from parastatal organizations such as IIROSA, and from private donors – often in controversial circumstances epitomized by the position of the I'tilaf al-Khair (Union of Good), the umbrella body of pro-Palestinian charities presided over by Sheikh al-Qaradawi of Qatar and which has been designated by the USA as a terrorist entity, while all its member institutions are outlawed in Israel. Amid such political polarization, wise policy interventions must be based on careful research, which in turn can only proceed incrementally through the earning of trust from all factions – unfortunately at the time of writing a disastrously scarce commodity among Israelis and Palestinians.

Following up the Islamic Charities Project

The Montreux Initiative/Islamic Charities Project was essentially an exercise in mediation by confidence building and a pilot project in 'diapraxis', that is, practical action as opposed to abstract dialogue, which is a specially innovative part of the FDFA's policies (Benthall 2012a). It was grounded in research, including a study in the 1990s by Jean-Nicolas Bitter, a former delegate of the International Committee of the Red Cross who subsequently became the responsible programme officer in the FDFA (Bitter 2003). Unfortunately, in its implementation, it turned out to be a somewhat one-sided process in that a major party to the disagreement, the US government, was reluctant to do more than register polite interest – possibly, one may infer, merely in order to keep themselves informed. The UK Foreign and Commonwealth Office joined the project as a co-sponsor in 2005, but withdrew the following year, probably as a response to adverse publicity in the UK regarding its contacts with Islamists. By mid-2013, the ICP was winding down.

Apart from the Palestinian intervention already described, further plans for following up what had been achieved were under discussion. There had also been a spin-off in activities launched by individual members of the core team. Benoît Challand, a Swiss political scientist now working at New York University (see Challand 2009), was leading an informal international network of researchers on zakat as it is actually practised in many variants, as opposed to religious teaching about zakat as an ideal.

There can be no doubt that future efforts will be made to bring Islamic charities fully into the international aid system, in view of the extent of suffering and poverty experienced by Muslims worldwide, the potential contribution of more materially fortunate Muslims to alleviating them and the pressure on the overseas aid budgets of major Western nations. Equally important […], a 'humanitarian vacuum' is created in complex zones of conflict such as Syria today, where bona fide Islamic charities are almost absent for political reasons and the field is left open for extremist groups to bring succour to victims. The experience of the Swiss project recorded here should help any future interventions by other governments or independent foundations to avoid certain pitfalls. And the growth of research on Islamic charities that we are seeing today – best seen as a subset of research on Faith Based Organizations more generally[10] – will also help give substance and credibility to future interventions.

Notes

1 INTRAC (International NGO Training and Research Centre) is a well-established support NGO based in Oxford.

2 'Objective' is the term used in the document (of course, a questionable concept in social research).

3 *Study on Recent Public and Self-Regulatory Initiatives Improving Transparency and Accountability of Non-Profit Organisations in the European Union*, commissioned by the European Directorate-General of Justice, Freedom and Security and submitted by the European Centre for Not-for-Profit Law (published in April 2009).

4 See for instance ACLU 2009, and the website of the Charity and Security Network (www.charityandsecurity.org); also the UCLA *Journal of Islamic and Near Eastern Law*, 20: 1, 2010–11, which contains six articles on Islamic charities, based on a seminar held at the University of California, Los Angeles, in 2010 [*including Chapter 6 here*].

5 *For an update on the Humanitarian Forum, see Chapter 1, n. 11.*

6 It is now generally agreed that the USA was sowing dragon's teeth in supporting the Afghan mujahideen in the 1980s. Saudi Arabia's commitment to the same cause clearly had comparable unintended consequences, as did its financial contributions to the rise of the Front Islamique de Salut (FIS) in Algeria, which gained popular support in large measure through its welfare and relief activities. Saudi involvement ceased when Algerian Islamists broke with Saudi Arabia in 1991, but played a part in the events that led to the Algerian civil war (Ciment 1997: 94–5). Annika Kropf (2014) speculates that Gulf monarchies may in the past have been in the habit of paying some degree of 'protection money' to Islamist extremists overseas. A milder interpretation is that they were buying off domestic opposition. Today, it is likely that the export of Saudi interpretations of Islam to Europe and elsewhere, through embassies and mosques, may well have future consequences that the more progressive leadership of the kingdom does not intend (Roy 2004: 235–43).

7 Especially the Comité de Bienfaisance et de Secours aux Palestiniens (France).

8 www.samaritanspurse.org/our-ministry/about-us/.

9 These issues are touched on in Barnett and Stein (2012).
10 See, for instance, Duriez et al. 2007; Clarke and Jennings 2008; Barnett and Stein 2012. The concept of 'value-based organizations' is more rigorous in that it allows non-religious agencies with strongly held humanitarian ideologies, such as Oxfam, to be considered within the same interpretative framework.

6

An unholy tangle: Boim versus the Holy Land Foundation

This chapter follows broadly the conventions of a legal journal, since it was first published in the UCLA *Journal of Near Eastern and Islamic Law* in 2010–11. It argues that the US legal system could do more to demonstrate its fairness with regard to Islamic charities.

To complement my argument, let us assume that the Palestinian zakat committees to which directors of the Holy Land Foundation (HLF) remitted charitable funds were indeed controlled by Hamas (though I do not accept that the evidence points that way: none of the zakat committees were 'designated' at the time when the funds were remitted and there is no indication that any funds supplied by HLF were applied otherwise than for humanitarian purposes). The former chairman of HLF, Ghassan Elashi, was sentenced to a sixty-five-year prison sentence in 2008 at the age of fifty-five and in 2015 was believed to be serving his sentence in the draconian conditions of a Communications Management Unit in a prison in Illinois reserved for hardened terrorists. In Britain, by contrast, whole-life sentences with no prospect of parole are given only to the worst murderers.

However, the US legal system has many redeeming features, exemplified in this case by what seems to me the impeccable reasoning of Judge Ilana Rovner in her minority finding.

It is not clear, at the time of going to press with this book, what has happened to HLF's frozen funds. The charity as such has not been allowed its 'day in court'. A post-conviction appeal on behalf of the directors has been launched, but it reportedly has little chance of success.

***

The United States Supreme Court's majority ruling in *Holder* v. *Humanitarian Law Project*[1] in June 2010 endorsed the government's decision that giving advice to designated terrorist entities on how to achieve their aims by peaceful means is a form of material support for terrorism. The ruling has been widely criticized in the American media as a threat to peace builders, from President Jimmy Carter down, and to journalists and academic researchers who set out to understand militant political groups.[2] An ethnography of the Supreme Court is clearly needed, though we have an approximation in Jeffrey Toobin's *The Nine: Inside the Secret World of the Supreme Court*.[3] My surprise at the ruling, albeit shared by others, was partly due to ignorance. I was unaware that, as a recently published paper by legal academics argues, '[the Supreme Court's] reliance on humanitarian law is often minimal and sometimes haphazard'.[4] If this is so, it should be no surprise that lower courts in the United States give humanitarian law and principles an attention that is equally sporadic. The following analysis of a holding delivered by a lower appeals court on a topic loosely related to the Humanitarian Law Project case, but civil rather than criminal, is written by a non-American and a non-lawyer. If it has any interest this will be because it is informed by some knowledge of the humanitarian world, by research conducted on the ground in impoverished and/or conflict-torn areas, and specifically by engagement with the legal and regulatory problems afflicting bona fide Islamic charities since 11 September 2001.[5]

On 13 May 1996, David Boim, aged seventeen, with dual Israeli and American nationality, was waiting at a public bus stop in Beit El, a religiously observant Israeli settlement in the central West Bank, where he was enrolled at the Mateh Binyamin Yeshiva High School. An intelligent and determined student, his ambition was to qualify as a doctor. Palestinians gunned him down and killed him during a drive-by shooting. One of the two alleged murderers was reportedly convicted and given a prison sentence by a Palestinian Authority tribunal. When the assailant was paroled, he absconded, and according to newspaper reports was eventually killed in 2005 by Israeli security forces during a raid in the West Bank town of Nablus (*Jerusalem Post* 2005). The other is said to have killed himself later in 1996 in a suicide bombing, having been released before his trial.

Unlike thousands of other victims of a conflict which has persisted, in various degrees of intensity, since 1948, David Boim's tragically short life will be publicly remembered. His memorial will be in the law books, because of the persistence of his parents, Stanley and Joyce Boim. They say that their aim in seeking retribution through financial compensation is not personal gain, but to dry up the funding sources of the Islamist movement Hamas as the presumed instigator of the murders.[6] As to whether Hamas did in fact instigate the crime, there is not complete certainty, but the allegation has, as far as I am aware, never been denied.[7] Hamas, however, has been as out of reach for the plaintiffs as were the individual murderers. The Boims shifted their attention to institutions and individuals within the purview of the US courts, claiming that they gave material support to Hamas and consequently share liability for David Boim's murder.[8] The principal defendant, the Holy Land Foundation (HLF), based in Texas and once the largest US Islamic overseas aid charity, remitted funds – raised from American donors for overseas relief aid – to a form of Islamic charitable committee, known as zakat committees, in the Palestinian Territories, which both the US and the Israeli governments have accused of being fronts or affiliates for Hamas. Funds were also remitted to a hospital in Gaza, which has also been accused of being a front for donating to Hamas. For the sake of simplicity, I will ignore in this analysis the other institutional defendants, none of whom would seem to have substantial funds to pay damages.[9]

President George W. Bush denounced HLF in December 2001.[10] Its assets were frozen and it was listed as a Specially Designated Global Terrorist. Separately from the Boim civil case, five HLF directors were prosecuted in a Dallas criminal court in 2007 for alleged material support to terrorism and on other related counts.[11] But the jury failed to agree that they were guilty and a mistrial resulted. As a result of a retrial the following year, most of the defendants were found guilty on all counts in November 2008.[12] Two of the directors, men in their fifties, were sentenced to prison for sixty-five years each and the combined total of the sentences was 180 years. The sentences were under appeal at the time of writing this article.[13] The verdict has been criticized on various grounds including the following:

> The zakat committees were not (and were still not in October 2010) designated in the USA as terrorist organizations.
>
> Defence attorneys presented evidence and testimony that some of the committees had received aid from the International Committee of the Red Cross, the US Agency for International Development, the European Commission and United Nations agencies.
>
> A former US Consul General at the US Consulate General in Jerusalem, who was also formerly a high-ranking intelligence official, testified that during his years working in the region he received daily CIA briefings and visited some of the zakat committees, and had never received information suggesting that the zakat committees aided by HLF were controlled by Hamas (with which all contact was forbidden).[14]
>
> Various alleged procedural irregularities, such as the appearance in court of an Israeli intelligence officer under a pseudonym; and the absence of any defence representation for HLF itself as opposed to its officers.

In 2004, a district court in the District of Northern Illinois awarded $156 million against HLF and other defendants and in favour of the Boims, because the United States Code allows US citizens injured by international terrorism the right to sue for treble damages.[15] The defendants appealed and in 2007 a panel of three judges in the Court of Appeals for the Seventh Circuit decided by a majority of two to one that the case should be remanded for further consideration in the lower court.[16] The majority decision, written by Judge Ilana Rovner, said that the Boims would have to prove a stronger chain of causation between HLF's remittance of funds and the murder of David Boim.[17]

The position of HLF here becomes extremely tangled, in that in 2003 another district court, in DC, had upheld the Department of Treasury's finding that HLF had knowingly provided funds for Hamas.[18] The Boims sought to prevent this point being relitigated, according to the principle of collateral estoppel or issue preclusion.[19] The 2007 appeal panel rejected this argument and decided that HLF should have an opportunity to defend itself on this issue in a lower court.

The Boims then applied for the appeal to be reheard by all the active judges of the Seventh Circuit Court of Appeals en banc, and this was granted. Their decision was published on 3 December 2008.[20] Ten judges heard the case; a majority of seven overturned the earlier panel's decision. Three judges (including the two who had formed the majority in the 2007 appeal decision) dissented. The nub of the majority decision was that both the test of intent and that of a chain of causation had been satisfied. Money is fungible, that is, it is transferable. If $100,000 is given to Hamas for social services, this releases $100,000 with which it can finance bombings. Much of the disagreement between the majority and the minority in the en banc hearing hinged on highly technical issues of primary versus secondary or indirect liability. A combative article on the case by Laura B. Rowe, published in a law journal, supports the majority decision, but criticizes both the majority and the minority in detail (Rowe 2009). She argues, in conclusion, that the majority decision does not go far enough: seeing that Congress has decided that material support for terrorism is equivalent to terrorism itself, which inevitably endangers innocent human life and incurs serious retribution in the criminal courts, it would be wrong to insist on a higher level of proof in the civil courts than the criminal courts require.

As a non-lawyer, it seems to me that the minority opinion, written by Judge Rovner, reflects a sensible balance between humanitarian principles and the rights of victims of criminal violence. It would appear that she paid some attention to the OMB Watch amicus brief submitted to the judges,[21] and/or to have personal acquaintance with humanitarian principles as they are enshrined in Geneva law and in internationally accepted codes of practice.[22] She did not favour dismissing the Boims' case, but asked for further proof as to causation. Perhaps most importantly, she refrained from assuming that the zakat committees and the Gaza hospital were in fact fronts for Hamas, as was alleged by the plaintiffs. She observes: 'HLF's ties to Hamas have yet to be evaluated in this litigation because the district court [in 2003] erroneously gave collateral estoppel to the D.C. Circuit's determination that HLF funded terrorism by funding Hamas and its affiliates'.[23] She and one of the other dissenters, Judge Wood, were evidently sensitive to the implications of the majority decision for humanitarian activities in general. This is not the first time, they must have reflected, that similar issues have arisen in conflict zones.

By contrast, Judge Richard Posner, former Chief Judge in the Court, who wrote the majority decision, does not mention the word 'humanitarian' once. He attempts to pre-empt the objection that the Red Cross or Doctors Without Borders could be sued for coming to the aid of Hamas casualties in an Israeli retaliatory strike: his solution is to acknowledge a special exception for medical aid to *individuals* by aid agencies. As Judges Rovner and Wood point out, this is a weak argument. Why should giving medical aid to the injured be exempted, while donating an X-ray machine to a hospital would not necessarily be? And what (one may add) of services other than medical aid, such as protecting children, digging latrines, or providing shelter and food for civilians who have lost their homes? The proper test should surely be whether the humanitarian services, medical or otherwise, are provided impartially and free of an intent to further the violent activities of the banned organization.

As it happens, I believe that, on the balance of probabilities, the Palestinian zakat committees[24] deserved, during the period when HLF was sending its donations (1997–2001), to be regarded as legitimate charities, operating in response to need, rather than as fronts for Hamas. My co-worker Emanuel Schaeublin has summarized as follows his view of the position with regard to the West Bank, before a programme of thoroughgoing reorganization that was implemented by the Fatah-dominated Palestinian Authority in Ramallah in 2007:

> Before the 2007 reform, the committees were efficient grassroot organizations that strengthened the local response system and self-reliance while minimizing dependency and victimhood. They were mainly composed of pious businessmen and academics with a good and honest reputation and close contacts to local governments and village councils. Committee members were working on a voluntary basis, and the businessmen on the committees contributed the necessary know-how to run the committees efficiently and provided for excellent financial reporting … [Z]akat committees have shown the capacity to work across clan, party and even religious boundaries. These factors can explain for the high degree of popular confidence in the zakat committees … A summation of the most reliable and best-informed interlocutors' views suggests that the majority of the zakat committees operated as genuine needs-based charities before 2007. (Schaeublin 2009: 60. See also Benthall 2008a [Chapter 4].)

If this was indeed a fair retrospective interpretation, there should have been no difficulty for these committees to be considered in the same category as the Red Cross or Doctors Without Borders. Attention was not given during the HLF criminal trial in Dallas in 2008 to the end use of the charitable funds collected by HLF from donors and channelled by HLF to these Palestinian charities – that is, investigating whether the charitable funds were used to finance Hamas operations, as opposed to purposes for which the donors intended: to help ordinary Palestinians in severe need. If such attention had been given, it might well be that the HLF directors would have been exonerated. However, Judges Rovner and Wood correctly went no further than to leave open this possibility.

It is a long-established principle that ownership of a trust fund belongs to its beneficiaries, on whose behalf the trustees are appointed stewards. Whatever the motives of HLF's promoters and fundraisers, there is little doubt that its many donors intended their contributions to be defrayed for the benefit of Palestinians in need. It appears to be true that the promoters of HLF had radical political views and were personally opposed to the 1993 Oslo Accords. However, this is not the same as espousing or sponsoring terrorism.

In the criminal trials in Dallas, the prosecution made much of the so-called 'Philadelphia conference', a three-day meeting of some twenty American Muslims opposed to the Oslo Accords, held in October 1993 in a hotel in Philadelphia, and monitored by the FBI.[25] Three of the HLF defendants attended. The government alleged that, on the evidence of the transcripts of this meeting, the defendants were more concerned to promote the political aims of Hamas than an apolitical humanitarian exercise. As regards the Boim case, this evidence was not referred to in the en banc Appeal decision, though it was touched on in the earlier Appeal hearing in 2007. One may speculate that the prosecutors in Dallas might have adopted a different strategy, of confining themselves to the allegation of 'attempting' and 'conspiring' to give material support to a designated terrorist organization, because 'attempting' and 'conspiring' to give material support for terrorism are caught by 18 U.S.C. 2339B ('Support of Designated Terrorist Organizations') as much as the actual provision of support.[26] Provided that the FBI transcripts passed the legal tests for quality of evidence, as well as quantity, such a strategy might have resulted in guilty verdicts without any examination of the actual operations of the Palestinian zakat committees. However, the hurdle to be surmounted would have been that the Philadelphia conference took place over a year before Hamas was designated in January 1995. Presumably this was an important reason why the prosecution presented detailed evidence as to the alleged culpability of the zakat committees. The majority in the en banc Appeal hearing of the civil case took for granted that the prosecution had proved their contention.

While much intellectual effort has been put into considering such questions of humanitarian ethics, going back to the foundation of the International Committee of the Red Cross in 1864, it seems strange to a layman that Judge Posner relies on such homespun analogies as the 1958 *Keel* v. *Hainline* case in Oklahoma. In a classroom melee, junior high school student A picked up erasers for other students to throw. Student B threw an eraser at student C, who was struck in the eye and sued. Student A was found liable for his bad behaviour even though there was no evidence of his having handed an eraser specifically to B. 'The court did not use the term "material support"', Judge Posner writes, 'but in handing erasers to the throwers Keel was providing them with material support in a literal sense'.[27] Aid agencies have to deal all the time with agonizing policy issues, such as whether to bring food aid to the immiserated people of North Korea when it is in practice impossible to do so without cooperating with, and implicitly supporting, a pariah regime. If anyone were to suggest adducing the case of *Keel* v. *Hainline* at an aid agency board meeting convened to decide such a matter, they would be met with incomprehension.

Looking at the detail of Judge Posner's text, I detect a lack of care in demonstrating his fairness. He is obliged to accept that HLF must have its day in court because there are no grounds for accepting that the principle of collateral estoppel should apply. But he cannot resist opining that it is 'implausible' that HLF did not know that Hamas was a terrorist organization,[28] when HLF's defence would be, not ignorance of the nature of Hamas, but confidence that its donations had been made to authentic local charities for the relief of suffering, in compliance with United States, Israeli and Palestinian law. Moreover, when giving examples of long-running terrorist campaigns in Ireland, Sri Lanka and elsewhere, Judge Posner cites 'Palestine, where Arab terrorism has been more or less continuous since 1920'.[29] He omits to mention the actions of the Stern Gang and Irgun in their efforts to evict the British from Mandatory Palestine in the mid 1940s or Baruch Goldstein's massacre of Muslims in Hebron in 1994.

It would be foolish to claim that the promoters of the Holy Land Foundation were charismatic humanitarian Muslims on a par with Hany El-Banna of Islamic Relief Worldwide, based in England, or Abdul Sattar Edhi of Pakistan's Edhi Foundation.[30] However, a justice system that hands down deterrent life prison sentences and punitive damages surely has an obligation to show that the scales carried by Justitia are evenly balanced. Judge Posner has as high a profile as any judge in the United States and a reputation for intellectual brilliance. But he is also a spare-time political commentator. The following is an extract from his contribution to the Becker-Posner blog for 2006, following Hamas's victory in the Palestinian parliamentary elections:

> Given Fatah's inability to suppress Hamas, Israel could not [until now] crush Hamas by bombing the government buildings occupied by Fatah. Once Hamas is the government, however, further violence toward Israel by Hamas members can be met appropriately by massive military force directed against the organs and leaders of the government. This threat may cause Hamas to avoid attacks on Israel. Hamas's victory may be the best thing that has happened to Israel in years. (Posner 2006)

The anthropologist Lawrence Rosen has written that the idea of distinguishing personality from public office is alien to the Arab cultures that he has studied, for Arabs tend to assess persons by enquiring about their connections in many contexts. Rosen's interlocutors, according to him, take for granted a continuity between judges' personal beliefs and their professional decisions (Rosen 2008: 23–5).[31] Judge Posner's integrity is beyond question. However, putting myself in the position of an Arab Muslim reading Judge Posner's decision and aware of his extra-professional writings, it would be easy to take the view that it reflects a determination on the part of the state to crack down hard on Islamic institutions, with inadequate attention to considerations of fairness.

Meanwhile, HLF's remaining assets of several million dollars remain frozen. As its former officers are in prison, it may not ever truly have its 'day in court'.

Acknowledgements

I am grateful to the organizers for their invitation to attend the symposium at UCLA on the 'Criminalization of Islamic Philanthropy' on 16 April 2010 and to numerous colleagues and the editors of this journal for their help in refining the arguments. Thanks are especially due to those associated with the Islamic Charities Project, Graduate Institute of International and Development Studies, Geneva, and the Charity and Security Network, Washington, DC.

Notes

1 *Holder* v. *Humanitarian Law Project*, 130 S. Ct. 2705 (2010).
2 See, for example, Guinane and Sazawal 2010; *New York Times* 2010; *Washington Post* 2010.
3 Toobin 2007.
4 Weissbrodt and Nesbitt 2010. It should be added that many other jurisdictions give equally inconsistent attention to International Humanitarian Law. Contrary to what many laymen probably believe, there should be no assumption that International Humanitarian Law can be drawn on to 'trump' domestic law.
5 *[Statement of publications, etc., omitted here to avoid duplication.]*
6 *Boim* v. *Quranic Literacy Institute*, 291 F.3d 1000, 1003–5 (7th Cir. 2002).
7 For discussion of this point, see *Boim* v. *Quranic Literacy Institute*, 291 F.3d, especially at 1004, 1024.
8 *Boim* v. *Quranic Literacy Institute*, 291 F.3d, 1003–7 (7th Cir. 2002).
9 They were the American Muslim Society and the Quranic Literacy Institute.
10 For the text see *Washington Post* 2001.
11 *United States* v. *Holy Land Foundation*, 2007 WL 4874763.
12 *United States* v. *Holy Land Foundation*, 2008 WL 524062.
13 *Their appeal was eventually rejected.*
14 ACLU 2009.
15 See *Boim*, 291 F.3d at 1001, 1003. The relevant provision in the US Code is U.S.C. 2332(a).
16 *Boim* v. *Holy Land Foundation for Relief and Dev.* 511 F.3d 707 (7th Cir. 2007).
17 *Boim* v. *Holy Land Foundation for Relief and Dev.* 511 F.3d at 711.
18 HLF was not given an opportunity to present evidence to the court. The same procedure has now been held to violate the Fifth Amendment right to due process; see ACLU, '*Kindhearts for Charitable Humanitarian Development, Inc.* v. *Geithner et al.*', www.aclu.org/national-security/kindhearts-charitable-humanitarian-development-inc-v-geithner-et-al (accessed May 2010).
19 The editors of the UCLA *Journal of Near Eastern and Islamic Law* have pointed out to me that the principle of collateral estoppel could not be applied because of the DC Circuit's almost total reliance on administrative law and agency deference in the *HLF* v. *Ashcroft* case. While the judiciary could not stop a government agency from freezing the charity's assets, this determination was insufficient for adjudicating the charity' total liability, leading to somewhat contradictory positions towards the charity's activities and, more specifically, towards its alleged involvement in the young man's death.
20 *Boim* v. *Holy Land Foundation for Relief and Dev.*, 549 F.3d 685, 687 (7th Cir. 2008) (en banc).
21 Brief of OMB Watch as Amicus Curiae Support Defendants/Appellants, urging Affirmation of Panel's Opinion, *Boim* v. *Holy Land Foundation*, 549 F.3d 685 (7th Cir. 2008), 2008 WL 3843624.
22 It appears that International Humanitarian Law cannot be directly adduced in such a case because: (1) it applies only to criminal, not to civil, law; (2) it covers the protection of humanitarian activities only, and is silent on the question of their funding. However, there is

an extensive literature on the ethical dilemmas that face humanitarianism. See for instance the website of the London-based Overseas Development Institute's Humanitarian Policy Group (www.odi.org/programmes/humanitarian-policy-group).

23 *Boim* v. *Holy Land Foundation for Relief and Dev.*, 549 F.3d 685 at 706, fn.3.

24 The Dar El-Salam Hospital in Gaza, also alleged to be a front for Hamas, is owned by the Al-Wafa Charitable Society. The research papers published by Schaeublin and by myself (see below) are confined to the West Bank. Schaeublin was writing up new field research, conducted in Gaza in September 2010, as the present paper was being prepared for publication (see Schaeublin 2012).

25 Government's Second Supplemental Trial Brief, *United States* v. *Holy Land Foundation*, CR No. 3-R-240-P (ECF) (N.D. Texas 12 Sept 2008).

26 For an authoritative summary of the most frequently prosecuted federal statutes relating to material support, see Doyle 2010.

27 *Boim* v. *Holy Land Foundation for Relief and Dev.*, 549 F.3d 685 at 697.

28 *Boim* v. *Holy Land Foundation for Relief and Dev.*, 549 F.3d 685 at 701.

29 *Boim* v. *Holy Land Foundation for Relief and Dev.*, 549 F.3d 685 at 700.

30 Cf. (on Hany El-Banna) Benthall 2009 and (on the Edhi Foundation) Benthall and Bellion-Jourdan 2003: 18–19.

31 This might be criticized as an 'orientalist' essentialization, but it tallies with the conclusions of a number of other researchers, including my own observations. True, the principle of judicial independence and impartiality has deep roots in Arab and Islamic culture. However, the fact that the principle has had to be demonstrated at length to contemporary readers suggests that it is not always self-evident; see Brown and Sharif 2002. By contrast, judicial independence and impartiality are an integral part of the doctrine of the separation of powers, which is particularly honoured in the United States constitution.

7

The Tariq Ramadan visa case

In February 2004, Tariq Ramadan, the well-known Swiss-born academic and commentator on Islamic matters, applied for a non-immigrant US visa on accepting a professorship in peace studies at the University of Notre Dame. He was granted a visa, but in July the State Department revoked it, citing the 'ideological exclusion provision' of the USA PATRIOT Act in justification. Ramadan resigned from his university appointment. In September 2005, he applied for a visa to allow him to accept invitations to speak at various organizations and universities. The government did not issue a decision. The American Civil Liberties Union (ACLU), supported by representatives of Ramadan's prospective hosts, filed a lawsuit against the government in January 2006. In September 2006, the government denied Ramadan's visa application, citing the decision of a US consular officer in Bern. Between December 1998 and July 2002, Ramadan had made donations totalling the equivalent of US$940 to a charity registered in Switzerland, the Association de Secours Palestinien (ASP). In August 2003, over a year after Ramadan's donations ceased, the US Treasury had designated the ASP as a terrorist fundraising organization, on account of its alleged connections to Hamas-linked charities. The ACLU continued its litigation, adducing the First and Fifth Amendments. District Judge Paul Crotty ruled in 2007 that the government's justification for denying Ramadan's visa was 'facially legitimate and bona fide', and that he had no authority to override the government's consular decision. In July 2009 a US federal appeals court ruled that a lower court should review whether the consular officer had properly faced Ramadan with the allegations that he had knowingly rendered material support to terrorism. In January 2010, the State Department decided, in a document signed by Secretary Hillary Clinton, to lift the ban against Ramadan's entering the United States, which he has since done on a number of times without incident.

Almost certainly, the real grounds for the exclusion of Ramadan were different. A grandson of Hassan al-Banna, founder of the Muslim Brotherhood, he was a critic of American foreign policy and believed in some American circles to be spearheading a campaign to introduce a caliphate in the United States. My role was to write an affi-davit pro bono for the ACLU in 2007 asserting that ASP was, when he made his donations, regulated under Swiss charity law and had not been designated by the US government; and giving my opinion that, though the 'designation' of ASP appar-ently relied on the fact that it had remitted funds to Palestinian zakat committees, there was no persuasive evidence that these committees were facades for Hamas. Judge Crotty's judgments included the puzzling comment that my evidence, 'while objectively illuminating, provides little comfort to the Court that Ramadan, subject-ively, lacked the requisite knowledge'. But on behalf of the ACLU I wrote the letter, reproduced below, reaffirming my opinion. Professor Nathan J. Brown, an American academic expert on Middle East politics, also wrote to Clinton in October 2010 in full support of the content of the affidavit.

It cannot be demonstrated that submissions on behalf of the ACLU actually caused Clinton to exercise her discretionary authority on account of 'national secur-ity and foreign policy interests', but it is noteworthy that the government refrained from having the affidavit rebutted.

***

19 October 2009

Hon. Hillary Rodham Clinton

Secretary of State

2201 C Street, NW

Washington, DC, 20520

Dear Secretary Clinton:

The American Civil Liberties Union, in connection with its representation of Professor Tariq Ramadan, has asked me to write regarding the expert declar-ation that I submitted in *AAR v. Napolitano,* Civ. No. 06-588, concerning whether Professor Ramadan's lack of knowledge that the Association de Secours Palestinien (ASP) was providing funds to Hamas (if indeed it was) was objectively reasonable. I am writing to reaffirm the opinions I expressed in that declaration and to affirm that subsequent information I have acquired through further research in the area only reinforces my opinion.

As set out in my original declaration, I am an Honorary Research Fellow in the Department of Anthropology, University College London, and an expert on Islamic charities. Since February 2007, when I submitted my declaration, I have continued to undertake and publish research on this topic, based both on publications and on fieldwork, and to act as an adviser to the Swiss Federal Department of Foreign Affairs on initiatives relating to Islamic charities. I have given presentations on Islamic char-ities to working groups at the United Kingdom Foreign and Commonwealth Office, the Charity Commission of England and Wales, the United Kingdom Home Office, and the French National Police Study and Training Centre (CNEF). I have also given advice to various legal teams and have given evidence pro bono in Appeals Court hearings in Copenhagen and Paris, both relating to Islamic charities. My book *The Charitable Crescent: Politics of aid in the Muslim world* (co-authored with J. Bellion-Jourdan) has been reprinted in a paperback edition with a new preface.

In my original declaration I set out, at the request of the plaintiffs, to assess the government's allegation that Professor Tariq Ramadan 'reasonably should have known' that ASP and or the Comité de Bienfaisance et de Secours aux Palestiniens (CBSP)[1] provided funds to Hamas, if indeed they did. I assessed two questions. First, whether there was evidence that ASP or CBSP did, in fact, provide funds for Hamas. Second, whether, if they did, Professor Ramadan reasonably should have know this.

As to the first issue, my opinion remains that there is no convincing evidence that either organization provided funds for Hamas. The publicly available information at the time of Professor Ramadan's donations indicated that ASP and CBSP were legitimate charities engaged in legitimate humanitarian work in the Palestinian Territories. Both charities remain registered charities permitted to operate today.

Moreover, to my knowledge, no one has alleged that ASP provided funds directly to Hamas as such. More frequently, the allegation of a support to Hamas is based on the US or Israeli government's belief that a particular organization is providing funds to zakat committees (Islamic charitable committees) in the Palestinian Territories, which these governments believe to be facades for Hamas. In my original declaration (at paragraphs 43–5), I cast doubt on this assumption that zakat committees should be presumed to be affiliated in some way with Hamas. Many zakat committees are not affiliated with Hamas at all.

Research that I and others have conducted since I submitted my original declaration only reinforces my opinion on this issue. Since February 2007, I have made as detailed a study as possible of the work since 1993 of the Palestinian zakat committees.[2] The first step of my research resulted in a publication, 'The Palestinian zakat committees 1993–2007 and their contested interpretations', published by the Graduate Institute of International and Development Studies, Geneva, in 2008 (PSIO Occasional Paper 1/2008). In this publication, I concluded that, on the balance of the evidence, the allegations against the zakat committees were unfounded and that the committees were, by and large, authentic charities motivated by religious and humanitarian considerations with a view to alleviating poverty and distress on the basis of need. I reviewed the contrary interpretation – that the zakat committees were fronts for Hamas – and I rejected it. My conclusions were based on my own fieldwork in Jordan and the Palestinian Territories in 1996; on specially commissioned research to obtain and analyze key documents; on interviews; on the published results of local public opinion surveys; and on the publications of other scholars and commentators.[3] A recent study written by Mr Emanuel Schaeublin, a researcher from the Graduate Institute of International and Development Studies, and funded by the Swiss Federal Department of Foreign Affairs, largely confirms my own findings in the 2008 Occasional Paper that the West Bank zakat committees were not fronts for Hamas. See Schaeublin 2009 'Role and governance of Islamic charitable institutions: The West Bank zakat committees (1977–2009) in the local context' [...]. This study, in which I assisted Mr Schaeublin, was based on analysis of documents and publications and on field research and interviews in the region, even more extensive than my own.

Thus, I continue to believe that a vast array of humanitarian aid is provided in the Palestinian Territories without the involvement of Hamas. I continue to believe that the mere fact that a European charity provides humanitarian aid in the Palestinian Territories does not mean that the organization works with or through Hamas, with or through Hamas-affiliated NGOs, or Hamas-affiliated zakat committees.

Even assuming ASP or CBSP were providing funds for Hamas at the time of Professor Ramadan's donations, I re-affirm my original opinion that it was entirely reasonable for Professor Ramadan to believe that these were legitimate charities. These charities were registered and legal in Switzerland and France respectively, were operating openly, and publicly raising much-needed funds for the alleviation of suffering in Palestine. I remain unaware of any information from the relevant time period that would have led a reasonable person in Professor Ramadan's position to conclude that these charities were supporting terrorism or Hamas.

Respectfully yours,

Jonathan Benthall

Notes

1 *The CBSP was included in the documents because it was earlier thought (in error) that Ramadan had made his donations to the French charity.*
2 What follows in this letter refers to the situation up to June 2007, when the takeover of Gaza by Hamas resulted in a political convulsion and in a radical reorganization of zakat committees in the West Bank. Also, my detailed research has been restricted to the West Bank, where the vast majority of the zakat committees were situated. I believe the situation was similar in Gaza during the period up to 2007, but I have not been able to verify this at first hand.
3 This Occasional Paper is available at *[web address now obsolete – March 2015]* and was made available online and publicized internationally to specialists in this field in September 2008. Printed copies were circulated in November 2008. Though the Occasional Paper has been referenced in a number of other publications by other authors, I have not seen any attempt to refute its arguments and to defend the view of the Israeli and United States governments with regard to the zakat committees.

8

Islamic philanthropy in Indonesia

This review of Amelia Fauzia's *Faith and the State: A history of Islamic philanthropy in Indonesia* (Brill, 2013) was originally published in the *Asian Journal of Social Science* 42: 1–2 (2014), 165–7.

An angle for comparative historical research is proposed here. To what extent did Christian institutions affect the development of Islamic charities in Indonesia, colonized by the Dutch, and in Jordan, under strong British influence during and after the period of the British Mandate for Transjordan (1923–46)?

***

Since the turn of the century, much has been published in English on Islamic philanthropy and humanitarianism, but almost exclusively concentrated on the Middle East, South and Central Asia, and Europe and the United States. In quick succession, however, the field has been widened by two publications on Indonesia: first, a doctoral thesis defended at the University of Utrecht by Hilman Latief in 2012 and available in print, 'Islamic charities and social activism: Welfare, dakwah and politics in Indonesia', and now this monograph by Amelia Fauzia. It derives from a doctoral thesis submitted to the University of Melbourne, and which has been skilfully converted into a book with the help and encouragement of Professor M. C. Ricklefs, the leading historian of Indonesia, who contributes a foreword. Fauzia is currently Deputy Director of the Research Institute at the State Islamic University, Jakarta, but she has previously been Global Director of a Ford Foundation-funded research project on philanthropy for social justice in Muslim societies, which studied six countries (Egypt, India, Indonesia, Turkey, Tanzania and the United Kingdom). The Ford Foundation project faced serious problems after 11 September 2001 attacks on the United States and the ensuing cloud that has hung over Islamic charities since then, together with the emergence of a school of politically influential, but academically dubious, counter-terrorist studies, developments that many observers believe were a regrettable overreaction to 9/11. Fauzia's book, however, has benefited from the comparative perspective she gained from her experience with the Ford Foundation and competes favourably with any survey published so far of Islamic philanthropy in other regions: for example, Amy Singer's *Charity in Islamic Societies* (2008), though authoritative on the Middle Ages and the Ottoman Empire, falls short of covering the turbulence of the present day.

In the Muslim world as a whole, we find a wide variety of different implementations of zakat, the Islamic tithe, varying from full incorporation in the tax system to informal giving to personal acquaintances. The entire spectrum of possibilities is found in Indonesia, where it has been the subject of energetic debates. Fauzia's guiding theme is the tension between the private or personal imperatives of the Islamic revelation – the strong injunctions to give zakat and *sadaqa* (optional charitable giving) – and public conduct where persuasion or coercion can be effective, including that exerted by the modern state. During Dutch colonial rule in Indonesia, the state was strong but decided to minimize its interventions in Muslim religious life, so that Muslim civil society strengthened – as manifested especially in the emergence of the 'modernist' Muhammadiyah, which celebrated its centenary in 2012 and must rank as the world's most important Islamic voluntary network with its over 11,000 non-profit institutions. After independence in 1949, the state was first weak, then strong under Soeharto's New Order (1965–98), then weakened again in the post-Soeharto era.

Fauzia begins her book with a short history of the implementation of zakat and *waqf*, the Islamic equivalent of the European charitable trust, during the pre-modern period in general and specifically in the Indonesian archipelago since the beginning of its Islamization in the thirteenth century. A chapter follows on the Dutch colonial period; then one on the efforts of reformist Muslims to modernize Islamic philanthropy under the secular Dutch government. Fauzia next discusses the development of Islamic philanthropy in Indonesia under the Old Order and then the New Order, when organized civil society was viewed with disfavour though community philanthropy was still practised in the rural grass-roots. Next, she shows how 'modernist' and 'revivalist' Muslims succeeded in pressurizing the *Reformasi* government to co-opt philanthropy according to their own vision of an Islamized state, while encountering covert resistance from religious traditionalists. This sometimes flared into the open, for instance in East Lombok Regency in 2005, when thousands of teachers went on strike in protest against deductions of zakat from their salaries; and since that date there has been strong contestation between the state and civil society with regard to the management of zakat. Finally, Fauzia brings her study up to date by showing how philanthropic practices have become a battleground for various interests and agendas.

Faith and the State is full of fascinating detail: for instance, on the Muhammadiyah 'charity stamps' that were put on sale in 1941 to raise funds and on the Japanese occupation (1942–45), which was the first period when for a short time the state officially sponsored Islamic charities. My own interest is specially attracted by the possibility of comparison with the recent history of zakat administration in Jordan and in the Palestinian Territories, which were under strong Jordanian influence until

1994. A similar tension between different visions of zakat can be identified: should it be centralized under the ministry of religious affairs or left for local communities to organize, as was broadly the case during the 'Oslo period' (1994–2007)? A survey in Indonesia in 2004 indicated that as many as 45 per cent of Muslims paid their zakat directly to beneficiaries. This seems to be a trend in the Palestinian West Bank today because of a shortfall in trust, despite the efforts of the Palestinian Authority, which set out to control zakat centrally after the secession of Gaza in 2007 but has more recently moved back towards accepting a measure of decentralization. If we look back at the history of the Jordanian zakat law, it appears to have been strongly influenced by British charity law, just as the structure of the Muhammadiyah seems to have been influenced by the Dutch law of associations. In both cases we may surmise, without belittling the central importance of zakat and ṣadaqa in Islamic moral teaching, that the Christian tradition of charity helped to shape the evolution of zakat practices in both the Jordanian and the Indonesian colonial encounters, mediated more recently by the post-colonial state.

Amelia Fauzia has already, at an early stage in her academic career, made an indispensable contribution to the study of Islamic philanthropy. The editing and presentation are of the high standard which used to be synonymous with Brill, though this is no longer guaranteed. If *Faith and the State* were published in paperback at a reasonable price, it should find its place in many reading lists.

9

Puripetal force in the charitable field

This chapter was originally prepared for a special issue of *Asian Ethnology*. I took the risk of coining a neologism, 'puripetal force'.

A further example to illustrate the theme of hyper-purism within Islam would be the distinction cited in the Introduction (pp. 13–14) between 'purist' and 'activist' Salafis in Kuwait, set out in Pall 2014.

***

The quest for purity

In 2009, I paid a visit with a Swiss colleague to the president of an Islamic charitable committee in the Palestinian West Bank, a Fatah nominee, shortly after a reorganization and centralization of the West Bank zakat committees that had been effected at the end of 2007 following the Fatah/Hamas split (Schaeublin 2009: 49). The president said that 'the new zakat committees are like a pool of water' and that one drop of ink would pollute the whole pool. The drop of ink was anybody with links to Hamas.

The following chapter will compare many different types of purity seeking. It is itself an attempt to clarify the muddy no man's land between religion and humanitarianism. I assume as axiomatic that all organized disaster relief is informed by values, whether publicly stated or implicit, that furnish some kind of moral order in the face of unlimited human needs. Some years ago, contributors to an edited book on this subject were asked to suggest a snappy title. I suggested 'Pure Aid' but this was turned down in favour of 'Sacred Aid', under which title the book was duly published (Barnett and Stein 2012). This leaves me free to use the idea of 'pure aid' to animate this chapter, which will argue that purity-seeking – which I shall call 'puripetal force' – is a more fundamental concept than sacralization and hence more useful for comparative analysis. Purity is at its most basic the maintenance of boundaries. Whereas in Newtonian physics 'centripetal force' draws bodies towards a central point, and is always balanced by centrifugal force, we may envisage puripetal force as a culturally universal resistance to social entropy or anomie.

'Sacred' is a word with complex connotations. It was the linchpin of Durkheim's theory of religion, referring to special kinds of beliefs and ritual activity that promote social cohesion, as opposed to the 'profane', by which he meant the mundane or everyday. It is true that some commonalities can be observed in religious spaces and timetables all over the world, but a number of social anthropologists have questioned the cross-cultural validity of the sacred–profane distinction derived from ancient Rome, arguing that it is 'vague and ill-defined' (Evans-Pritchard 1960: 12) and 'unusable' (Stanner 1967: 229), and may have limited usefulness even in interpreting the Christian tradition. In Arabic, the same verbal root *ḥa-ru-ma*, to be forbidden, gives us *al-ḥaramain*, the two most sacred places in Islam, Mecca and Medina; the *ḥarīm*, that part of a house reserved for women; and *ḥarām*, prohibited actions such as gambling. In Buddhist thought, the nearest we find is the distinction between *samsara*, the Conditioned, and *nirvana*, the Unconditioned, but these are both categories of *dharma* that merge into one another, so that they cannot be called a mutually exclusive dichotomy (Orrú and Wang 1992: 54–8); moreover, in Buddhist practice we find great emphasis on the salvific possibilities of everyday actions.

The quest for purity is, I suggest, a universal component of ideological systems. My intention here is to use the concept to enable us to avoid using 'religion' or 'faith' as analytical terms – thus sidestepping the difficulty which these terms present, considered by some scholars such as Jonathan Z. Smith (1982) and Timothy Fitzgerald (2007) to be insuperable. I am not of course claiming that religion can be reduced to purism – though the values of chastity, abstinence, asceticism and general obedience to rules may be loosely called 'puritan' and probably have homologous tendencies in all religious traditions. There is a 'paradox of purity', as pointed out by the literary critic Kenneth Burke, in that purity can be logically defined only by its opposite (Burke 1966: 323).[1] He also called it the 'paradox of the absolute' (Burke 1945: 34–5). Moreover, purity is arguably sterile. Much is summed up in the very title of Mary Douglas's anthropological classic *Purity and Danger* (1966). Purity goes with cleanliness, control, coherence, precision and asexuality, whose antonyms are all dangerous but all essential to life and creativity. Hence, as another anthropologist, Edmund Leach, pointed out, the figure of the ascetic monk in religious traditions is balanced by that of the ecstatic shaman who has some kind of access to the supernatural powers that can bring peace, fertility and blessings – but also disasters in the form of earthquakes, epidemics and wars (Leach 2000a: 348–51).

The aim of this chapter is, by drawing on the meditations on purity by Burke, Douglas and Leach, to facilitate discussion of various traditions of ethical order, including religious ones, without having to distinguish sharply between the religious and the secular. It will juxtapose two traditions of ethical order that function at a global level and interact with each other, Islam and humanitarianism; but will close by briefly considering other purisms so as to sketch a multi-dimensional map of rival ethical orders that try to impose their own definitions of purity, sometimes generating conflict and sometimes finding common ground. I shall argue finally that the common ground between humanitarianism and the major religious traditions is expanding.

Purity in Islam

Islam since its foundation inherited a world in which all the major religious traditions were imbued with strong prohibitions and rites of purification surrounding the bodily functions of ingestion, evacuation and sexual activity. This applied even to Christianity, despite the priority that Jesus gave to purity of heart as opposed to ritual practices (Katz 2002: 3–4). Such a tenet necessarily entails an extensive overlap between moral and material values. We find in the Qur'an two important lexical fields concerned with purity. One is centred primarily on the body but also on rectitude, the other on the intellectual principle of monotheism and the rejection of idolatry (into which category was subsumed Christian Trinitarianism as understood in the Qur'an).[2] It is debatable to what extent there was a crossover between the two lexical fields, but if we see Islam as an historical offshoot of Judaism, it is helpful to adduce the precedent of the Hebrew Bible, where Mary Douglas has shown that idolatry was classed together with other defilements: corpses, falsehood, betrayal and shedding of blood (Douglas 1993: 152). Denial of God, polytheism and apostasy have always been strongly rejected and condemned in Islam. One scholar of Islam identifies it as the 'pure religion', meaning that this was how its original followers saw it (Ringgren 1962). More precisely, Islam was especially explicit in asserting its purism, and the purity affirmed by foundational Islam pertained more to a prior ideal condition than to a messianic future (Wansbrough 1978: 147–8).

Islam owed much of its expansionary success over the centuries to its ability to accommodate local belief systems without compromising the commitment to monotheism. Yet within the doctrines and practices of historical Islam we may identify tendencies of varying 'puripetal force'. Of these, the most powerful today is Wahhabism,[3] the version of Islam which has strengthened that force from its pact with Arab petromonarchies. This has mutated more widely into jihadi extremism among a small and toxic minority, through interactions with the tribal Muslim periphery and its discontents (Ahmed 2013), though there is no inevitable historical connection between 'tribal' Islam and political activism.

Purity in philanthropy

The ideological system that I want to spotlight alongside Islam for purposes of analysis is the whole sphere that we call philanthropy or humanitarianism, considered as a complex of social relationships, irrespective of its historical roots in religious traditions. The word 'charity' may also be used here provided that, for this purpose, its strong Christian associations are set aside, for it is one of the English words used to translate the Greek New Testament word for spiritual love, *agapē*, the highest Christian virtue. Charity in a universal sense may be seen as grounded in compassion, the *pitié* that Rousseau saw as a restraint on our *amour de soi*. Charity at its most basic is a bodily act: extending a hand to a stricken traveller or sharing food with a neighbour. All such acts imply an inequality between donor and beneficiary, which opens the way to political relations as soon as actions coalesce into institutions. Yet great efforts have been made to ring-fence areas of charitable activity as distinct from politics and commerce: examples are the Charities Acts in England and the French Law of Associations of 1901, and the recently fashionable idea of 'humanitarian space' – the scope for independent action available in conflict zones (or not, as the case may be) to relief agencies, on the analogy of physical safe zones and corridors.

It is now a commonplace that charity and humanitarian aid have, and have always had, an inescapable political dimension in practice (Donini 2012). But this does not detract from the ideological power of the principle of ring-fencing, which amounts, for liberal Western society, to what the anthropologist Roy Rappaport has called an 'ultimate sacred postulate' (1999: 263). The 'space' allotted to charity is conceived as being unadulterated by either politics or economics. The holding of institutional religion at arm's length from charity is more ambiguous. Organizations that combine religious and humanitarian goals have always been widespread and influential, and are still legal under most jurisdictions. Nowadays, however, under widely accepted codes of conduct, proselytizing among the recipients of aid, and religious discrimination by aid agencies within a given territory, are both prohibited as abuses of power. Hence, overtly evangelical aid agencies (such as the US-based Southern Baptists and Samaritan's Purse) have become outliers in the Christian world whereas they used to be mainstream.

Within the broader charitable sphere we may identify what I have called puripetal tendencies. One such tendency is exemplified by the demand of a recent author, Shawn Flanigan, that aid and evangelism should be legally decoupled, and that international NGOs seeking partnerships among local NGOs should select only the secular ones (Flanigan 2010, 140; 145–6). This view, that the values of 'development' – a euphemism for the now discredited term 'modernization' – are essentially inimical to religion, is probably widely held among many aid professionals, though it is seldom articulated with such candour. Philip Fountain diagnoses Flanigan's assumption, that secular development values are neutral and superior, as deriving from 'the Enlightenment zeal for binary purifications' (Fountain 2013a: 20).

A puripetal tendency of great historical importance has been crystallized in the institutionalization of the International Committee of the Red Cross (ICRC), founded by Henry Dunant and others in 1864, and in the specialized meaning given to the word 'humanitarian' in the Geneva Conventions and other branches of International Humanitarian Law (IHL). Much confusion has been caused by IHL's restrictive understanding of a word that is also used colloquially, often encompassing human rights and 'development' and sometimes meaning no more than 'compassionate'.[4] Geneva law, embodied institutionally in the Swiss government and in duties delegated to the ICRC, is mainly concerned with the protection of people in situations of conflict when they have lost their normal protector. 'Within the humanitarian community', write Michael Barnett and Janice Stein, 'the ICRC is routinely referred to as the "high priests," a designation that simultaneously mocks a holier-than-thou attitude while also paying respect to venerated status' (Barnett and Stein 2012: 26). The ICRC, as part of the International Red Cross and Red Crescent Movement, is officially non-confessional, though the semiotics of the red cross and red crescent emblems has a complex history (Benthall and Bellion-Jourdan 2003, 45–68). An important trend in debate about humanitarianism today calls for a restoration of the original clarity of Dunant's vision of aid givers as neutral third parties in the battlefield, as set out in his *Un Souvenir de Solferino*. But Rebecca Gill has convincingly shown that the history of modern relief aid was much more messy than the retrospective myth of Dunantism allows. Before World War I, the red cross was better known in Britain as the blazon of its military ambulances and VAD (Voluntary Aid Detachment) than as the emblem of the Swiss committee, whose members were widely disparaged by British diplomats as sentimental utopianists. Only after that war did the ICRC successfully establish itself as the moral conscience of the Red Cross movement, and Dunant's masterpiece was not available in English translation till 1947 (Gill 2013).

Médecins Sans Frontières (MSF), which had a turbulent relationship with the ICRC for many years after its foundation in France in 1971, is loyal nonetheless to Dunantist principles of neutrality and independence and, after its expansion into a transnational agency, it has earned almost equal respect (Redfield 2013). It is as puripetal in its own way as the ICRC, and satisfies many of the criteria of a Faith Based Organization (Benthall 2008d: 96–107).

I have already illustrated how the purism of humanitarianism can overlap with the purism of one religious tradition, Christianity, and it can do so in many different ways, for there is a world of difference between the fundamentalist Southern Baptists and the UK-based Christian Aid, which has more in common with the non-confessional Oxfam. But the interface that I will review here in some detail is with Islam.

Islamic charity

The central concept in this interface between the two purisms is that of zakat, the Qur'anic tithe, which is literally central in that it is the third of the five 'pillars of Islam', an affirmation of faith as well as an act of social solidarity. The word is derived from the verb *zakā*, which means to purify, but also with connotations of growth and increase. By giving up part of one's wealth – in broad terms, one-fortieth of net assets per year – one purifies that portion which remains, and also oneself, through a restraint on one's selfishness, greed and imperviousness to the sufferings of others. Likewise, the beneficiary is purified from jealousy and hatred of the well off. Zakat is mandatory and, if it is neglected, no amount of prayer will be efficacious. It is distinguished from *ṣadaqa*, which is optional or voluntary, but closely associated with it: the Arabic *ṣadaqa* had connotations of moral rectitude. Zakat is conceived as the opposite of usurious interest or *riba*, which is essentially corrupting. The most important historical institutionalization of *ṣadaqa* was the *waqf* (plural *awqāf*), the Islamic equivalent of the European charitable trust, which meant literally a 'stopping' or 'tying up' of property for good causes under legal guarantee.

All schools of Sunni Islam are agreed on the importance of zakat, which has inspired many idealistic tracts expounding its potential to generate a society free from the disadvantages of both capitalism and socialism, and linked to the casuistic subtleties of 'Islamic economics', which unlike zakat is entirely a modern construct. There is in practice a wide variation ranging from administration of zakat by the State, as in a few countries including Pakistan, to informal payment of zakat to individuals whom one knows personally.

I will show how the interface between the two purisms is handled in different ways, with special reference to disaster relief in Asia, by British Islamic charities and by their counterparts in the Arabian Gulf. Marie Juul Petersen has elaborated a neat contrast between the two types of charitable ideology, characterizing the former as 'secularizing Islam' and the latter as 'sacralizing aid', though she abstains from evaluating their operational effectiveness (Juul Petersen 2014). My own formulation is similar to hers, but I would see both 'secularizing' and 'sacralizing' as forms of purity seeking that come into conflict with each other. A third example I shall take, drawn from Indonesia, does not fit into Juul Petersen's dichotomy and will be treated here as an intermediate case.

Islamic Relief Worldwide

Of the British Islamic charities, easily the largest is Islamic Relief Worldwide (IRW). It would be enlightening to trace the exact process whereby conservative interpretations of the Qur'anic zakat rules were replaced, in at least two respects, by the more liberal interpretation observed by IRW. The first point is whether all in need are eligible to receive zakat funds or only Muslims. The traditional view was 'only Muslims', and this rule is by no means extinct. But some time during the first eight years after the foundation of Islamic Relief in Britain in 1984, the decision was made to extend its aid to all communities without distinction, and indeed to target that aid to those in the greatest need. The change of view enabled this new charity not only to gain a favourable reputation in Britain and subsequently worldwide, but also to benefit from funding from the British government and European Community institutions. (Muslim Aid, the second largest British Islamic charity, founded in 1985, followed suit later in about 2003.) The test as to whether this principle of non-discrimination has been observed can only be set within the confines of each operational territory where there are mixed religions and ethnicities. In practice, all Muslim aid agencies devote most of their resources to working in Muslim-majority countries, which they justify by drawing attention to the high levels of deprivation and political unrest in large swathes of the Muslim world (De Cordier 2009b).

The second adaptation to the modern charity environment has concerned the understanding of jihad. The seventh of the eight categories of beneficiary eligible for zakat, according to Qur'an 9: 60, is those 'in the way of God', which is interpreted as meaning 'those in jihad'. This is a highly equivocal term whose meaning always varies with its context. One sense of jihad is that it is a striving to overcome one's own weaknesses of character, and an important manifestation of this striving can be taking practical steps to alleviate the suffering of others. But the military sense of jihad has also survived the centuries and some Islamic authorities still maintain that it is admissible for zakat funds to be spent on military efforts in the cause of true religion.[5] For this reason, scholars such as Timur Kuran have been able to argue that zakat is not the same as Christian charity, since a proportion of the resources which it raises can legitimately be spent not only on 'good works' but on various other authorized purposes including the military defence of religion (Kuran 2004). It has thus been extremely important for IRW, Muslim Aid and the other British Muslim charities to display their unequivocal attachment to humanitarian values – non-violence and also abstention from 'political activities' according to the dictates of the Charity Commission of England and Wales, which has set out 'red lines' (subtly changing over the years) that accredited charities have to steer clear of in their campaigning. (Current English charity law, however, like the historic Islamic rules of zakat, accommodates military objectives to some extent in that one of the charitable purposes permitted under the Charities Act 2011 is 'the efficiency of the armed services of the Crown', which includes the subsidy of officers' messes.[6]) IRW has claimed that it 'intentionally and explicitly integrates Islam's perspectives with professional relief and development' (Abuarqub 2010).

A third decision made by IRW was to refrain from any religious activities:

> Da'wa, or inviting others to Islam, is obligatory for each Muslim, always through reasoning rather than luring and coercion. But da'wa has very little to do with international development and should remain a separate activity from humanitarian work. Therefore, while it is important for IR to demonstrate and maintain its faith identity and meet the expectation of its religious donors, the primary focus of the organisation will always be the needs of the poor and vulnerable. (Abuarqub 2010)

This resulted in a policy that has sometimes puzzled: an abstention from building or repairing mosques, whereas members of the Caritas family of Catholic aid agencies have been willing, on occasion, to repair damaged mosques on the grounds that they are cultural assets valuable to a suffering community.

IRW's efforts to balance competing principles have been well explained in a study by Victoria Palmer of the agency's short-lived operation to assist unregistered Rohingya refugees around Teknaf in the Cox's Bazar District, the southernmost point of mainland Bangladesh (Palmer 2011). In the summer of 2013, only some 30,000 refugees who had fled from persecution in the Rhakine State of Myanmar were registered with UNHCR; between 200,000 and 500,000 were unregistered. Since Palmer's field visit in 2008, their plight deteriorated. In July 2012, the Bangladesh government not only decided to turn back these Muslim refugees from its borders with Myanmar, but also ordered European NGOs to suspend their services to unregistered refugees in the region. The result was (at the time of writing this) an increasingly serious crisis in shelter, public health, nutrition, schooling, and law and order (Refugees International 2012).

Palmer's field visit took place two weeks after IRW undertook the planning and management of a new unofficial camp, known as the Leda Camp, to which some 9,600 refugees were moved from Tal Camp, which had been condemned by human rights groups as unsatisfactory. Funding came from the European Commission. MSF had moved on and handed over its healthcare services to IRW, which also took responsibility for water and sanitation, a feeding centre for young children and mothers, and camp management, though the government was responsible for the camp as a whole and deliberately provided only a minimum of services in order to try to make camp life less attractive to prospective refugees. (IRW left in June 2010 and handed over to Muslim Aid.) Palmer examines critically the postulate of 'cultural proximity', which proposes that Faith Based Organizations have an operational advantage when working with beneficiaries who are co-religionists. 'Culture' in the current debates is in effect a euphemism for religion, but Palmer aptly draws attention to other commonalities – of language, diet, dress and physical appearance – between IRW's staff, almost entirely recruited in this case from the local area, and the refugees. Her conclusion (in which she is not alone) is that there is no automatic advantage in cultural proximity, religious or otherwise: it has to be worked for through superior performance. While one should be careful not to generalize from the specific case of this refugee camp, which evidently presented particular difficulties, it is noteworthy that, according to Palmer, most of the fifty Muslim staff members (out of a total of sixty-five) claimed that the religious character of IRW was not a motivating factor for them, and some had transferred from the employment of MSF.

IRW in Bangladesh was caught between two stools: regarded with suspicion politically by the secular government (which has generally been hospitable to every kind of NGO) and criticized by others as not Islamic enough. The question of mosques was specially significant: 'ECHO [the European Community Humanitarian Office] prohibited the building of purpose-built mosques in Leda Camp (in line with their policy of not supporting religious institutions)' (Palmer 2011: 103). IRW designated some community centres as alternative spaces, but they were inadequate: far too small, with no pulpit, no *mihrab* showing the direction of Mecca, no carpet, no loudspeaker for the call to prayer, no nearby water facilities for the obligatory ablutions. 'It is very much a shaming issue for us', the project coordinator told Palmer. 'We are Muslims, our name is also in the name of Islam, but there is no mosque.'

Any aid agency that takes on the responsibility of running a refugee camp runs into the problem that they are almost by definition authoritarian institutions – Michel Agier (2010) uses the phrase 'humanitarian government' – and even in the nearby camps for UN-registered refugees it was found by a Danish fact-finding team that until 2008 they were run by a mafia system (Danish Immigration Service 2011: 21).

My own field experience of IRW's work in Asia, its participation in reconstruction in Aceh, Indonesia, after the great tsunami in 2004, showed it in a favourable light, especially with regard to its rebuilding of houses and schools. But this success seemed largely due to its having committed on a relatively small scale (compared to the over-extension by some larger agencies, which led to costly humiliation) and to its effective management practices. The religious motivation was there in the background, however, engendering an impressive solidarity among their staff and also facilitating cooperation with other faith-based aid agencies [... *see* Chapter 3].

I would also argue that, apart from the contribution that IRW makes to British overseas aid, it has been a force for integration within Britain itself, following the lead of Christian agencies such as Christian Aid and CAFOD, which are held in great respect even by those who are critical of traditional religious leaders. Though founded by Egyptians, who in general have not played a prominent role in the British charitable scene, IRW has achieved an astute, if sometimes contentious, balance between the two purisms of Islam and humanitarianism, but with a leaning towards the latter. It has even been able to do the same in the United States, where several other Islamic charities ran into serious problems after 9/11 (ACLU 2009).

The Muhammadiyah

Another factor that facilitated IRW's early and energetic response in Indonesia to the tsunami was its prior links with the two leading Indonesian Islamic organizations, the reformist or modernist Muhammadiyah, founded in Jogjakarta by Ahmad Dahlan in 1912, and the more traditionalist Nahdatul Ulama (NU). In general, the domestic Indonesian contribution to humanitarian relief after the tsunami was grossly underrated by Western evaluators, but recently it has begun to be documented.[7]

Unfamiliar to most Western commentators, the record of the Muhammadiyah in humanitarianism goes back much earlier in time than the late twentieth century 'Islamic resurgence'. It is better known in Indonesia for its network of schools, universities and health and welfare institutions – some 11,700 in number (Fauzia

2013: 264).[8] But its subsidiary PKU – standing for Penolong Kesengsaraan Umum, 'Assistance for the Relief of Public Suffering' – was first founded by Muhammadiyah members in 1918 as an independent organization to provide emergency services for victims of the eruption of Mount Kelud. Relief work was subsequently undertaken for victims of floods, famines, epidemics and earthquakes. Amelia Fauzia, the historian of Islamic philanthropy in Indonesia, records that the early work of the PKU was influenced by 'al-Ma'un theology' – which alludes to Surah 107 of the Qur'an, 'The neighbourly assistance', a stern warning to those who fall short in their charitable obligations – but also more practically by the examples of the Al-Azhar *waqf* in Cairo, of Christian orphanages, poorhouses and hospitals, and of the Red Cross. The secretary of the PKU wrote in 1929:

> Muhammadiyah's PKU works for and assists the alleviation of public suffering without looking at other parties' work, and without serving other people who want to obtain public influence. It works solely because of the instruction of Islamic teachings brought by our Prophet Muhammad, peace be upon him, and following his tradition.
>
> So, Muhammadiyah's PKU aims to be like an oasis that is pure (*jernih*) and clean, located in a place accessible to everyone no matter what nationality and religion they have. It is there for whoever wishes to drink the water as long as they do not deliberately destroy the stream and close the oasis. Muhammadiyah's PKU does not aim to act like a dragnet to attract people to become Muslim or join Muhammadiyah, but it solely fulfils the Islamic obligations for all nations, irrespective of religion.[9]

Though one of the motivations for the original foundation of the Muhammadiyah had been to provide a counterbalance to Christian missionary activity, the PKU subordinated *da'wa* to humanitarian principles and was fully committed to non-discrimination, and also to cooperation with the Dutch colonial authorities, for which it was criticized by Islamic hardliners. Since 1939, however, according to Fauzia, the inclusive principle became attenuated and was later comprehensively replaced by an exclusive concern for the welfare of the Muslim *umma*. This change was correlated with the ascendancy of what is often called a 'puritan' (or 'Salafi') form of Sunni Islam, which was always strongly represented in the Muhammadiyah, notably in its opposition to syncretism and *takhayul* ('superstitions' such as magical healing), but which never took on the political colours of Wahhabism such as became dominant in Saudi Arabia. The Muhammadiyah always included a strong modernizing and outward-looking tendency. The movement, which claims a membership of some twelve million, is currently split between a conservative backlash, especially with regard to the role of women, and projects for revitalization (van Bruinessen 2012; Burhani 2013). The anthropologist Mitsuo Nakamura has noted that the Muhammadiyah has been successful in 'purifying' the worldview and practice of Javanese Muslims from *kejawen*, that is to say Javanese-ness, including pre-Islamic elements both indigenous and Hindu–Buddhist; but the result may be a spiritual or cultural 'dryness' that needs to be refreshed (Nakamura 2012: 331). Much of the debate within the Muhammadiyah is in fact framed around rival ideas of religious purity: whether cultivation of the self or good deeds should have priority. Nakamura argues that the ethical principle of *ikhlāṣ*, the name of a Qur'anic Surah,[10] embraces both (Nakamura 2012: 200–1).

In the Muslim world as a whole, as noted above, we find a wide variety of different implementations of zakat, varying from full incorporation in the tax system to informal giving to personal acquaintances. The entire spectrum of possibilities is found in Indonesia and has been the subject of energetic debates. In recent years, the tension between hierarchic state control and civil society has assumed warlike proportions (Fauzia 2013: 248), and government efforts to channel Muslim citizens' zakat payments into official funds have met with resistance. In 1978, the Muhammadiyah founded its own zakat institution, Bapelurzam (Badan Pelaksuna Urusan Zakat Muhammadiyah), in the Kendal region of northern Java. Insisting that zakat should be given to institutions rather than to the poor, it is committed to non-discrimination and accountability (Fauzia 2013: 203–10). However, according to a survey carried out in 2004, 45 per cent of Indonesian Muslims claimed to pay their zakat directly to individuals and 51 per cent through local zakat committees (Fauzia 2013: 244).

In 2007, the Muhammadiyah's disaster relief operations, which had risen to prominence after the 2004 tsunami, were brought together as the Muhammadiyah Disaster Management Centre (MDMC), which cooperates with every kind of national and international organization. Among its strengths one may single out two. First, in a country of 17,000 islands, 30 per cent of whose roads are unpaved, MDMC has been able to draw on the Muhammadiyah's huge network of branches to scale up a community's response at the grass-roots to an emergency and thus to increase the efficacy of external aid (Husein 2012). Second, MDMC's knowledge of local cultures gives them a sensitivity to varying interpretations of disasters. According to Mohammad Rokib, the conviction of Muhammadiyah members that a disaster such as the Mount Merapi eruptions of 2010 was a test of moral and spiritual strength – as opposed to mere bad luck or a punishment for past sins – came to be a source of social cohesion, both in recovery from the disaster and in practical steps taken to mitigate its recurrence in future. Moreover, whereas professional psycho-social counsellors left the area soon after the immediate crisis, the Muhammadiyah provided teachers, preachers and prayer leaders to help survivors overcome long-term post-traumatic shock (Rokib 2012).

In its scale and experience the Muhammadiyah should be better known globally as a model for Islamic social activism.[11] The strength of the Muhammadiyah and that of its slightly larger sister organization, the Nahdlatul Ulama (NU), are unique in the Islamic world, and the Muhammadiyah is specially notable for the density of its nationwide networks and degree of administrative rationalization and internal democracy. Their ethos may be distinguished from that of the welfarist networks which emerged in the Middle East and North Africa under the inspiration of the Muslim Brothers of Egypt, who always commingled welfarism, religion and political opposition. Martin van Bruinessen has suggested that the Muhammadiyah's pattern of organization is partly due historically to the demands imposed by the Dutch law of associations during the colonial period (personal communication, 2013). I suggest that the Muhammadiyah has realized a remarkably firm congruence between Islamic purism and humanitarian purism.[12]

The cordon sanitaire of Saudi charities

Reverting to what Juul Petersen calls the 'sacralizing of aid' by Gulf-based Islamic charities, we will take as examples the World Assembly of Muslim Youth (WAMY) and the International Islamic Relief Organization (IIROSA), both based in Saudi Arabia and both affiliated to the Muslim World League. A third major Saudi Islamic charity, Al Haramain, was closed down in 2004 after allegations of supporting terrorism, which remain contentious since it is probable that the main offenders were local operatives who were given latitude by ineffective head office controls to commit nefarious acts (Bokhari et al. 2014).

In August 2012, WAMY announced a programme of relief and rehabilitation for the Rohingya minority of Myanmar, victims of abuse including murder, rape and forcible expulsion (Ali Khan 2012). WAMY was following the lead of King Abdullah of Saudi Arabia, who had recently allocated US$50 million for aid to the Rohingya. The head of WAMY coupled his announcement with a plea to the international community to defend the Rohingya's human rights, calling specially on Arab and Islamic countries and lamenting that the Western media had been largely silent about the massacre of Muslims in Myanmar. Western governments and even Aung San Suu Kyi had turned a blind eye. (This was before President Obama's speech in November 2012.)

WAMY, founded in 1972, claims to have branches in fifty-six countries and affiliations with some 500 youth organizations all over the world. It is an educational and humanitarian charity whose declared aims include preserving 'the identity of Muslim youth' and helping them overcome the problems they face in modern society; introducing Islam to non-Muslims 'in its purest form as a comprehensive system and way of life'; and promoting dialogue between Muslim and non-Muslim societies.[13] What is seen in Saudi Arabia as the purest form of Islam appears to outsiders as a strict variant that adheres to literalist readings of the Qur'an, emphasizes dress, bodily deportment and gender segregation, and excludes popular traditions such as the cult of local saints. [...] In common with many other humanitarian institutions in the Gulf states, both governmental and private or semi-private, WAMY gives de facto preference in allocation of its resources to Muslim populations.

WAMY's two principal commitments are to youth education, including practical warnings about the dangers of addiction, integrated with religious teaching, and to the care of thousands of orphans – a category of beneficiary that is invariably given special attention by Islamic charities (Benthall 2012b: 79–81). WAMY's ability to intervene after disasters has been much reduced by measures taken by Gulf governments in response to the 'war on terror' (Lacey and Benthall 2014) and, in any case, none of its programmes have as far as I know been the subject of serious research. But linguistic analysis of a speech by the secretary general published in English in 2005 gives a revealing hint of the WAMY world-view. Looking back on the year, he recalls the 'natural disasters' that 'emphasize the need for cooperation among nations to face the challenges of time, and thus ease the sufferings of the masses of the world': the Indian Ocean tsunami, refugee movements in Darfur, famine in Niger. Finally, just before earthquakes in South Asia, he mentions, 'It pains me immensely to illustrate the tragic events that rocked the London city subway, Sharm-el-Sheikh and more recently Bali, which resulted in great loss of innocent lives'. The secretary general's train of thought could impel us to adapt for the Salafi context the theory advanced by some sociologists that cultural categories are routinely 'naturalized' as part of a strategy to dominate.[14] 'Islam is without flaw', the subtext seems to run; 'the perpetrators of the "tragic events" of 2006 claimed to be Muslims; therefore rather than allocating responsibility we will characterize them as destructive forces of nature'.

IIROSA, founded in 1978, more pragmatic than WAMY but still deeply grounded in Salafi Islam, was particularly active in Afghanistan in 1980s and later in the former Eastern bloc during the 1990s, when it saw its role as repairing the divisive damage done by Communism to the Muslim religion and culture. In a largely critical interpretation of Saudi charities, the francophone author Abdul-Rahman Ghandour described them (2002: 242) as implementing a cordon sanitaire to maintain ideological influence on the Middle East. The IIROSA in its heyday was the most powerful of these charities, strongly committed to 're-Islamization' (*i'ādat aslamah*), that is to say protecting the identity of Muslim communities from the twin evils of secularization and Christian proselytism. Material relief was sometimes used, for instance in the Bosnian conflict of the early 1990s, to undertake *da'wa* or spiritual relief (Bellion-Jourdan 2003: 142–4), for instance, by distributing militantly anti-Christian videocassettes.

In the 1990s, the IIROSA developed innovative fundraising techniques and opened communications with Western humanitarian organizations through the energy of one of its co-founders, Dr Farid Yaseen Quraishi. In 1996, however, he was dismissed and IIROSA reverted to a discretion more palatable to its Saudi sponsors. After 9/11 and the 'designation' or blacklisting of two of its branches, in Philippines and Indonesia, it went through a lean period and its annual budget, formerly of the order of $85 million, is thought to have been at least halved. More recently, it has

undertaken a revival: not yet through implementing large-scale emergency programmes, but through reaching out energetically to interact with environmental-
ists and agronomists, also with diplomats and non-Muslim aid agencies. In 2013,
IIROSA seemed to be struggling to escape from isolation, as in the 1990s under
Quraishi. For instance, a regular columnist in its magazine *Egatha* presented futur-
istic ideas such as the application to emergency relief operations of artificial intelligence, and the quantification of the needs of each hundred victims of a disaster as
Relief Units (Ezz Eldin 2011; 2012). The relationship with international humanitarianism was still awkward, though likely to be eased in future by the search in the
West for so-called 'new humanitarian donors' to compensate for pressures on aid
budgets.

Peering into purity of motives

IIROSA has come up against another form of purism: that currently espoused by
the US government and judiciary with regard to humanitarian activity. Whereas
IIROSA's head office, as opposed to two of its former branches,[15] is not 'designated'
as a terrorist entity, it was still in the spring of 2015 regarded with suspicion in the
USA, for the US government places high priority on probing into the purity of
motives as opposed to that of effects.

Imagine a major earthquake such as the one that hit the Kashmir region in 2005.
One voluntary association, let us call it Al-Aleph,[16] has much the best local knowledge to reach isolated mountain villages to bring help to survivors. It happens to be
affiliated to a group that has been designated by the USA as a terrorist organization.
You are the leader of a foreign rescue unit with technical resources but no knowledge
of the region. Is it your priority to cooperate with the voluntary association to help
search for survivors, dig them out from the rubble, give them medical attention, and
secure a proper burial for the dead? Most people would answer 'yes', and indeed in
2005 international agencies were quite willing to cooperate with such a group; but
if you have any connections with the USA you would now risk being prosecuted in
the criminal courts for giving 'material support' to terrorism, which is considered
equivalent to terrorism itself and can be punished by a life sentence in prison.

Let us take another hypothetical example, a hospital called Al-Ba' located in
the Gaza Strip. It specializes, let us say, in obstetrics and mother and baby care. It
provides its services without any enquiry into the religion or political affiliations
of patients, that is to say it functions on the basis of need – with graduated fees
depending on the patient's ability to pay, sometimes without charging any fee at all.
But it is deemed by the enemies of Hamas to be part of the Hamas network on the
grounds that it is controlled by, or affiliated with, an Islamic charity. Whether the
supposition is justified is another matter. This is a delicate matter and according to
research in which I have participated, until the split between Hamas and Fatah in
2007 the Islamic charities in the Palestinian Territories were much less politicized

than the Israeli and American counter-terrorist advisers believed – though by 2013 such a hospital has been much more likely to be directly controlled by the Hamas government in Gaza (Schaeublin 2012).[17] If the hospital were turning away patients who rejected Hamas's political ideology, or using medical care as a way of recruiting Hamas supporters, then it would probably be more justifiable for the Al-Ba' hospital to be blacklisted, and for any donor who sent it money to risk criminal prosecution. But I have hypothesized that the evidence is that Al-Ba' provides its services 'without adverse distinction', as the Geneva Conventions put it,[18] thus making it eligible for protection as a humanitarian institution. Current US law, however, will have none of this. It is less interested in the actual provision of humanitarian services than in the question of whether or not the motives of the hospital managers and its donors are tainted, to which it adds the doctrine of fungibility or convertibility, which holds that $10,000 sent to Al-Ba' hospital liberates money that Hamas would otherwise have spent on medicines, so that it can spend $10,000 on bombs, with the result that the hospital's entire medical activities are deemed to be beyond redemption.

Actually the US government and Islamic *ulama* would be in agreement as to the all-importance of purity of intention – *nīyah* in Arabic. The US government goes further and argues that even if one's intention is pure, one is still liable to be criminalized if one allows one's acts to be corrupted by the intentions of others. Proof of this is the much-criticized decision of the US Supreme Court in 2010 (*Holder* v. *Humanitarian Law Project*), which makes it illegal for a peacebuilding or mediating NGO to try to persuade a terrorist organization to put down its weapons and have trust in the political process. Why? Because it could be lending that terrorist organization legitimacy. Yet in Northern Ireland, peace would surely not have come without decades of work by church groups, women's groups, youth groups and others to take the initiative away from the paramilitaries.

One danger of clamping down on decent Islamic charities is that a humanitarian vacuum is left which can be filled by extremists including those of the Al-Qaeda persuasion. Ultimately, we need to form balanced judgments on the basis of outcomes, which I suggest are more important than purity of intention, especially because, despite the best efforts of our law courts to 'read' the states of mind of individuals, this is not an exercise where certainty is possible. The UK Charity Commission's approach to problems relating to terrorist abuse of charities seems to strike a sensible balance, based on the concepts of risk reduction and proportionality and on the core principle that funds raised for charitable purposes must be spent faithfully for those purposes and protected from abuse. Purity is ascribed to the verifiable conditions on which the funds were solicited (generally in the context of concessions by the taxation authorities).

Unresolved tensions are currently in play between the international NGO sector on the one hand, which observes that an overreaction against Islamic charities has put at legal risk the operations of all NGOs in countries such as Syria, Sudan and Somalia (in addition to the physical risks of working in conflict zones), and on

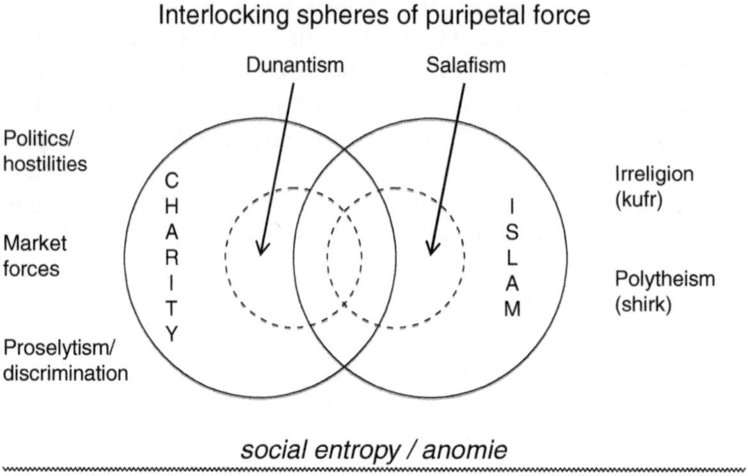

Interlocking spheres of puripetal force

social entropy / anomie

Figure 1 Interlocking spheres of puripetal force.

This figure is a visualization of the quest for purities as analogous to competing gravitational forces. The Dunantism of the ICRC and the Salafi trend are forms of intense puripetalism within their respective spheres. The figure could be expanded multidimensionally to include other religious and quasi-religious movements, and various schools of law.

the other hand the US government position which dominates the policies of the Financial Action Task Force (FATF), a powerful organization under the OECD, effectively controlling the compliance procedures of the international banking system.[19]

I have chosen to describe and interpret the relationship between the purisms of humanitarianism and Islam. Figure 1 is intended to schematize the relationship between these two spheres, each rough-hewn at their edges but including concentrations of puripetal force. The sphere of Christianity could be added with ease in this scheme, embracing a wide variety of contemporary puripetal movements including conservative evangelicalism, the Eastern Orthodox Churches, and conservative tendencies in Roman Catholicism – though we may go further back in time to include the Reformation, the Religious Society of Friends, and Unitarianism.[20]

The interactions are multidimensional. For instance, a key concept in Christian moral theology is service – in Greek, *diakonīa*. The social teaching of the Gülen Movement – founded in Turkey but now markedly transnational – has been realized in such organizations as the Istanbul-based international relief organization Kimse Yok Mu (Is there anybody there?)[21]. It is consistent with modern interpretations of the Qur'anic zakat prescriptions, but gives much more emphasis to the concept of *hizmet* – a common Turkish word meaning 'service', used in both secular and religious contexts – which is indeed an alternative name for the Movement (Harrington 2011: 11–13). Arabic Bibles translate the Greek *diakonīa* as *khidma*, which does not appear in the Qur'an (unlike the term *'abd*, 'slave', whose derivative *'ibāda* is used to signify devotion to God). It is as if the intention has been to purify Islam of the contentious resonances of jihad and (in some anti-Muslim circles) zakat, with the unacknowledged aid of New Testament theology.[22]

The main pressure points today between the spheres of institutional religion and the sphere of humanist ethics are at the level of individual autonomy: where theological principles are brought to bear on legislation concerning sexuality, reproduction and euthanasia – issues that secular liberals prefer to regard as belonging to the domain of individual choice, provided only that the vulnerable are protected (Perreau-Saussine 2012: 37). The chosen stand of the Abrahamic monotheisms against the tide of secular humanitarianism will be to defend the purity of theological principles, variously formulated. Yet with regard to issues of social justice and responses to disasters and extreme deprivation, the points of tension are now reduced. All these systems of thought face the same dilemma: that they are in practice subordinate to the ungentle and impure realities of the 'structurally violent' world whose sufferings they hope to alleviate.[23] In some limited compensation for the sharpness of these class and sectarian divisions, I would argue that there is a significant convergence between the institutions of international humanitarianism and religion – exemplified in the work of Islamic Relief Worldwide and the Muhammadiyah, Caritas and Christian Aid – or, in schematic terms, an enlargement of the area of overlap between competing puripetal forces. Which gives some grounds for hope.

Acknowledgements

I am most grateful to the editors and all the Asia Research Institute, National University of Singapore, team for stimulus and comments on drafts, to Martin van Bruinessen for advice on Indonesia, and to Emanuel Schaeublin and Christian Lekon for commenting on a near final draft. The usual disclaimers apply.

Notes

1 I was led to Burke's writings on purity by Grano and Zagacki (2011), who analyze the reopening of the New Orleans Superdome for Monday Night Football in September 2006 as a purification ritual to purge post-Katrina guilt, because in the aftermath of the hurricane 'poor, predominantly African American evacuees [had been] cast as an animalistic mass' in the same space.

2 The key Arabic roots of the former are *ṭ-h-r*, *ṭ-ī-b* and *z-k-t* (Katz 2002); of the second, *kh-l-s* (Ringgren 1962), as in the title of Surah 112 of the Quran, *Al-Ikhlāṣ*, 'The Purity of Faith'. For further analysis see Benthall and Bellion-Jourdan (2003: 24–5). See also Gauvain (2013). Neither he nor Katz makes a connection between the two lexical fields, but there appears to be such a connection with the root *ṭ-h-r* in Qur'an 3: 55.

3 Wahhabis generally prefer to call themselves Salafis, an extremely protean term. The original Salafiyya of the late nineteenth century, based in Egypt, had modernizing aspects, for instance in insisting that Muslims free themselves from the 'imitation' (*taqlīd*) of traditional authority. Samira Haj has argued persuasively that Ibn Abd al-Wahhab (1702/3–91/2), the founder of the Wahhabi movement and its alliance with the House of Saud, when viewed in his historical context, 'differed from other reformers both in his condemnatory attitude toward certain practices [such as the veneration of saints and shrines] and his reliance on force to correct them. However, neither his alliance with the Saudi tribal chiefs nor his restrictive attitudes can be attributed, as mainstream scholarship does, to a violent, fundamentalist, or traditional strain in Islamic thought' (Haj 2008: 65–6). Yet her study confirms that the Wahhabiya was essentially a purification movement, the pursuit of *ikhlāṣ* (ibid.: 51).

4 A lucid history of the word 'humanitarian' is given in Davies 2012.

5 Cf. Qaradawi n.d.: vol. 2, 57–73. Similarly, the fourth category of eligible beneficiary, 'those whose hearts are made to incline to truth', can be understood to legitimize spending on proselytism and religious propaganda; and the fifth category, 'captives', to legitimize support for anti-colonial movements or Muslim minorities living in non-Muslim tyrannies.

6 E.g. the Royal Air Force Coningsby Officers' Mess, registered charity no. 1137559.

7 See Ratcliffe (2007) for early recognition of this, and Husein (2012).

8 *My review of Fauzia 2013 is republished here as Chapter 8.*

9 Translated from the Indonesian and cited by Fauzia (2013: 152).

10 See n. 2.

11 In November–December 2012, the Muhammadiyah organized a large centennial research conference at one of its universities, in Malang, East Java, reviewing 'a renewed identity for its post-centennial era'. Remarkably, the convenors allowed and encouraged candid criticism of the organization as well as praise for its achievements and academic analysis, recognizing new challenges such as the threat of infiltration by violent extremists.

12 These two important organizations are not alone in providing humanitarian services in Indonesia, for '[W]e can assume that there is a wide ideological spectrum of Islamic humanitarian agencies that have emerged in response to communal conflicts, and that their political orientations are as varied as the social and educational backgrounds of their founders and volunteers' (Latief 2012: 106). Jihadi groups in Indonesia such as Laskar Jihad have followed a mixed agenda of religious militancy and humanitarian relief, but not to the same extent as some similar groups in, for instance, Pakistan.

13 www.wamy.co.uk/index.php?sub=subpage&mod=about.

14 Cf. Bourdieu 2003: 105.

15 In Philippines and Indonesia. Given that Saudi society is hierarchic, the situation seems anomalous.

16 Pseudonyms have been used here for the names of organizations in order to draw attention to the issues of principle that are raised, irrespective of ethnographic data which may be contested.

17 As for the West Bank, the actual outcome was that in 2013 the new Fatah-controlled zakat committees had sacrificed most of the trust, and funding flows, built up over many years before 2007 by the until then decentralized, and relatively unpoliticized, zakat committees which the PA and Fatah decided in 2007, under pressure from the US government, to dismantle.

18 Additional Protocol II (1977), Article 18.

19 For sustained coverage of these issues, see the website of the Charity and Security Network, Washington, DC: www.charityandsecurity.org.

20 I must leave others to test the applicability of the model to other ideological movements, both religious and political, some of them highly contentious, especially where Judaism and Israel are concerned. But here we may note the importance of another ideological sphere, that of jurisprudence, which impacts on humanitarianism and charities but is also bound up in religious teaching through Halakha, Sharia and ecclesiastical law.

21 The name was inspired by the call made to identify survivors in the rubble after an earthquake.

22 Michael Feener points out, however, that in Indonesia and some other post-colonial contexts, Christian *diakonīa* has been viewed by many Muslims as a form of enticement to lead Muslims astray (personal communication, 2013). I have not come across this pejorative association of the word in Arab contexts.

23 Key texts for understanding the general crisis of humanitarianism include Duffield (2001), Donini (2012) and Fassin (2012). I have tried myself to analyze the 'stable system' or disaster–media–aid nexus, whereby representations of misery in the South are turned into consumables for the North, which reciprocates with aid flows (Benthall 2009: ix–xxvii).

Part II

Islamic humanism

10

Confessional cousins and the rest: the structure of Islamic toleration

This chapter attempts to bring to bear some insights from cultural anthropology on the question of religious toleration, a cornerstone of modern humanism. It concludes, from examining in particular the respective historical attitudes of Christianity and Islam towards 'polytheistic' belief systems, that they both can claim their own tradition of toleration. A starting point for all such discussions ought to be that the history of Christianity has been blemished by episodes of intolerance which have almost exceeded what Islam is blamed for. In particular, too, the Ottoman Empire achieved a kind of multi-religious and multi-ethnic equilibrium until it unravelled after the mid-nineteenth century. But the genocide of Armenians between 1915 and 1917 was a scar on Turkish history, for which the old *dhimmi* system described in this chapter must bear some responsibility.

The specialist debate about toleration within Islam has developed in the ten years since this chapter's publication in *Anthropology Today* in February 2005. Though I cited three papers by Yohanan Friedmann, I was not aware when going to press of his important monograph, *Tolerance and Coercion in Islam: Interfaith relations in the Muslim tradition* (Friedmann 2003). According to him, this is 'not a book of political or social history and does not try to compare the treatment of religious minorities in various civilizations ... It rather deals with the laws themselves ... It is a book concerned with Muslim ethos rather than Muslim history' (ibid.: 11–12). He makes clear that the exaltedness of Islam is an undisputed theme during the period of classical Islam, reflecting the positive self-image maintained at the time by all religious groups. Yet, in 'some sources', hierarchy between the non-Muslim religions may be discerned, in descending order: Christianity, Judaism, Zoroastrianism and polytheism (of which a loose translation is *shirk*[1]) (ibid.: 38–9). There was no authoritative resolution of the ambiguity as to whether Christians and Jews were or were not *mushrikūn* (ibid.: 72). As regards Muslim rule in India, Friedmann reiterates his position that was drawn on in my article: 'The only way a small Muslim garrison could govern an area inhabited by a non-Muslim and idolatrous population was to allow that population to retain its traditions and interfere as little as possible in its affairs' (ibid.: 85).

Two scholarly monographs on the broad topic of Islam and other religions have appeared since 2005.[2] Anver E. Emon in *Religious Pluralism and Islamic Law* (Emon 2012) rejects the concept of tolerance as a useful analytical tool and refuses to take sides with those who argue that the institution of the *dhimma* – roughly equivalent to the 'People of the Book' – was a mechanism either for interreligious harmony or for the persecution of minorities. According to him, Sharia is best understood as a 'claim space' delimiting what can be counted as legal argument. Different schools of Islamic thought in its heyday debated such questions as to whether Christians should be allowed to ring church bells and whether Zoroastrians were 'People of the Book'. The *dhimmi* rules do survive today in some Muslim majority countries such as Saudi Arabia, but the old pluralism of Islamic legal doctrines has been replaced by competition with the modern bureaucratic state, the international order, and customary and local norms. Emon also draws an arresting parallel between pre-modern treatment of the *dhimmi* and the arguments deployed in Euro-American courts today when the rights of religious minorities – for instance, with regard to dress or observance of holidays – clash with the imperative of social cohesion.

Jerusha Tanner Lamptey's *Never Wholly Other* (2014) is a learned analysis of the Qur'an's treatment of religious diversity, written explicitly within the context of a feminist Islamic scholarship that flourishes particularly in the United States, facilitated by academic institutions of Christian theology. Lamptey notes that the Qur'an varies between positive evaluation of religious otherness and blatant scorn. She argues persuasively that the 'proximate Other' presents more of a challenge than the 'distant Other'. In the case of Islam, Christianity or Judaism is 'the Other-who-can-never-be-wholly-other'. Lamptey considers towards the end of her book (2014: 246) the predicament of those born outside the purview of 'People of the Book', whereas the Qur'an assures that 'every community [*umma*] has been sent a warner' (35: 24). For her, there are two options. One is to restrict the denotation of 'People of the Book' to the groups named in the Qur'an and accept its relative silence as regards other communities. The other choice is to 'reconceive this term as more inclusive and even possibly wholly inclusive. The latter may seem to be a radical supposition, but if revelation is truly universal and the term *kitāb* [book] refers to both a physical book of scripture and also to revelation in general, then this conclusion is viable. Moreover, inclusion within this category cannot be based upon perfect adherence to *taqwā* [piety] or absolute monotheism, since the Qur'ān criticizes some of the People of the Scripture for failing in both these categories'. This is the same conclusion that I reach in the following article, though from the perspective of cultural anthropology, and in particular the study of indigenous cosmologies, rather than from that of Islamic theology.

A more wide-ranging writer, Gerard Russell, in his *Heirs to Forgotten Kingdoms: Journeys into the disappearing religions of the Middle East*, shows that 'whereas Christians had no hesitation about putting an end to the Norse or Celtic religions and relatively quick success in doing so', some Middle Eastern 'pagans' were deeply learned in Greek philosophy and Babylonian astronomy, and were able to cling on for much longer. Several of these groups survived because they managed to secure the label of 'People of the Book' for themselves: one example being the Mandaeans, indigenous to southern Mesopotamia, who were able to slip into the elusive Qur'anic category of 'Sabians' (Russell 2014: xxii, 10, 40, 60). The purist movement of thought initiated by Ibn Taymiyyah and Ibn 'Abd al-Wahhab was responsible for the later stigmatization of these religious systems.

In 2014, the so-called Islamic State (or ISIS), that gruesome distorting mirror of religion, persecuted the Christians under its control on the grounds that they were *dhimmis*. In the Iraqi town of Mosul, ISIS threatened death to those Christians who refused to pay a poll tax (*jizya*) and abide by strict regulations, or to convert to Islam, or to flee the city within forty-eight hours. Within three days, the vast majority of Christians (and also Shia Muslims) had fled. But the Yazidi minority were classified as polytheists (*mushrikūn*) and treated even more ferociously as Satanists who could be enslaved and whose women could be made ISIS concubines (Lister 2014: 26–7).

Sadly, the hopes expressed at the end of this article for a positive resolution of the political impasse in Sudan were frustrated. But my argument stands, that there is evident scope for flexibility in Islamic teaching about other belief systems.

A secondary theme is the proposition that there is no equivalent in Islamic social thought to the radical self-questioning of the Christian West which dates back to Bartolomé Las Casas and Michel Montaigne and to which cultural anthropologists have contributed since the nineteenth century. I pondered here on whether there can be a Muslim equivalent to Lévi-Strauss, who treated Amerindian myth as equally worthy of respect as European philosophy and psychology. For instance, in *The Jealous Potter* (Lévi-Strauss 1988) he contended that psychoanalysts merely rediscovered symbolic connections relating to the human body that groups such as the Jivaro of the Amazon, formerly regarded as savages, were perfectly aware of and dramatized in their mythology.

There are two possibilities. Either I was right in diagnosing a subtle inhibition that confines Muslim social scientists to the study of monotheistic cultures or else it is simply a matter of time before cultural anthropology as a global discipline extends its influence into Muslim education and scholarship. Indonesian and Malaysian anthropology may well be an exception that tests the rule: that is to say, they provide examples of Muslim anthropologists, such as the eminent Javanese scholar Koentjaraningrat (1923–99) who undertook the hajj with his wife in his mid-seventies, after suffering a series of strokes (Fox 2001: 244). He had no difficulty in accepting the precepts of late twentieth century Western anthropology and applying them to the cultural mosaic of insular South East Asia, which includes many examples of so-called paganism or polytheism. I have the impression that it is more common in Malaysia than in Indonesia for young Muslim anthropologists to undertake ethnographic fieldwork with groups other than monotheists. But in the Arabian heartlands of Islam, all the social sciences – and in particular cultural anthropology and the sociology of religion – are still extremely weak. For those who believe that 'Islam is the answer', natural science, medical science and technology are legitimate objects of study, but the social sciences are basically redundant.

Another exception that tests the rule is the distinguished personal career of the Turkish anthropologist, Professor Nur Yalman of Harvard University. His remarkably broad scholarly interests include ethnographic studies of Hindus and Buddhists in South Asia. He describes his values today as 'pan-humanist', drawing attention especially to the influence of Indian spiritual traditions on Sufi Islam. Though there may not yet have been a 'Muslim Lévi-Strauss', Yalman has been entirely at one with the intellectual centre of gravity in social-cultural anthropology during the second half of the twentieth century, praising for instance Lévi-Strauss's 'creative originality … in alerting us to the importance and complexity of the life of the imagination of "peoples without writing" … He deserves full credit for destroying the very concept of "primitive peoples" and "primitive mentality"' (Yalman 1996). But the imprint of Islamic doctrine on Yalman would seem to have been exceptionally mild. He was born into a highly intellectual and libertarian family, including his grandfather, who was a publisher and a senior Freemason, and an uncle, Ahmet Emin Yalman, who had a doctorate from Columbia University and was President of the International Press Institute. Nur Yalman's secondary education was at the American school in Istanbul, Robert College, before he studied anthropology in Cambridge, England, with such mentors as Edmund Leach, Meyer Fortes and Jack Goody (Yalman 1967; 2004). In any case, he predicts that Turkey with its tradition of free debate and enquiry, and its approximately 200 universities, will soon provide a home for a humanistic anthropology unconfined by regional or confessional limitations (Yalman personal communication, March 2015).

The equally cosmopolitan Tunisian-born social anthropologist Professor Mondher Kilani of Lausanne University has published widely on a variety of anthropological topics including cargo cults in Papua New Guinea. His secondary education was at the Lycée Carnot in Paris, followed by university studies in Lausanne and Paris. He is specially noted for his critical approach to the universalist bias of anthropological discourse, holding that, while an absolutely non-ethnocentric viewpoint is both theoretically and practically impossible, anthropologists need to reflect on the unexamined assumptions underpinning Western universalism. I should add that in response to an earlier article on 'the religious provenances of anthropologists', which set out to recognize non-Western intellectual sources on the discipline (Benthall 1996), Kilani has charged me with a tendency to 'confessionalize' the discipline. He questions 'why anyone should feel obliged to establish a close connection between the formulation of a position that is critical or dissident with respect to mainstream anthropology – a position that in and of itself is more than welcome – and the author's "religious" or "cultural" origin'. 'Benthall seems to have assumed that my own critical approach to the universalist basis of anthropological discourse must necessarily be mediated by my supposed affiliation with the Islamic tradition' (Kilani 2012: 99–101).

Complex and sensitive questions are raised here which deserve to be considered in more depth. But they may have some traction in the light of Fenella Cannell's suggestions: 'Christianity has functioned in some ways as "the repressed" of anthropology over the period of the formation of the discipline' (Cannell 2006: 4). Discussion of the religious provenances of anthropologists is not off limits: the intellectual biography of Mary Douglas, for instance, gives careful attention to her upbringing as a 'cradle Catholic' and to the Catholic elements in the work of her mentor Evans-Pritchard (Fardon 1999).

***

Religious toleration is a topic addressed by several anthropologists, especially in the contexts of insular South East Asia (Geertz 1960; Beatty 1999; Hefner 1985; Bowen 1996) and the Middle East (Dwyer 1997). In a study of India, too, Peter van der Veer has unveiled the ideological content in the reputation of modern Hinduism for religious toleration, in the sense of pluralism under a secular state. He suggests that this Westernized concept does not correspond exactly with the Hindu tradition of 'hierarchical relativism' – that is to say, the contention that there are many paths and gods, but in a hierarchical order (van der Veer 1994).

But toleration is not yet a standard topic in anthropology, or one to which other disciplines look for guidance. Toleration, in the strict and historical sense followed in this article, rests on a 'double negation' – I negatively appraise something that others do, but decide not to interfere with it (Galeotti 2002) – and also on a relationship of dominance. It may be distinguished from cultural pluralism and relativism, with their egalitarian, anti-hierarchic leanings.

One of anthropology's achievements is to recognize subtlety and philosophical insight in many belief systems once disparaged – with such disastrous consequences for the colonized – as 'pagan' or 'animist'. It questions whether Eurocentric distinctions between religion on the one hand and social and environmental relations on the other are always applicable to them. It also recognizes 'powerful cosmic explanatory systems, proto-scientific in their bio-zoological classificatory scope and analogical in their method of reasoning' (Parkin 2000: 13). The anthropological critique of Christian proselytism led to this, but the modern principle of religious toleration did at least prepare the ground.

Let us take as a working assumption that Judaeo-Christian preconceptions remain even with those who have dropped or diluted their Judaeo-Christian beliefs. To get a comparative bearing on Christian and post-Christian toleration, we may consider the history of Islam, which like Christianity is a universalizing ideology with a long tradition of imperialism and proselytism, though with significant differences. Both Islam and Christianity inherited the ancient Jewish abhorrence of idolatry, which in Jewish theology is held to relate to true religion as adultery relates to marriage (Halbertal and Margalit 1992).

Toleration in Islam

Selective quotations from the Qur'an are inconclusive, ranging from the apparently belligerent 'sword verse' (9: 5) to the famous 'Let there be no compulsion in religion' (2: 256), which, though often interpreted today as enjoining tolerance, was traditionally taken to refer to the right of non-Muslims to convert without impediment (Urvoy 1996: 25). The classic Islamic doctrine of toleration is concentric. In the middle is Islam, resting on the revealed words of God. At the periphery are the feared and despised forces of *shirk* and *kufr*, polytheism and rejection of God – *kufr* having more shocking connotations than our 'unbelief', since it has overtones of ingratitude and infidelity. Occupying the intermediate, liminal position are the People of the Book or scriptuaries – mainly Jews and Christians – given recognition as *dhimmis*, who paid a poll tax in return for qualified rights and protection (Tritton 1930; Fattal 1958; Ye'or 1994). According to Bernard Lewis's model, there were three basic inequalities in classical Islam: between master and slave, man and woman, believer and unbeliever. However, the lower status of the unbeliever, unlike those of the slave or the woman, was essentially voluntary (Lewis 1984). People of the Book had the choice of converting to Islam or accepting *dhimmi* status. And the intermediate statuses of *dhimmi* and *musta'min* (temporary non-Muslim resident) once had their structural counterparts with the freedman or *mawlā*, who was halfway between a free man and a slave, and the eunuch, who could move freely between the male and female worlds (Lewis 1988).

There is no equivalent to this in Christendom. It is fair to recognize the institution of the *dhimma* as the Islamic precursor of the public international law that emerged in Christian Europe in the early seventeenth century and it was the foundation of the *millet* (religious community) system of the Ottoman Empire (Masters 2001). However, scholarly interpretation of the *dhimma* has been affected by a strong monotheistic bias.

All anthropologists know that, despite the ideology of the undivided Islamic *umma*, or 'community', Muslim societies have displayed much variety and much compromise between official doctrine and local belief systems – just as the original Revelation may be seen as an expression of Near Eastern monotheism in an Arab garb. This polymorphism was the norm in the Muslim belt of Africa, in insular South East Asia and other regions where Islam spread to be the dominant religion – until the advent of reformist movements such as the Wahhabists and Mahdists who sought to revive what they claimed was an original strictness of doctrine.

Michael Lambek, in his discussion of Islam in the French island dependency of Mayotte in the western Indian Ocean (Lambek 2000), prefers to write of 'acceptance' of Islam rather than 'conversion', indicating a process that is gradual and collective, not so much a rejection of the past as 'a cumulative embracing of opportunities'. Indeed, it may be that the indigenous belief system has incorporated or converted Islam, just as much as the other way round, a similar dialectical process to that which generated the much more complex mosaic of devotional practices to be found in south India, sometimes described as fully integrated 'Indian' religious systems (Ahmad 1981; Bayly 1989). In Mayotte, *'ilim dunia* is the 'this-world' tradition of knowledge concerned with what Lambek calls 'cosmological' (or astrological) Arabic texts and possibly even predating the penetration of Islam, which dates back to the eleventh century CE, as opposed to *'ilim fakihi*, the learned tradition concerned with Islamic texts. *'Ilim dunia* 'does not dispute Islam so much as disregard it' (Lambek 1993: 228). The two traditions are discordant, especially with regard to such fundamental issues as death, fate and individual accountability, yet 'the two systems exist side beside without an obvious sense of contradiction' (ibid.: 397). A trajectory of three stages in the penetration of Islam in Africa has been suggested by one historian (Fisher 1973; see also Peel 2000): quarantine, mixing and reform.

But what of the regions where substantial non-Muslim and non-monotheistic populations have survived under Muslim rule? What happens when populations reject the insurance policy of conversion while continuing to revere their own local spirits (Gellner 1988)? Key places to look for this today are southern Sudan, where it is said that the majority of the population have not converted to either Islam or Christianity (though I can find no firm data on this), and Indonesia, which is a religious state though not an Islamic state, and one where many small 'animist' communities survive. It has built its nationalist *pancasila* ideology around an explicit idea of toleration with belief in one god as a major element (Ramage 1995).

India, however, must provide the historical *locus classicus*, for there the contact with indigenous Indian belief systems became dramatic with the extension of Islamic rule to North India under the Delhi sultanate in the early thirteenth century. Two and a half centuries have gone by since the fall of Muslim rule in India, making any direct comparison with Muslim states of the early twenty-first century impossible. Just to note the most obvious difference, there are no states today in which a Muslim court rules over a large non-Muslim majority. But perhaps some broad generalizations may be hazarded.

Islam in India

The text-based authority of the *ulama* had to contend both with the political commitments of rulers and with other objects of popular respect such as holy lineages and Sufi orders and saints (Bayly 1989; Gopal Krishna 1995). Some anthropologists have drawn attention to the continual reworking of a 'folk theology' that may float almost free from formal doctrine (for a debate on which see Das 1984; Robinson 2000). The historian Richard M. Eaton has given sustained attention to the various reasons for the spread of Islam in India, especially Bengal, emphasizing that in the pre-modern period the line separating Islam from non-Islam was porous and shift-ing (Eaton 1993). A leading Indian historian of thirteenth century India concludes that the Turkish governing class were more racially than religiously exclusive, the Sufi mystics' attitude was one of 'sympathetic understanding and adjustment', while Muslim merchants respected Hindus for their trade ethics (Nizami 2002: 332).

But it is likely that the various cults and devotional traditions now known as Hindu would have been legally classified with the pagans of the Arabian peninsula, had the Arab conquerors been less outnumbered (Friedmann 1972). The recogni-tion in the Qur'an of the shadowy Sabians (2: 62; 5: 69; 22: 17) and Magi (22: 17) was extended to include the Zoroastrians of Persia, thanks to a hadith according to which the Prophet authorized this. The categories of People of the Book and *dhimmi* ceased to be synonymous and began to diverge (Friedmann 1998). The Arab con-querors of Sind in the early eighth century treated the Indian temples on a par with churches and synagogues, and the Hindus were generally accepted as *dhimmi*s by the Hanafi school of law that came to predominate in India (Jackson 1999).

Al-Biruni, the great eleventh century Iranian Indologist, came to the conclu-sion, in those parts of his *Kitāb al-hind* dealing with beliefs and customs, that the Hindu elites worshipped God alone and only the common people needed objects of worship or idols. Some later Muslim scholars followed al-Biruni in adopting a con-ciliatory approach to Hinduism. For instance, Dara Shikoh (1615–59), son of the Moghul Emperor Shah Jahan, held that all heavenly books, including the Vedas, stem from one source and constitute commentary on one another. Explanation of cruxes in the Qur'an might thus be found in the Hindu sacred texts. Idolatry was needed by those not yet aware of the inner *(bāṭin)* meaning of religion (Friedmann 1975).

These conciliatory approaches were balanced by other views, those of the Shafiʻi and Hanbali schools of law. The heresiographer al-Shahrastāni held that all Indian sects were polytheists. Some other medieval Muslim thinkers living in India advo-cated violence against Hindus. It is recorded (by a virulently anti-Hindu chronic-ler) that the early thirteenth century sultan Iltutmish was approached by leading scholars who asked him to withdraw the status of *dhimmi* from the Hindus and treat them as *kāfirs*, to be offered 'death or Islam'. According to this account, he sent his vizier to reply to the *ulama* that their view might become realistic after a few years, with a more secure military presence in India, but at present 'India has newly been conquered and the Muslims are so few that they are like salt [in a large dish]' (Barani, *Sana-i-Muhammadi*, cited in Nizami 2002: 332). One of the Muslim kings of Kashmir, Sultan Sikandar (1389–1413), almost wiped out its Hindu population, though his revered successor Zain-ul-Abidin (1420–70) was to reverse the policy of the previous hundred years in Kashmir by taking a keen interest in Buddhist and Hindu philosophy and appointing followers of these religions to high positions (Madan 1981).

As accurately reported by al-Biruni, the Hindus reciprocated by rejecting contact with Muslims as polluting. The schism between Muslims and Hindus has indeed been one of sharpest dividing lines in the history of the subcontinent, despite the Indian republic's achievement in building itself a reputation for toleration and peaceful coexistence (Gaborieau 1985). In the late twentieth century, long after the disappearance of the Moghul Empire, a few voices could be heard calling for a revival of the doctrine that Hindus are People of the Book, on the grounds that they possess sacred texts of divine rather than human origin, the Vedas and the Gita, and that 'idolatry' came late to Hinduism and Buddhism. This, one writer argued, 'would remove one of the major psychological obstacles between the two communities' (Kabir 1969: 133).

Nineteenth-century India's remarkable intellectual and polymath, the Bengali religious and social reformer Ram Mohan Roy (1772–1833), chose to present his first arguments on the need to reform Hinduism in the languages of Islam. His earliest publication was published in Persian in Calcutta in about 1804, with the Arabic title *Tuhfat ul-muwaḥḥidīn*, 'Gift to monotheists', and a preface in Arabic. He seems to have proposed a reworking of Hinduism in response to various influences: classical Islamic teaching, the Moghul Emperor Akbar's short-lived syncretic court religion *dīn-i Ilāhī*, the deism of the European Enlightenment, British orientalist scholarship, and perhaps Christian missions. At the same time as some open-minded Europeans were discovering Asian religions, Roy had considerable success in purging Hinduism of what he saw as Brahmanical distortions – the historical cost being some loss in the epistemological relativism of traditional Hinduism in favour of logical certainty (Mitter 1987). A whole modem tradition of elite Hinduism under Western influence has sought to emphasize its monotheistic aspects.

Some Indologists such as Gaborieau (1985) use an overarching parallellist model to describe Muslim–Hindu relations, not far from a Lévi-Straussian structural inversion. If non-Muslims are doctrinally *kāfir* for Muslims, non-Hindus are *mleccha* or 'barbarians' for Hindus: Muslims can provoke Hindus by killing cows, Hindus can provoke Muslims by desecrating their mosques with pigs, and so on. Ethnographic evidence naturally presents a far more complex picture. For instance, T. N. Madan, describing fieldwork in a village in rural Kashmir between 1957 and 1975, tells how the Kashmiri Brahmans or Pandits invited Muslims from outside to perform services from which they themselves were ritually debarred on principle, thus introducing a source of pollution on which they became practically dependent. The Muslim exclusion of Pandits, by this time a minority in the village, stemmed not from ritual pollution but from 'moral abhorrence'. The relationship between Muslims and Pandits, though mutually dependent, was asymmetrical because the Muslims were free to make their living by attending to the needs of fellow Muslims alone (Madan 1981).

Redoubts of the 'pagan' in Muslim states

Many surviving examples of small 'pagan' communities in Indonesia and Malaysia can be identified. The last outpost of 'paganism' in the Himalayas, the Kalasha of the Islamic state of Pakistan, has been well documented (Lievre and Loude 1990; Parkes 2000). As for Sudan, it is clear from Sharon Hutchinson's monograph that the Islamic central government in Khartoum strongly rejects the indigenous religious traditions of the South as *shirk*, and even uses a disparaging term, the equivalent of our 'gibberish', for indigenous languages (Hutchinson 1996). The government's policies during the 1990s were at times near genocidal. In her fieldwork during the early 1980s, Hutchinson met only one rural Nuer who was a practising Muslim, despite the government's determined policy of Arabization and conversion. Christianity, given qualified protection as a religion of the Book, was fast gaining Nuer adherents through various missionary churches.

In a study that focuses on how the Nuba Mountains of southern Sudan have been left out of the process of modernization, Andrew Davidson gives a rare ethnographic sketch of a contemporary Nuba mountainside farming village, Shatt Damam, whose inhabitants have resisted the calls of both Islam and Christianity. They retain a strong attachment to their ancestral *dār*, or homeland, and also, despite government pressures, to matrilineal inheritance. The Shatt are suspicious of all outsiders, especially Arabs, and in return are considered backward and peculiar. They do not resist the belief in one god as revealed to the Prophet Muhammad so much as the Islamic prohibitions on nudity, alcohol and eating pork. Government agencies implement a tacit state policy of Islamic proselytization in exchange for services. The indigenous religion, with its seasonal festivals and ritual specialists, is still a significant constituent of village life. Davidson portrays a village threatened by male out-migration, indebtedness to local merchants and inadequate rains, resulting in a mood of rancour which can no doubt be traced back to the history of the Nuba as victims of Arab slavers (Davidson 1996).

Traditions of toleration

Let us return to the comparison of Islamic and Judaeo-Christian toleration, bearing in mind that, of course, admonitions against prejudice in a society do not prove its absence, but on the contrary its presence. Incidentally, the standard word used to translate 'toleration' in modern Arabic, *tasāmuḥ*, has the same overtones of generosity from a position of dominance (Taibi 1995).

Landmarks in the history of Christendom such as the Peace of Westphalia in 1648 and the Toleration Act of 1689 in England, established after lengthy internecine religious conflicts, remind us how long it took for the principle of toleration to be accepted even *between* Christian denominations. Some historians have suggested that one reason why Christendom became more tolerant within its own borders was fear of the apparently powerful and integrated Ottoman Empire to the east. Europeans generally characterized non-Christian religions as 'idolatrous' until the early seventeenth century, when the term 'polytheism' came into favour in scholarly discourse. It has been argued by Francis Schmidt that until twentieth century

developments in anthropology, the polytheisms have nearly always been appre-
hended in counterpoint to the monotheisms. A major reversal took place at the time
of the Enlightenment, when Hume proposed that the first human beings must have
been polytheistic rather than, as previously assumed, monotheistic (Schmidt 1987).
(It was not yet realized that whereas the term polytheism may be applied with reasonable accuracy to Hinduism, it cannot be to Buddhism or Jainism, or to most
African religions.) These insights, and those of de Brosses and Sir William Jones,
though followed by the condescending Victorian theories of progress, prepared
the ground for the modem anthropological approach to religion that in the second
half of the twentieth century began to influence Christian theology and missionary
practice.

Equally important, we may trace a humanitarian concern for the welfare of polytheists back to the sixteenth century missionary Las Casas, who devoted much of
his life to trying to secure better conditions for the Amerindians governed by the
Spanish, and to Montaigne's essay on cannibals, in which he asked whether eating a dead man's flesh was really worse than common European practices of penal
torture. We may see Las Casas as prefiguring centuries of colonial paternalism and
Montaigne as prefiguring Romantic primitivism (Leach 2000b). Nonetheless, by
comparison with the Islamic tradition these European thinkers initiated a slow
counter-current against the unquestioning supremacism of the Christian West.

There is no obvious analogue in Islamic thought, in al-Biruni or elsewhere.
Even today, though many Muslim social scientists have done excellent research on
Muslim societies – often looking back to the fourteenth century's Ibn Khaldun, who
has been called one of the greatest of all sociologists – and sometimes on Christians
or Jews, it is rare indeed to find a Muslim social scientist embarking on a study of
'pagan' groups. There are no Muslim equivalents known to me of W. E. H. Stanner's
writings on Australian Aboriginal religion or Lévi-Strauss's on Amerindian myth.
To some extent this might be attributed to the devastating effects of Western colonialism on Arab–Islamic civilization, but the extreme lack of examples to contradict
my case suggests that the reasons are deeper. The reason cannot be the absence of a
freethinking tradition within Islam, for – contrary to some received opinion – this
has existed. For instance, one of the most celebrated Arab poets, the blind Syrian
al-Ma'arri (973–1057), wrote: 'Each generation of men follows another and turns
the old lies into the new religion. Which generation was given the right path?'
(Urvoy 1996: 172; Meddeb 2003: 39–40).

Many Christian missions have recently adopted a sophisticated approach to indigenous belief systems and have found ways of working with secular organizations to
protect indigenous rights (Benthall 1995). Although this analysis will not convince
either historical materialists or ethnographic particularists, I think that if we look
back on the history of Christianity, the teaching of universal love of human beings
irrespective of ethnic origin – give or take sideswipes against powerful Jewish sects
such as the Pharisees – characterized the religion almost from the start. But there

was no structural bedrock of toleration analogous to the Islamic concentric scheme. The Jews came to be more criticized for rejecting Jesus than accepted as confessional cousins, which led to a European anti-Judaism much fiercer and more disastrous than Islam's, hence indirectly to the current historical tragedy in Israel–Palestine. Muhammad was widely held to be a false prophet. The Christians experienced sporadic persecution under the Roman Empire, as well as competition from such competitors as Mithraists and Manichaeists, thus acquiring a strong taste for suppressing ideological deviation.

We are reminded by Louis Dumont's writings that hierarchy can be implicit or insidious rather than formal. Indeed, if the diagnosis of 'monotheistic bias' is accurate, this might imply a deep-seated hierarchic attitude on the part of Christians in their perceptions of monotheistic as opposed to non-monotheistic belief systems. For instance, though the Vatican today makes regular diplomatic overtures towards Hindus and Buddhists, its inclination seems more to be towards what I have called a cousinly or concentric preference for Jewish and Islamic theology, with deep reservations about New Age religiosity (Vatican n.d.). But Christendom, unlike Islam, has never formulated this hierarchy into a system of protective law.

'Noble spiritual beliefs'

Caution must be observed against oversimplifying monotheistic systems. As Mary Douglas notes, 'The tolerance of the one and the many as non-contradictory or a mystery is common to many religions at different levels – Islam, Buddhism, and popular Christianity [...] One upshot of the exercise [of interpretation] is to make the words "polytheism" or "monotheism" not be lightly used, so immense the labour of ethnography that goes into determining their sense' (Douglas 1980: 111–12). Nonetheless, let us try to sum up the relative propensities within Islam and Christianity for toleration of indigenous cultures, and hence for their protection when they appear to stand in need of it.

Christianity seems to have developed a far more powerful counter-tradition than Islam's of questioning its own messianic and universalizing leanings from within. It has led to forms of post-Christian humanism, one of whose manifestations is modern cultural anthropology, whose preferred subject matter has been marked by positive discrimination in favour of the marginal and local, including the stigmatized. This is not to deny that universalizing forms of Christianity, affording little respect to unfamiliar belief systems, can still be powerful.

Within Islam, though an overall process of self-criticism has been pioneered by many outstanding individuals and is gradually gathering institutional support, this rarely extends to a sympathy with the Qur'anically abhorred forces of *shirk* and *kufr*. Yet the lesson of the past is clear. First, Islam has proved to be just as flexible as Christianity in accommodating popular forms of belief and practice. Second, its scholars were able to recognize Hindus as People of the Book, though on most objective criteria they would have fallen more naturally into the category of *shirk*.[3] If this leap of toleration could be made for the Hindus, albeit for reasons of state, why not today for other belief systems such as the indigenous cosmologies of Africa, Indonesia and Malaysia?

The Indonesian *pancasila* – now threatened by militant Islamism – has been seen by some as a step in this direction, though still committed to the monotheistic principle. The fundamental moral tenet of *pancasila* is held to be religious toleration (Ramage 1995), and reference to Allah was replaced by *Tuhan* ('lord') in order to accommodate the Hindu Balinese, who had formerly been seen by the Indonesian government as being just like the other 'animists' of the archipelago (Darmaputera 1982; Vignato 2000). Others interpret *pancasila* as largely a political compromise aimed at discouraging any discourse deemed to be socially divisive, while encouraging poetry, dance and plastic arts specific to each ethnic group (Bowen 1991) – the real aim being to head off the threat of an Islamic state. In practice, *pancasila* has served more as an instrument of state control than as a charter for toleration.

To give another example of what might be possible, during peace negotiations in 1993 that tried to end the prolonged civil war in Sudan, an apt phrase, 'noble spiritual beliefs', was introduced to recognize the southern 'pagans'.[4] Such magnanimity deserves to be taken up as an auspicious reference point for the future.

* * *

As for the academic debate about 'Islamic anthropology', which got under way in the mid-1980s but soon ran into the ground (Ahmed 1984; Tapper 1995), it never faced the theme of the present article – but the debate should be resumed, especially in the current political climate.

Acknowledgements

This article is an expanded version of a paper given on 22 November 2003 in a session of the American Anthropological Association Annual Meetings in Chicago, organized by Vinson Sutlive in honour of George and Laura Appell, entitled 'Human rights and cultural preservation in the interest of peace'. I am grateful to the Royal Anthropological Institute for inviting me to represent it at the AAA meeting, to Jean La Fontaine for her comments on an earlier draft, and to a number of extremely helpful anonymous referees.

Notes

1 More precisely, *shirk* is associating other entities with God. The original accusation of *shirk* was probably part of an intra-monotheist polemic (Hawting 1999).
2 Another erudite work, Mun'im Sirry's *Scriptural Polemics* (Sirry 2014) is an analysis, from a modernist–reformist point of view but also grounded in traditional commentaries, of the polemical passages in the Qur'an, arguing that they were part of the religious currency of the day

as Islam emerged from a monotheistic matrix. Sirry argues in favour of a much less exclusivist exegesis of the Qur'an than many other interpreters, but he confines his discussion to relations with Christians and Jews, i.e. within the monotheistic enclave.

3 Another historical example may be the pagan Vikings who appeared in the Spanish and Moroccan coasts in the ninth century and were called *Mājūs*, that is Magians or Zoroastrians, not because they were thought to be Persians but because as a people recognized by law they did not have to be fought and were eligible for a truce for the purposes of trade (Brunschvig 1986; Brett and Fentress 1996). However, this is disputed (Melvinger 1986).

4 From the National Democratic Alliance's Resolution on the Issue of Religion and Politics in the Sudan, passed at a conference in Asmara, capital of the state of Eritrea in June 1993 (Wöndu and Lesch 2000: 234). I am grateful to Alex de Waal for drawing this to my attention.

11

Religious persecution and conflict in the twenty-first century

This review of *The Price of Freedom Denied: Religious persecution and conflict in the twenty-first century*, by Brian J. Grim and Roger Finke (Cambridge University Press, 2011) appeared in the *Times Literary Supplement* on 1 June 2012, under the heading 'Repression by numbers'.

Most cultural anthropologists are sceptical about the value of vast global comparisons such as are presented by Grim and Finke, but such an approach is defensible provided that one is alert to possible bias or misjudgements that can warp the whole enterprise. I suggest here that the authors may have underestimated the disrupting impact of colonization on the Muslim world and overstated the continuing global extent of expansionist Muslim theology.[1] However, they deserve credit for facilitating evidence-based discussion on an issue where sensitivity has been aggravated by the plight of Christians and other religious minorities in numerous Muslim-majority countries, and since publication of their book by the rise of ISIS in the Middle East and Boko Haram in Nigeria.[2] Important books by Rupert Shortt (2012)[3] and Gerard Russell (2014) have developed the theme in the form of narratives rather than statistics.

I also mention Chris Hann's critique of what he has called 'religious human-rightsism'. Hann has been fighting a rearguard action against the commitment to 'religious equality' which has been generally adopted by most social scientists, and which he diagnoses as the market ideology of a 'level playing field'. While recognizing that making value judgements about other people's spiritual commitments is a delicate task, Hann argues that historical religious institutions dominating in a given country deserve a measure of protection from more aggressive rivals, on condition that they respect the rights of minorities. Put another way, this is a plea for selective religious toleration. It is at odds with the demands for religious equality that are gaining ground in social science as well as in the law (as in Beaman 2012). Hann's 2000 article reads in retrospect as an appeal to anthropologists for corroboration, or at least discussion, of his position. It seems to have so far fallen on stony ground. But he and his mentor, the late Ernest Gellner, have the merit of approaching the problem from a more comparative perspective than most of the 'religious human-rightsists'. Hann's ethnographic examples in this article are Poland and Turkey, but he has also carried out fieldwork in China. Gellner was specially interested in North Africa and the former provinces of the Ottoman Empire, where citizens were born into millets or confessional communities, originating from the Islamic rules on the treatment of non-Muslim 'People of the Book'. In all these regions the management of religious diversity has been accepted as a necessary duty of government. In China and India, a laissez-faire policy towards religion is unthinkable.

***

In 1995, five members of the wealthy Aum Shinrikyo religious group coordinated an attack with the nerve agent sarin on five subway trains during the morning rush hour in Tokyo, causing twelve deaths and hundreds of illnesses. The Japanese government's response was to act against all individuals involved with or supporting criminal behaviour, to begin surveillance of Aum Shinrikyo and to revoke its status as a religious organization. But the government refrained from criminalizing it or in other ways submitting to public hysteria about 'brainwashing'. The result was to defuse the violent side of Aum Shinrikyo, whose membership is now sharply reduced. Such has been the policy of religious freedom since Japan disestablished state Shinto after the World War II. Japan's level of violent religious persecution and conflict is now rather low, despite an earlier historical record of severe restriction of religious activity dating back to the late sixteenth century. The Chinese government, by contrast, banned the Falun Gong spiritual movement in 1999 as an 'evil cult', though it was entirely peaceful. The intensity of violent religious persecution in China is now on a par with that in Burma, and exceeds the estimates calculated by Brian J. Grim and Roger Finke for Saudi Arabia and Pakistan.

Their dense and thought-provoking book *The Price of Freedom Denied: Religious persecution and conflict in the twenty-first century* (supported by a grant from the John Templeton Foundation) highlights this kind of contrast with the dispassion and technical sophistication of a NASA camera photographing Earth. Their statistical analysis of indicators for 'government restriction of religion', 'social restriction of religion' and 'average persecution levels', for the years 2000 to 2007, in all except the world's smallest countries and the United States itself, is based on the International Religious Freedom Reports published annually by the US State Department. (Since the main vehicle for collecting the data is US embassies, the evidence for three countries without them is limited.) 'Social restriction of religion' includes restrictions imposed by what the authors call 'the culture at large' – a formulation that drills deeply and widely into atavistic memories. It is uncontentious that such restrictions are correlated with high levels of religious persecution. The more challenging part of Grim and Finke's thesis is that high levels of religious persecution are aggravated by restriction of religion by governments. They endorse the view shared by Voltaire, Adam Smith and Hume that religions must be protected from both the state and one another. With whom are they arguing? One of their targets is Samuel Huntington's recommendation that, as a result of the purported 'clash of civilizations', a country can best avoid international conflicts by reaffirming its commitment to a single civilization. True, this is a position frequently adopted by ideologues all over the world, whether or not citing the authority of Huntington. However, *The Clash of Civilizations and the Remaking of World Order* was published in 1996 and, after numerous critiques, it has become an academic Aunt Sally.

With more originality, Grim and Finke also specify as targets those government officials who see religious regulations as necessary for controlling conflict within a country's own borders. In China, for instance, the question for the state is not whether or not to regulate religion, but how much regulation is the right amount to maintain a 'harmonious society'. Grim and Finke are surely right to point to China's state policies on religion as closely linked to the survival of a political system still nominally based on Communism.

In Chinese history, state power was frequently challenged by religious or quasi-religious movements, some of the more important being the Shandong Rebellion of 1774, the Taiping Rebellion of 1850–64, and the promotion by the anti-Communist Japanese of Shinto, Buddhism and Christianity in the parts of China that they occupied during the World War II. Later, an ironic outcome of the Cultural Revolution's attempt to annihilate most vestiges of organized religion was, in Grim and Finke's words, that 'the cult of Mao soon arose, granting him divine qualities and making him an object of prayer and confession' – to which one may add the effervescence of the Red Guards. Grim and Finke prescribe religious freedom guaranteed by governments as the only antidote to religious persecution. If, however, religion, especially in its more millenarian forms, has been as integral to the political configurations of China as these authors suggest, a change of state policy in favour of thoroughgoing faith libertarianism would be likely to have immense political repercussions. It would have been even more satisfying if Grim and Finke had engaged with articulate apologists for the present Chinese state policies on the question of religious freedom, or indeed with apologists for restrictions on freedom of religion in any other countries.

They would have found a worthy foil in the social anthropologist Chris Hann, who criticized 'religious humanrightsism' in an important article (Hann 2000), and has not retreated from that position in his more recent writings on religious politics. Hann wrote that he knew of no country 'where all groups formed on the basis of common beliefs are treated alike by the secular authorities, irrespective of their size and their historical significance', yet this is the implied goal of the libertarian campaign. He appealed to fellow anthropologists to agree with him that in countries where a particular religion has made a major contribution to the dominant collective identity, it may be held to embody valuable traditions and to deserve protection from religious entrepreneurs such as Scientologists and Hare Krishnas.

Hann is at odds with the 'religious economies' perspective favoured by Grim and Finke, which he calls a supermarket model. Hann is attracted by Ernest Gellner's view that, because secular rationalism is not enough to bind human communities, the 'lukewarm' preservation of traditional institutions with their symbols and rituals, long after the cognitive foundations of society have moved away from religious doctrine, offers the best chance for tolerance. (Japan is a good advertisement for this argument.) More recently, Hann has written of the former Eastern bloc countries with dominant Orthodox or Catholic confessions that, while religious monopolies cannot be defended, it would be better to draw attention to ecumenical tendencies within these dominant Churches, following approximately the pattern of the Established but now open-minded Church of England, or the Lutheran Churches of Scandinavia, rather than force them into defensive fortresses to rail against well-financed foreign missionaries. For Hann, religiosity is intimately entangled with national and collective identity, and hence necessarily with government. Governments have to build their current policies on historical accretions and all interventions relating to religion can backfire in unexpected ways. Hann's style of social science is more useful to policymakers than Grim and Finke's, just as charts and geolocation aids, rather than NASA's Blue Marble, are useful for navigators.

The future of religion in China, given the weight of the Chinese economy, is surely of high importance for the world at large. Grim and Finke show that, in the absence of a single national faith, there is a grey area of organizations and practices that are neither 'officially permitted' by the Religious Affairs Bureau nor banned. Moreover, the threat of Tibetan secession has caused the atheist government to select a young man, now aged twenty-two, as a reincarnation of the Panchen Lama, the second-highest figure in Tibetan Buddhism. In the almost equally sensitive Xinjiang-Uighur Autonomous Region, north of Tibet, the state imposes strict controls on the large Sunni Muslim population, for instance forbidding government employees from attending religious services. Grim and Finke, despite the lucidity of their analysis, miss a unique point about contemporary China: that it has turned Marxism upside down. For whereas Marx contended that religions were veils obscuring the reality of brutal capitalist power relations, an intellectually threadbare communism is now in China the veil itself. The decision of the authorities to erect a ten-metre-high bronze statue of Confucius in Tiananmen Square in January 2011, and then remove it two months later, is emblematic of their difficulties in reinventing a national ideology, difficulties that have perhaps been underestimated by political commentators. *The Price of Freedom Denied* may be, then, of only limited use as a guide to policy in specific cases. But, we may read it in another way, by putting on one side its hortatory mission and considering it as a purely descriptive analysis. The authors have developed a system of numerical coding extrapolated from recent US State Department reports and have correlated these with a study of religious freedoms throughout the world published in 1945 by a Yale professor, M. Searle Bates. They have considered the possibility that their codings are flawed by observer bias in these published reports, but they state that other comparable studies have yielded broadly similar results.

It may be objected that giving France and Rwanda the same code for 'government restriction of religion' – both scoring around the middle of the range – is applying too broad a brush. But Grim and Finke's aim is to test their correlations at such a high level of generality that questioning a few of the codes for specific countries would not affect the statistical whole (nor does the omission of the United States). And, as far as I can judge, the correlations they infer are factually justified. Government restrictions on religion do go with high levels of physical persecution.

A thorny question remains, which the authors face with scientific composure: is lack of religious freedom specially salient in Muslim-majority countries? Their statistical conclusion is that 'while religious persecution and conflict can potentially occur in any country, religious persecution is more likely to occur in Muslim-majority countries than in other countries' and that 'the levels of religious persecution are far more severe, with the contrast between Christian-majority and Muslim-majority countries being especially striking'. Governments in Muslim-majority countries harass Muslims of minority sects, such as the Ahmadiyya in Pakistan, much more than Muslims are harassed in Christian-majority countries. Muslim-majority countries in West Africa, however, show low levels of religious persecution.

Seeking to explain these imbalances, Grim and Finke give less weight to the impact of colonialism in politicizing Islam than to the battle within Islam over the interpretation and enactment of Sharia law. Minor slips (Pakistan did not become an Islamic republic till 1956) are immaterial in such an astronautical depiction of the world, but the coverage of Islam is blemished by one serious error. The authors take the classical Islamic division of the world between *dār al-islām* (domain of submission to God) and *dār al-ḥarb* (domain of war) to be part of mainstream Islamic doctrine today. But only fringe groups such as Al-Qaeda and Hizb ul-Tahrir now adopt this rigid division of humanity. As Fred Halliday observed, no Arab newspaper organizes its news sections in this way.

Are high statistical levels of religious oppression in Muslim-majority countries due to an inherent feature of the faith? One cannot be certain, but probably what is needed is time for religiosity to become more lukewarm. It is often forgotten that St Augustine came to believe, albeit reluctantly, in the pedagogy of fear to convert heretics, and St Thomas Aquinas taught that they were so dangerous to the common good that if they refused to be persuaded to retract, it was best to execute them. In the case of Islam, the process of cooling is rapid in some places today, but in others slowed down by many political factors.

Notes

1 A thoughtful review of the book by Ahmet T. Kuru makes similar points, and adds some factual criticisms (Kuru 2011).

2 Grim and Finke give no attention, however, to a small Muslim majority country, Oman, where the extent of religious toleration is somewhat greater than that shown by its equally autocratic Gulf neighbours, no doubt because it follows the Ibadhi form of Islam which is distinct from both Sunnism and Shiism (US State Department International Religious Freedom Report for 2013).

3 Shortt's *Christianophobia* also covers persecution of Christians in a number of non-Muslim-majority countries.

12

What makes Islam unique?

This review of Michael Cook's *Ancient Religions, Modern Politics: The Islamic case in comparative perspective* (Princeton University Press, 2014) and Akeel Bilgrami's *Secularism, Identity, and Enchantment* (Harvard University Press, 2014) was published in the *Times Literary Supplement* on 10 September 2014 under the heading 'What makes Islam unique?'. Cook's brief reference to a remark by Bilgrami provided the peg on which to hang a review of the two books.

Juxtaposing Cook's masterly imaginative scholarship with Bilgrami's 'roving and unconfined habitus', it concludes by noting that the influence of Edward Said, which suffuses Bilgrami's book, is conspicuously absent from Cook's. I agree with the anthropologist Lawrence Rosen in his appraisal of Said's critique of orientalist scholarship that 'Said got much of the substance wrong, but his method – looking at discourse as an artifact of its writers' contexts – was basically sound' (Rosen 2007). In Cook's case, my justification for invoking the shade of Edward Said is to warn against the possible misuse of his scholarship by propagandists who would use it to anathematize Islam. For Cook concludes that, though not one of the features of the late twentieth century Islamic revival, with its high political profile, is unique, the combination of features that makes it up is unique: 'No heritage is a reliable predictor of the behavior of those who inherit it, but just as surely heritages are not interchangeable.'

***

In 1977, Patricia Crone and Michael Cook gatecrashed the sober world of early Islamic studies with their *Hagarism: The making of the Islamic world*, self-described as 'a book written by infidels for infidels'. Hagar was in biblical tradition the handmaid of Sarah who bore Abraham their son Ishmael. The authors presented Hagarism as a messianic irredentist movement that became Islam. Their mentor at London's School of Oriental and African Studies, John Wansbrough, whose own books were equally subversive of Islamic 'salvation history' though stylistically impenetrable, praised Crone and Cook's erudition and ebullience but questioned their historical rigour. They have since modified their youthful hyperbole and both are now eminent professors.[1]

Michael Cook is admired for his masterly *Commanding Right and Forbidding Wrong in Islamic Thought* (2000). His new synthesis, *Ancient Religions, Modern Politics: The Islamic case in comparative perspective* (2014), addresses a vital present-day issue on which many have offered opinions, all unsupported by the historical scholarship that he has been able to apply. Is the high political profile of Islam, compared with its competitors, due to special characteristics of the heritage itself, or can it be principally ascribed to other factors, such as the domination of so many Muslim majority populations by Western powers during the colonial period? Cook sets out to examine the role of Islam in modern politics compared with that of Hinduism and Christianity, the latter mainly in the Latin American context, since his focus is on religions with a major presence in developing countries. His conclusion is clear: 'no heritage is a reliable predictor of the behavior of those who inherit it, but just as surely heritages are not interchangeable'. He carries through his comparison across the three faiths with steely thoroughness and precision, covering in turn the themes of identity, social structures, militancy, credal exclusivity, political power and fundamentalism.

The core of the matter is the Islamic revival since the latter part of the twentieth century. (His study is largely restricted to Sunni Islam, with occasional references to the Shia tradition.) Cook identifies partial non-Muslim parallels: as regards the increase in religiosity, in the rise of Pentecostalism and Charismatic Catholicism; as regards identity politics, in the Hindutva nationalist movement; as regards the imposition of social values, in the mainstream Christian Right in the United States; as regards the campaign to restore the Caliphate, in a Christian Reconstructionist fringe (also in the United States); as regards the rise of jihadism, in the intermittent militancy of Sikhs. Hence not one of the features of the Islamic revival is unique. But the combination of features that makes it up *is* unique. Moreover, two of these movements – Hindu nationalism and militant Sikhism – first emerged in contentious emulation of Muslim stances.

A summary of Cook's comparative discussion of the theme of warfare will exemplify the strengths of his method while also raising some minor questions. He postulates a spectrum of doctrines on warfare, with Sikh militancy and Buddhist pacifism at opposite ends (though he acknowledges the pugnacity of Buddhist monks in the war against the Tamil Tigers in Sri Lanka). Hinduism shares with Buddhism a norm of non-violence but its canonical texts are full of martial violence, and its legal tradition set out ideals and standards for the conduct of hostilities, embodied in the Kshatriya ruling and warrior caste. It was assumed that conflict would be between Hindus: non-Hindus were for the most part simply ignored. The Hindutva nationalists of today have chosen the Muslims as their opponents, but get little satisfaction from the old Hindu law of war. As for Christianity, extreme violence is commended by God in the Hebrew Bible or Old Testament, which was never repudiated by the

Church, and some passages in the Book of Revelation are ferocious; but the Jesus of the Gospels was on the whole close to the Buddha in his pacifism. It was not until the eleventh century that the idea of the crusade solidified. It remained a secondary development, without direct endorsement in the foundational texts of Christianity, and it was eventually thwarted by military failure on account of the long supply lines between Western Europe and the Muslim front.

At this point Cook jumps across many centuries to modern Latin America and describes the cult of martyrdom among the pious Cristeros, 'unreconstructed conservatives' who rebelled in the late 1920s against the anti-clerical Mexican state. But he argues that the Cristiada was only a marginal event in the history of Latin America. By contrast, the liberation theologians, whose influence has spread over many countries, were constrained in their approaches to violence by their attention to the unfiltered message of the Gospels, and, to the extent that they accepted the necessity of violence, their inspiration was more Marxist than Christian. Here it must be noted that Cook skips over the ravages inflicted by the conquistadors. Moreover, his focus on Latin America absolves him from having to consider the exaltation of death in battle as a strand in European oratory, harking back to Ancient Rome (as in Thomas Babington Macaulay's poem 'Horatius'), which must be counted as part of what would now be called 'cultural Christianity' – certainly, Christianity as it has been perceived and represented from outside.

Turning to Islam, Cook observes that the Prophet Muhammad is recorded as having mounted about seventy military expeditions against unbelievers during his rule in Medina, all quite small by the wider standards of the day, some offensive and others defensive, many of them commanded by himself. He was also willing to declare a truce on occasion. There was no military structure, but making war came naturally to most Arabian tribesmen. The theme of warfare against unbelievers, 'jihad in the name of God', is prominent in the Qur'an and Sunna. This heritage has remained vivid throughout the centuries. Many Muslims today are embarrassed by what is frequently criticized as a medieval survival and seek to reinterpret jihad (literally, 'striving' in Arabic) so as to tone down or remove its objectionable features. One solution is to limit the scope of jihad to defensive operations. Alternatively, Muslim apologists revive a strain in pre-modern tradition that elevated spiritual striving, the 'greater jihad', above war-making. Here Michael Cook cites an important book by his namesake, David Cook, *Understanding Jihad* (2005), which outlines the history of this irenic sub-tradition but insists that it was only a derivative form and that it is difficult to find historical examples of when the 'greater jihad' has been used to reject the possibility of aggressive warfare.

Michael Cook then traces expertly how, in reaction to Western criticism of jihad, two of the most influential twentieth-century Islamists, the Pakistani Abu A'la Maududi and the Egyptian Sayyid Qutb, presented jihad in apologetic mode, as a selfless mission to destroy all the world's corrupt structures of power. By contrast, the leaders of Al-Qaeda have reaffirmed without qualification the principle of offensive military jihad, though in practice they justify their attacks on the West as retaliations for earlier attacks on Muslims. This jihadi ideology looks back with enthusiasm to the martial side of the Prophet's life. Another difference from the earlier Islamists is that the jihadis turned their attention to semi-autonomous tribal areas, no longer having in mind regular armies under governmental control. *Ancient Religions, Modern Politics* was published before the sudden emergence of the would-be 'Islamic State'. While Abu Musab al-Suri (now believed to be in a Syrian prison) calls for adaptation to a secret, cellular form of terrorism, Ayman al-Zawahiri, Al-Qaeda's current leader, and its splinter groups set their sights on restoration of the Caliphate at the core of the Muslim world.

At the conclusion of his sustained comparative exercise, of which the above is only a specimen, Cook reflects on the dilemma facing all populations of the developing world: the need to choose on the one hand between defiance towards the richer nations and cooperation with them, and on the other hand between conservation of heritage and adoption of Western institutions and values. 'Against this background the Islamic heritage provides resources for a considerable – and antithetical – range of stances.' It is the wide choice of possibilities that Cook is concerned to bring out. Extreme rejectionism and absolutism are dramatically expressed in some areas of the Muslim tribal periphery. But there is another form of Islamism that is much more selective, an Islamic way of being 'modern'. It emphasizes, for instance, the egalitarianism of foundational Islam, opportunities for women in the public sphere, and outlets in Sharia for peaceful relations with non-Muslims – but without risk of confusion with the philo-Western liberalism of the nineteenth century Indian reformer Sir Sayyid Ahmad Khan. By contrast, the Hindu heritage has only a weak contribution to make to political ideology in the global 'South', and the Catholic heritage even less. Cook adds that Confucianism is too elitist to compete seriously, and that Communism, because of its lack of spiritual appeal, was unable to survive the setback of devastating economic failures, which religions have regularly been able to do.

Looking ahead, Cook speculates on possible futures for Islamism, including the probability that over time people tend to tire of the politicization of religion. He deprecates the notion that Islam should undergo a reformation comparable to the one that produced Protestant Christianity, reminding us that this unleashed forces of fanaticism and intolerance in Europe not unlike those to be found in Pakistan or Iraq today. If he had included Judaism in his comparative study, he could have adduced the history of another reform movement that would be more pertinent to present-day Islam. In the early nineteenth century, liberalizing synagogues in Germany and the United States began to correspond and eventually consolidated as Reform Judaism. The main movements within Judaism – Orthodox, Conservative and Reform – are recognized institutional focuses for debate and limited consensus within the overall Jewish community.[2] By contrast, individual Islamic reformers have made their mark for more than a century, such as the circle of Muhammad Abduh and Rashid Rida in Egypt, but they did not establish durable institutions – leaving a gap for the anti-Western Muslim Brotherhood to fill, and a resulting crisis of authority within Islam. An exception is Indonesia, a major Muslim-majority nation almost ignored by Cook, where the Muhammadiyah, founded as long ago as 1912 under the influence of Muhammad Abduh, is a highly structured modernist organization with a huge and successful network of educational and welfare activities, avoiding direct political involvement.

Another hopeful sign for Islamic reformism today is the legacy of the Sudanese Sufi religious leader Mahmud Muhammad Taha, who was executed in Khartoum after a conviction for apostasy in 1985. Cook does not mention the distinction that Taha sought to make – in which he is followed by his translator and editor, Abdullahi Ahmed An-Naim, a professor at Emory School of Law in Atlanta – between the universal revelation conveyed in the Qur'an during the Prophet's early period in Mecca and the legal dogmatism expressed in the later Medinan chapters. The difficulty, as Malise Ruthven has observed in *Encounters with Islam* (2013a), is for such progressive views to entrench themselves in the face of fourteen centuries of cultural programming. On the positive side, however, so many mainstream Muslims are horrified by the vicious excesses of the 'Islamic State' that reformist programmes are likely to be pursued with more energy than hitherto.

Michael Cook declares that his purpose is descriptive and analytical. One name is significantly absent from his impressive bibliography: that of Edward Said. And we find in *Ancient Religions, Modern Politics* no reflections about the author's own standpoint or the anticipated effects of his own writings as public interventions. This does not detract from the excellence of his monograph, but it may be that, in such a supercharged political context, when his overall message is amplified via the mass media some of its more subtle tones will be lost.

Cook cites the words of the Indian-born philosophy professor Akeel Bilgrami on the dilemma of moderate Muslims who are opposed to 'Islamic absolutists' but are inhibited by defensiveness: they fear that 'such criticism would amount to a surrender to the forces of the West, which have for so long shown a domineering colonial and postcolonial contempt for their culture'. Bilgrami's *Secularism, Identity, and Enchantment* (2014) was commissioned fifteen years ago by the late Edward Said for a Harvard University Press series, 'Convergences: Inventories of the present', and it includes a touching and humorous tribute to his erstwhile colleague at Columbia University. Bilgrami has assembled here a number of published essays on the relationship between religion and politics, nearly all of which he has revised and added to, often with outsize endnotes. The format is unenticing. Too often an essay ends by regretting that there is not enough space left to continue the argument: tighter writing and editing could have released more space. But, whereas Cook, with his lucid analytical matrix, shows us the world as it is, Bilgrami shows us how the world might be otherwise. His is the roving and unconfined habitus appropriate to a visionary.

One of the central aims of his wide-ranging and ambitious book is to establish intellectual affinities between Karl Marx and M. K. Gandhi. At first sight there is not much convergence between historical materialism and Gandhi's belief in the power of example to create a moral community. But for Bilgrami, they have in common their diagnosis of human 'alienation', that well-chewed bone of contention in Marxist exegesis, which has fuelled many critiques of scientism and industrial expansion. Bilgrami sets out to frame the concept of a sacralized nature, which Gandhi espoused in his religiously eclectic way, as merely one specific manifestation of a broader underlying tradition which holds that nature is suffused with values. Another manifestation of the tradition was Marx's atheistic concept of humanity's 'species being'. Both Marx and Gandhi were inheritors of the German and English Romantic movement, in particular its 'natural supernaturalism', a term Bilgrami borrows from the literary critic M. H. Abrams. Bilgrami conducts his discussion at an abstract and speculative level, though some practical conclusions emerge in his praise of the indigenous anti-capitalist politicians of Bolivia and Ecuador.

His book catches fire when he considers the dilemma of a secular (in his case atheist) Muslim vis-à-vis religious absolutism, his reflections on which have come, as mentioned above, to the attention of Michael Cook. Bilgrami insists that the Islamist critique of Western supremacism should be taken seriously, even when it spills into violence. This critique has historical affinities further back than Gandhi: with European Romanticism and even with the radical dissenting sects of the seventeenth century. (Charles Tripp has gone further to argue that much of the Islamist critique is a rebranding of Western sources.) For Bilgrami, academics writing on political issues for a public readership in the United States have a duty to concentrate on exposing the wrongs of the US government and its allies, just as during the Cold War Jean-Paul Sartre concentrated on criticizing the West rather than the Soviet Union. But he accepts the need to oppose Islamic absolutism. He recommends that liberals, recognizing the defensive nature of many Muslims' everyday commitment to their faith, should look for sympathetic tendencies within the Muslim population rather than imposing condemnation from outside. The distinction between the early, inclusive, Meccan chapters of the Qur'an, and the later, more hardline, Medinan chapters, provides one possible opening for the depoliticization of doctrine from within the faith.

It could be added to Bilgrami's argument that radical reinterpretations of Islamic doctrine in favour of feminism and religious pluralism are currently being explored and debated – especially by female Muslim scholars based in United States universities, such as Aysha A. Hidayatullah, author of the recently published *Feminist Edges of the Qur'an* (2014), which even questions the inerrancy of revealed Scripture. It remains to be seen if these innovations will spread to the conservative heartlands of Islam, where training and status are as important as what a scholar says, and where the social sciences as understood in the West are extremely weak. The field is thus left free for an ambiguous figure such as Yusuf al-Qaradawi, the Qatar-based spiritual leader of the Muslim Brotherhood, to occupy what he claims is a 'middle ground'.

Cook's comment on Bilgrami, referred to above, concludes that it is 'clearly the demise of the Soviet Union and the waning prestige of Marxism that have rendered the predicament he describes so acute: before that intellectuals could criticize aspects of their Islamic heritage without the stigma of surrender to the West'. This explanation neglects the repercussions of the Six-Day War of 1967, of the failure of Arab nationalism, and more recently of the 'war on terror', opening a chink in Michael Cook's otherwise impregnable scholarship to warrant the thought that a touch of post-Saidian reflexivity would have made his towering work even more definitive.

Notes

1 Patricia Crone died on 11 July 2015.
2 For a more detailed presentation of this argument, see Benthall 2015.

13

Tariq Ramadan

This review of Tariq Ramadan's *The Arab Awakening: Islam and the new Middle East* (Allen Lane, 2012) was published in the *Times Literary Supplement* (*TLS*), 12 October 2012, under the heading 'Splits at the seams?'.

Chapter 7 of this book describes the successful efforts of the American Civil Liberties Union to secure a non-immigrant visa to enable Tariq Ramadan to visit the United States. The issue at stake was not evaluation of his work, but intellectual freedom, and the US government evidently decided – after reflection – that American values were robust enough to withstand Ramadan's wish for exchanges of ideas with US citizens. In this review, I tried to elucidate Ramadan's complex intellectual position, especially his relationship with the Muslim Brotherhood (less positive than is often assumed), while also defending him against unjust criticisms and saluting his personal courage. There was no room in the *TLS*'s pages to acknowledge that the expression 'doing the splits' was a translation of *faire le grand écart*, which was a descriptor applied to Ramadan's position by Ian Hamel (2007: 22). The *TLS* sub-editor who devised the heading linked this idea with the characteristic Islamist doctrine that Islam is, or ought to be, a seamless whole.

In the summer of 2015, most of the hopes for the 'Arab awakening' have been dashed, except in Tunisia.

After all his previous difficulties in entering the USA, Ramadan decided in 2014 to decline publicly two invitations for conventions of the Islamic Society of North America (ISNA) in Detroit and Reviving the Islamic Spirit (RIS) in Toronto.[1] He accused ISNA's leadership of remaining silent in the face of unconscionable US foreign and domestic policies and RIS of projecting a Sufi version of Islam as 'above politics', whereas in fact Sufi leaders gave spiritual support to Middle East autocracies, in particular the al-Sisi regime that has taken power in Egypt. As regards ISNA, he had in mind especially the White House *iftar* (the evening meal during the holy month of Ramadan) on 14 July 2014, when President Obama spoke in support of Israel's assault on Gaza without protest from his guests. As regards RIS, Tariq Ramadan probably alluded to Habib Ali al-Jifri, founder of the Tabah Foundation in

Abu Dhabi, who controversially gave a prayer of *tawfiq* (success) for the Egyptian President Abdel Fattah al-Sisi.[2]

In his explanation of this decision, Ramadan, who was born in 1962, writes:

> I am also a member of a generation that is passing on. It is up to the new generation to produce leaders who have understood that in bending over backwards, in saying 'Yes sir!' they sacrifice not only their dignity, but forget and betray their duty. I dream of a new feminine and masculine leadership, educated, free and bold, a leadership that does not confuse the concept of dialogue with the authorities with unacceptable compromise and intellectual surrender, a leadership that does not transform Sufism, the historical underpinning of so many liberation movements, into a school of silence and cowardly calculation. As I look around me, I see the first premises of a dream come true, alhamdulLilah.[3]

***

In an iconic bout on French television in 2003, Tariq Ramadan tangled with Nicolas Sarkozy, then Interior Minister. Sarkozy – after recalling that Hani Ramadan, Tariq's older brother, had recently defended the stoning under Sharia, in certain countries such as Nigeria, of women convicted of adultery – asked Tariq whether he agreed with this 'monstrosity'. Ramadan replied that he disagreed with his brother: such a punishment was 'not applicable'. But he added that this was a minority view among Muslims and he was in favour of a moratorium to make possible a debate. 'Un moratoire!' snapped Sarkozy. Ramadan refrained from pointing out, as some modernist Islamic scholars do, that there is no authority for lapidation in the Qur'an itself: he fell back instead on the need for a consensus of interpretation of traditional texts among the community of accredited *ulama* – to which, for all his intellectual sophistication, he does not actually belong.

Ramadan, Professor of Contemporary Islamic Studies at the University of Oxford, has often been accused of being two-faced, saying one thing to Muslims and another to non-Muslims, but the criticism seems misplaced. Anyone is entitled to change their views over time. (He used, for instance, to argue that the French legal tradition of *laïcité* was in need of revision to accommodate Islam, but more recently he has conceded that the French laws enable Muslims to be loyal citizens without contradiction.) A more accurate depiction of his posture is that he is constantly doing the splits, as he apparently tries to reconcile his loyalty to Islamic orthodoxy with the humanities as they are understood in the West.

Tariq Ramadan has loyal followers, especially among young Muslims in Europe, but he also attracts extraordinary hostility. He is frequently identified as a spearhead of the Muslim Brotherhood, charged with spreading Sharia to Europe and North America, but in an insidious way that permits him to be intermittently critical of the Brotherhood. The principal evidence supporting this theory, which cannot be decisively refuted because the Brotherhood does not publish the names of its leaders in Western countries, is that Ramadan is the scion of an important Egyptian

Islamist family. His maternal grandfather was Hassan al-Banna, the Brotherhood's founder, and his father was Said Ramadan, a prominent member who settled in Geneva when the Brotherhood was banned in Egypt. His brother Hani, director of the Islamic Centre in Geneva, has been justly described as a 'neo-fundamentalist'. Tariq does not disown his lineage, which has no doubt contributed to his prestige in parts of the Muslim world. Study, however, of his prolific writings and of his life as recorded by the Swiss journalist Ian Hamel in *La Vérité sur Tariq Ramadan: Sa famille, ses réseaux, sa stratégie* (2007) must lead to the conclusion that he is essentially an individualist. Articulate in French, English and Arabic, he has compiled an impressive personal website, but he has shown no talent for institution-building – unlike another charismatic Islamic leader, the Turkish-born Fethullah Gülen, who has founded a redoubtable international movement.

Born in Switzerland in 1962, Ramadan began his career as a teacher of literature and completed dissertations on Nietzsche and on his grandfather, al-Banna; he also spent some time in Cairo studying Islamic law. He first became well known in Switzerland, but sought a larger platform in France. Since moving to Oxford in 2009, he has remained an activist, pedagogue and preacher, with a high media profile. Because no classically trained Islamic scholar in Britain has stepped into the shoes of Sheikh Zaki Badawi (1922–2006), who was influential at the highest levels as a mediator between the state and Muslim minorities, Ramadan has sometimes been treated as a spokesman for his religion on a par with the most senior Christian and Jewish clerics.

Ramadan was briefly banned from entering France in 1995; but after 2004 the United States government was more resolute. [*The passage on Tariq Ramadan's US visa difficulties and their resolution has been omitted here to avoid repetition; see Chapter 7.*]

Ramadan has always condemned both terrorism and anti-Semitism: various allegations that he has had contacts with violent extremists have never been substantiated. Perhaps his early interest in the career of Malcolm X was remembered by the American authorities. But the main reason for his exclusion from the USA over five years, apart from his family connections, must have been his criticisms of American foreign policy regarding Afghanistan, Iraq and Israel. In 2009, he stated that he was also banned from entering Egypt, Saudi Arabia, Tunisia, Libya and Syria, because he had criticized their governments' records on human rights. Ramadan evidently sees himself as a man of destiny with a bridging role. His sincerity need not be questioned and his courage in a world dangerous for activists should be acknowledged. (Hassan al-Banna and Malcolm X were both assassinated.) The virulence of the attacks on his reputation in France and the USA may reflect resentment that the case for Islam's rightful place in the West, coupled with a leftist orientation, should be advanced by an elegant Swiss. In the Christian world, spiritual leadership and political activism are usually undertaken by separate personalities, by means of an unspoken division of labour that the example of Jesus did not necessarily enjoin.

Ramadan has both held to the characteristic position of the Muslim Brotherhood that Islam is a seamless whole and also exercised entrepreneurial flair in answering a demand for culturally sensitive cosmopolitan leadership, which is otherwise scarce in the Islamic world. Among his many writings, some are vulnerably bland (see the *TLS* review by Simon Blackburn 2010) in contrast with his sharpness in polemic. Others, such as *Les Musulmans d'occident et l'avenir de l'islam* (2003), seem to play down differences within Islam, especially the Sunni–Shia divide – an omission he has now corrected, noting that the swathe of energy resources located in Shia regions exacerbates geopolitical tensions in the Middle East. One cannot read a new book by Tariq Ramadan without bearing in mind the background of contention that his name evokes, but the proper approach is to pay him the compliment that his thinking has evolved over time and to engage with his text afresh.

The Arab Awakening: Islam and the new Middle East (Ramadan 2012) is his response to the complex drama that has unfolded in the region since Muhammad Bouazizi, a young street vendor in the Tunisian town of Sidi Bouzid, set himself alight in December 2010 and died of his injuries. Twenty-six of Ramadan's blogs and newspaper articles are reprinted as appendices. In part, this is an *altermondialiste* critique of Western policies from a Muslim point of view. What has probably attracted most attention is Ramadan's claim that youthful cyber-dissidents who stimulated mass protest in Tunisia and Egypt had since 2004 been given training in non-violent strategies by NGOs, such as Freedom House, funded by the US government. Advice on electronic communications was included in the US-funded manual *Nonviolent Struggle: 50 crucial points*, published online in Serbia in 2006 as a result of the mass non-violent movement led by a group called Otpor ('resistance') that had played a part in the deposition of Slobodan Milosevic in 2000. Ramadan is right to notice the existence of such training programmes, but it is doubtful whether they were extensive enough to justify his inference that the US government was systematically hedging its bets by backing dictators and training dissidents. The background to his remarks is the widespread suspicion among Arab intellectuals concerning ever-present American interference in Middle East politics. With these interlocutors in mind, Ramadan takes issue with their conclusion 'that the uprisings were directed by outside forces, and that public opinion was manipulated', but he has probably exaggerated the actual importance of these sporadic American interventions. Autochthonous debate in the Middle East about the possibility of effective non-violent campaigns has been circulating for many years and one can point to numerous historical examples to show that Islam, contrary to stereotypes, is compatible with non-violence. One is the Khudai Khidmatgar ('servants of God') movement of Pakhtun nationalists in what is now Afghanistan and Pakistan, led by Khan Abdul Gaffar Khan, known as the 'Frontier Gandhi', who conducted a non-violent campaign against British rule between the two world wars. Another is the Iranian Revolution in 1978–9 (until the return of Ayatollah Khomeini), in which the communication media of the day such as audiocassette tapes played a major part.

One of Ramadan's strongest themes is his warning to the petroleum-hungry United States and Europe that the era when they can protect their privileges in the Middle East and North Africa is coming to an end. Among the rising countries of the Global South and East, China in particular has invested mightily in the region while making a point of non-interference in local politics, with the effect that much Arab opinion now favours Beijing over Washington, despite China's military cooperation with Israel. China's repression of its own Muslims in Xinjiang province, and its lack of internal democracy, do not affect the way it approaches the Middle East: 'the Chinese government is unlikely to be embarrassed by human rights rhetoric contradicted by facts'. Ramadan admits that 'there can be no room for idealization', drawing attention to the risk of new forms of dependency and a regression in social and human rights. Since he makes much of the parallel between the politics of Islam in the West and religio-political issues in the Middle East, one would like to hear him expand his thoughts on how Chinese foreign policy towards Muslim majority countries is likely to develop and on how those countries will evaluate Chinese intervention if American and European influence becomes less decisive.

Much of Ramadan's commentary might have been written by other left-leaning observers of Western foreign policy. Its conclusion on the agonizing problem of the uprising in Syria, where substantial minority groups support the regime's brutal repression, is the Delphic pronouncement that 'the people's bravery and determination have forced history's hand'. In the religious dimension, he is more at home. His criticism of the American authorities for burying Osama bin Laden at sea, in defiance of all Islamic teaching, will seem sentimental to many readers, but spiritual leaders in other religions would agree that the bodies of even the most culpable human beings should be treated with traditional respect after death, and in common with Ramadan they would deplore the barbaric killings of Saddam Hussein and Muammar Qaddafi.

The originality and importance of Ramadan's new book lie in the challenge he puts to his fellow Muslims: 'The time has come to stop blaming the West for the colonialism and imperialism of the past, or for today's attempts at manipulation and control. Arab and Muslim majority countries must jettison their historic posture as victims'. Addressing young people in particular – weighted towards them as the demography of the Middle East is – he urges that opposition factions should work together and overcome the differences between secular and religious affiliations. The uprisings turned out not to be controlled by Islamists (contrary to some initial expectations), but to draw together people from all social classes and groupings; yet it is a mistake to forget that most of the activists made their political demands 'as Muslims – and not against their religion'. According to Ramadan, the 'Islamic reference' unites people of the region as a cultural as well as a religious source of meaning, including non-practising Muslims and the Christian minorities – though the latter are exposed to stigmatization, which he condemns. In Ramadan's view, Arab and

Muslim majority peoples must reconcile themselves with their own 'genius': 'to be free, they must reproduce what already exists'.

Ramadan argues that secularism as a political programme in the West – in the sense of the separation of religion from the state – was an outcome of Enlightenment philosophy associated with pluralism and freedom, but, when imported to Turkey by Atatürk, and to a number of Arab countries during the post-colonial period, it became a means to subject religion to state control, so that the association with pluralism was lost. Ramadan accuses the secularized elites of the Arab world of being both blind to the dysfunctionality of Western societies and cut off from the memories and traditions of their own peoples. Ramadan also has harsh words for Salafi formalists – enforcing strict codes for food, dress and ritual – and equally for Sufi groups, whom he decries as preoccupied with self-cultivation and abstracted from the realities of political controversy. In the Middle East, it is Turkey that Ramadan singles out as exemplary, in that the Islamist government led by Recep Tayyip Erdoğan has committed itself to uniting the loyalties of secularists and Islamists by putting forward a policy of all-round reform. But Ramadan has mixed feelings about the move in Turkey towards integration with Europe, at the expense of a new 'Islamic' power bloc, leaning to South and East, that was discussed in the late 1990s and now survives only as a loose-knit organization for economic cooperation, the 'Developing Eight'.

Ramadan glosses over the authoritarian tendencies of the founders of the Muslim Brotherhood (family loyalty, perhaps), but he emphasizes that its early history must be seen in the context of the worldwide anti-colonial cause. Islamist groups are now heterogeneous, splitting along similar faultlines to those in the Christian world that divide liberation theology (on the left), Christian democracy (more centrist) and conservative or fundamentalist movements (on the right). Ramadan does not spare criticism of Islamists. 'Islamic economics' has no grounding in religious ethics; rote memorization in schools, and downgrading of the humanities, result in spiritual poverty and a deficit in cultural innovation; rhetoric in opposition is followed, when political office is gained, by ineffectiveness; the Brotherhood's slogan 'The Qur'an is our Constitution' is both incomprehensible and unrealizable. In short, the movement as he represents it is ossified. He feels free to question the motives of the Qatar-based Sheikh Yusuf al-Qaradawi, the most prominent spiritual guide of the Muslim Brotherhood, when Qaradawi condoned the repression of opposition in Bahrain and described the Shia as a 'sect' whose influence should be restricted. If Ramadan is really delegated to be the principal propagandist of the Brotherhood in the West, he must indeed have a character of serpentine subtlety.

Rather than serving up stale assertions from the past, Ramadan's critics should take issue with his recent arguments. His authority in attempting to distinguish 'the bedrock of Islamic belief … the core of Islam for all the world's Muslims', from a 'second level', that is to say the way the scriptural sources are read and interpreted,

is open to question. For he includes the whole of the Prophetic tradition, as well as
the Qur'an, in this core, ignoring the fact that the hadiths (sayings and actions of
the Prophet) have been subjected to selective critical analysis since the end of the
nineteenth century by Ignaz Goldziher and others. Ramadan has never shown any
interest in historical research on foundational Islam such as has long been accepted
for Judaism and Christianity, but if he is as serious as he says about promoting 'free,
analytical and critical thought' in the Arab world, scholarly examination of the ten-
ets of religion should surely be encouraged. Moreover, when Ramadan writes, as a
beacon for religious toleration, that religious pluralism should be extended 'beyond
the monotheism of the "People of the Book"' – that is, to 'pagan' or 'polytheistic'
belief systems – he would himself be regarded by many fellow Muslims as deviat-
ing from the 'core', which singles out any association of God with other entities (in
Arabic, *shirk*) as one of the worst offences.

The Arab Awakening yields glimpses – as when Ramadan writes of Islamic 'culture' and of the 'monopoly on heaven and dogma' exerted by religious institutions –
that he may be moving towards a more anthropological view of religion than has
informed his earlier work. In that case, he will no doubt be impelled to do the splits
with even more elasticity. But that does not make him a sinister fifth columnist.
The most interesting question is whether the Islamic world at large will treat Tariq
Ramadan's work as merely idiosyncratic or as a dramatic internalization of objective
tensions that he has brought to light.

Notes

1 http://tariqramadan.com/blog/2014/08/12/pourquoi-je-ne-participerai-pas-a-isna-a-
   detroit-aout-2014-et-a-ris-a-toronto-decembre-2014/; www.facebook.com/official.
   tariqramadan/posts/910290628985234.
2 See Azad 2014.
3 See n. 1 above.

14

Mona Siddiqui

This review of Mona Siddiqui's *Christians, Muslims, and Jesus* (Yale University Press, 2013) was published in the *Times Literary Supplement* (*TLS*) on 29 January 2014, under the heading 'Abraham's children'. As well as being a senior academic in religious studies, Siddiqui is well known to the British public as a frequent contributor to the 'Thought for the Day' religious slot in the early morning *Today* programme broadcast by the BBC's Radio Four.

The question 'Do Muslims and Christians worship the same God?' is indeed a brainteaser, which Siddiqui sensibly does not tackle head-on. This is not, however, just a scholastic matter: in Malaysia, Muslim rioters have attacked churches in protest against the use of 'Allah' to denote the God worshipped by Christians (which has always been the case among Arabic-speaking Christians). Curiously, few Christians regard the God of the Old Testament as incompatible with the triune God of Christianity.

Nor does Siddiqui offer a comprehensive comparison between Christianity and Islam, about which sweeping generalizations are often made. In a work such as John Renard's *Christianity and Islam: Theological themes in comparative perspective*, which covers historical, institutional, credal, spiritual and ethical aspects of the subject, we find that, despite fundamental differences between the two traditions, the reality has often been more nuanced (Renard 2011). For instance, the deity that Muslims worship is often thought of by non-Muslims as severe and judgemental, but many Christians have such a concept of God, whereas many Muslims believe that God's mercy always takes precedence. Again, one might expect images of transcendence to be the hallmark of Muslim prayer, since Islamic doctrine denies the divine–human intimacy of the Incarnation, and images of immanence to be more typical of Christian prayer, but in fact, images of both transcendence and immanence permeate devotional prayer in both traditions.

Siddiqui focuses tightly on the persons of Jesus and Mary as they appear in the New Testament and in the Qur'an, and more broadly in the two religious traditions as they evolved. She also reflects on the specifically Christian semiotics of the Cross, which is foreign to Islam. Her aim is to raise the standard of theological debate.

***

Mona Siddiqui is a notable practitioner of interfaith dialogue from a Muslim standpoint, and one might expect her *Christians, Muslims, and Jesus* (2013) to make a self-assured case, as did Miroslav Volf in his *Allah: A Christian response* (reviewed in the *TLS*, 20 January 2012) – that Muslims and Christians worship the same God. The stimulus for Volf's book was the 'Common Word' project, launched in 2008 by Prince Ghazi of Jordan and endorsed by several hundred other Muslim theologians and intellectuals with a view to improving Muslim–Christian relations (www. acommonword.com). Siddiqui reveals near the end of her book that she does not think that Muslims and Christians worship a different God, 'whatever that question means to some'. But her case is shot through with qualifications, testifying to her honesty and intellectual empathy as well as a depth of scholarship to be expected of the Professor of Islamic and Interreligious Studies at Edinburgh. Her book concentrates on the life and death of Jesus according to both Christianity and Islam – literally the crux of the matter.

In the Qur'an, Jesus ('Isa) is revered. He is acclaimed as one of the Righteous, the 'Word of God', the only prophet and messenger 'of end times' (among twenty-four other prophets and messengers mentioned by name), also a miracle-worker, ascetic and renouncer. The nativity stories in the Gospels and the Qur'an are comparable. According to the Qur'an, Jesus was taken to heaven by God after his death; according to post-Qur'anic tradition, he will return as a judge before the Day of Resurrection. Some Christian theologians today support the Islamic view that Jesus did not profess his own divinity, which was also consistent with the understanding of the early Jewish Christians.

The Qur'an repudiates the doctrines of the Trinity and the Incarnation that form the heart of mainstream Christian belief. Siddiqui devotes two chapters to an even-handed exposition of Christian and Islamic apologetics and polemics since the seventh century. Christian writers recognized Islam as a monotheistic belief system but deplored it for denying Jesus's salvific status and were sometimes shocked by what they saw as the Qur'an's acceptance of carnality. Some of them were implacable: in the twelfth century, Peter the Venerable condemned Muhammad as halfway between the heresiarch Arius and the Antichrist. For their part, Islamic writers followed two verses of the Qur'an that explicitly reject the Trinity, which is viewed by Christians as a description of the fecundity of God, completely distinct from tritheism. A conversation is recorded between the Nestorian Patriarch Timothy I and the Caliph al-Mahdi in Baghdad near the end of the eighth century, in which Timothy says: 'We believe in Father, Son and Holy Spirit as one God. And as the sun with its light and its heat is not called three suns but one sun, so also God with His Word and His Spirit is not three Gods but is and is called one God'. Some five centuries later, Thomas Aquinas defended against Muslim ridicule the dogma that Christ was the

Son of God. God, being of the highest intellectual nature, did not need to generate like earthly organisms, but did so through spiritual means that the limited human intellect is able to glimpse only dimly.

Little has changed today, in that Islamic theology rejects the Trinity and the mystery of divine Sonship. A verse in the Qur'an (3: 55) establishes Jesus as the only prophet who is made to distance himself from the doctrines that his community is said to hold about him. God will cleanse Jesus from his followers' corrupted belief that he is divine. Another verse (4: 157) denies that Jesus was crucified by his persecutors, 'but so it was made to appear to them'. Siddiqui quotes the New Testament scholar Heikki Räisänen: 'In sum, the Qur'anic Jesus, unlike any other prophet, is embroiled in polemic'.

As well as the Trinity, the doctrines of original sin and the atonement are rejected in Islamic thought. Here Siddiqui's book would have been enriched if she had noted the similar positions held by Jewish theology. But she explains that without the tragic, transcendental dimension of sin in Christianity, evil for Muslims is not a state but, more prosaically, actions that corrode the individual and society. All human beings are capable of taking responsibility for our actions and overcoming the passions that may lead us astray, symbolized by Iblis (Satan), so that through God's gift of faith and freedom we may attain a state of higher consciousness.

Mary the virginal mother of Jesus – Maryam in the Qur'an – might seem at first sight to provide an opportunity for harmonization. In the Qur'an, only Moses, Abraham and Noah are mentioned by name more frequently than Mary, and Mary herself is mentioned more times than in the entire New Testament: God chose her 'above women of all peoples', and Surah 19, with its ninety-eight verses, is dedicated to her. Siddiqui omits to note that Gibbon, following the orientalist George Sale, held that the Roman Catholic doctrine of Mary's own Immaculate Conception, according to which she was born free of original sin, was borrowed from the Qur'an; and as far as I know this theory has not been refuted by historians.

But Siddiqui shows that what she calls the 'doctrinal density' associated with Mary in Christian thought has no equivalent in Islam. Whereas Catholic and Eastern Orthodox theology exalts Mary for herself as the Mother of God, building on the sparing references to her in the New Testament, in Islam her story is an example of virtue, obedience and chastity, and the virgin birth of Jesus is explained by a straightforward recognition of divine omnipotence and will. The purity of Mary's conception of Jesus does not become an ideal for ordinary Muslim women to aspire to, for their most virtuous and socially desirable role is motherhood. It is not Mary but Fatima, the Prophet's daughter and mother of the tragic heroes Hassan and Hussain, who is specially venerated in popular Muslim piety. Siddiqui concludes her chapter on Mary by suggesting that the late Sri Lankan Catholic theologian Tissa Balasuriya, who was briefly excommunicated in 1997, might offer a way forward for Christian–Muslim understanding, both in his questioning of the doctrine of original sin and in his interpretation of Mary as a model for political activism on the basis of her words in the Magnificat: '[the Lord] has brought down the powerful from their thrones, and lifted up the lowly' (Luke 1: 52). Such an interpretation would resonate on the one hand with the Islamic principle that none are called on to bear the burdens of others, and on the other hand with egalitarian and feminist movements in the Muslim world. But Siddiqui leaves us with the reflection that the nature of the divine Word born by Mary is certain to remain contested between the two traditions.

Another move for narrowing the gap is to emphasize Sufi spirituality, in which Jesus is often associated with wisdom, asceticism and divine love. Siddiqui observes that some medieval Muslim philosopher-poets saw the Trinity and the Incarnation as symbolic ways of speaking about the unknowable Absolute. For Ibn al-Arabi, love became a universal principle encompassing the actions of all creation, which is strikingly similar to the Christian concept of universal *agapē* – whereas God in the Qur'an reserves the prerogative to withhold his love from transgressors. Jalal al-Din Rumi presented Jesus as 'the perfection of humanity', endowed with life-giving breath. The implication here, which Siddiqui does not confront head-on, is that mystical traditions of this kind, with their undoubted imaginative power, are not confined to the Abrahamic monotheisms. Rumi, for instance, seems to have subscribed to a version of the much older tradition of belief in reincarnation; and the famous Persian mystic al-Hallaj – whom Siddiqui mentions approvingly, if only in passing – was executed for heresy in Baghdad in 922, having preached on the union between the soul and God and declared 'I am the Truth'. The Sufi tack must surely lead away from the harbour of strict monotheism towards open waters of metaphysical or spiritual experience, especially the 'oceanic' feelings that have inspired so much religious practice and creative art alike. If one suggests it is probably a residue from humanity's evolutionary past, that need not exclude theological explanations.

In the conclusion to her book, Siddiqui summarizes personal statements collected from some of her Christian friends about their thoughts and feelings when they look at a cross or crucifix. For one of them, it has become a successful marketing brand for the Churches. Others read into it symbols of suffering, compassion, tragedy and atonement, but also military conquest. Siddiqui admits that, though she is moved when contemplating the cross in a local church, she cannot incline towards 'a God who undergoes this inexplicable agony for an inexplicable act of mercy'. But the message of the cross has helped her, she says, to understand the need to forgive more readily, forgiveness in the Qur'an being more an attribute of God than an ethical injunction to believers. One sympathetic study of Islam by a Catholic, Marcel Boisard's influential *L'Humanisme de l'Islam* (1979), goes further than Siddiqui and generalizes that the Gospel injunction to pray for one's persecutors and love one's enemies seems to Muslims 'absurd and shocking to reason'.

'I have not ventured', Siddiqui writes, 'into political, sociological and civilisational aspects of the Muslim or Christian world because Christological doctrines are in my mind, the most disputed and perhaps the most intriguing area of Christian–Muslim debate.' In her furthering of interfaith understanding, she is not satisfied with recognizing that both Jesus and Muhammad are world historical figures revered as ultimate exemplars of ethical living; nor with documenting the deep commitment in both traditions to charitable giving and the practical relief of suffering. But her method leads to a kind of impasse.

A more positive message might have emerged if she had drawn on the concept of 'orthopraxy', as opposed to orthodoxy, which has gained some currency in religious studies. Whereas it is true that Salafi–Wahhabi Islam appears to be more concerned with right conduct than with right belief, the view that Islam as a whole emphasizes ritual at the expense of intellectual content is now criticized by scholars as a Christian misrepresentation. It is more productive to think of orthodoxy and orthopraxy as mutually entwined in all religious traditions. Thus, even the Nicene Creed is not only a statement of doctrine, but also a hymn of collective praise that enacts or performs the Holy Trinity. Interfaith understanding might be promoted more easily if assent or submission to doctrine, expressed by participation in ritual, were accepted as the practical criterion for membership of a faith, rather than the more elusive 'belief' whose ardour or intensity is so variable.

Siddiqui does give attention in her first chapter to the shared genesis of both Christianity and Islam in Judaism, but, whereas Christians emphasize the fulfilment of Judaism through Christianity, the Islamic claim is that, by means of the Qur'an, Judaism and Christianity are restored to their primordial truths. Islam had to legitimize itself in 'the heavily competitive sectarian milieu of seventh-century Arabia'. Siddiqui does not mention the story in Genesis 22 of Abraham's willingness to obey God's command to sacrifice his son, who is then replaced by a ram. This story, known in Judaism as the Akedah, or 'binding' of Isaac, made Abraham the definitive model of faith for the three monotheisms and – as discussed by Carol Delaney (1998) in her provocative book *Abraham on Trial* – is a common foundation for the three theologies.

But the sharp focus of *Christians, Muslims, and Jesus* is Mona Siddiqui's own choice. She deserves recognition as one of the most imaginative leaders of contemporary Islamic thought.

15

Akbar Ahmed

This was published as a guest editorial in *Anthropology Today*, 29: 4, August 2013. An authoritative review of Akbar Ahmed's *The Thistle and the Drone* was published by Malise Ruthven (Ruthven 2013b). This book seems to me the finest of Akbar Ahmed's many publications, blending a literary and religious sensibility with political and historical analysis, a model for engaged anthropology.

I was only able to touch here on Ahmed's discussion of Osama bin Laden (1957–2011), which is the subject of a whole chapter in his book, 'Bin Laden's dilemma: Balancing tribal and Islamic identity'. In bin Laden's youth, as an economics student in Jeddah, Saudi Arabia, he absorbed the ideas of the Egyptian scholar-activist Sayyid Qutb (1906–66) and later, after joining the jihad against the Soviet Union in Afghanistan, he was mentored by Abdullah Yusuf al-Azzam (1941–89), the Palestinian theorist of Islamic radicalism. With characteristic originality, Akbar Ahmed compensates for what he sees as excessive emphasis by commentators on Bin Laden as a religious sectarian. When there was conflict between Bin Laden's inherited Yemeni values, based on honour and revenge, and Qur'anic injunctions in favour of mercy and reconciliation, it was his tribal identity that took precedence.

***

Social anthropology has intermittently succeeded in claiming a seat at the top tables of international affairs, but its spiritual home remains at the margins. Hence the temptation to become a sectarian enclave. An alternative response – because so many of the peoples that have been its traditional focus of enquiry are suffering severely – is to engage in activism, like Survival International. Suppose, though, that an intellectual formulation were found that could bring anthropology to the heart of momentous discussions in Western foreign ministries and the White House, while also foregrounding the predicament of marginal peoples as a reproach to the West's moral conscience?

Akbar Ahmed's new book *The Thistle and the Drone: How America's war on terror became a global war on tribal Islam* (Brookings Institution Press, 2013) seems to fill the bill. During a week in June it was the centrepiece of a number of panel discussions at London venues, including the House of Lords (27 June) and the School of Oriental and African Studies (29 June). There was no rigorous examination by specialists, but opportunities will come up in the future, as well as for a broader appraisal of a book that includes some forty ethnographic case studies – carried out with a small team of young American researchers – and sustained reflection on the geopolitical decisions reached by Osama bin Laden and the former President of Pakistan, Pervez Musharraf, as well as on the current dilemmas that still face President Obama. Ahmed, now the Ibn Khaldun Chair of Islamic Studies at the American University in Washington, DC, is one of the most media-savvy and self-conscious of writers and he will no doubt be following up the publication of his book with an account of its reception, which varies at this early stage from the admiring to the hostile and is handicapped in that probably no single person is qualified to review it adequately.

Some of the discussants in London concentrated on the literal issue of drones, or Unmanned Aerial Vehicles (UAVs), which have victimized Muslim tribal societies disproportionately. According to Ahmed, even if the rate of civilian casualties can be shown to be lower than that resulting from the use of more traditional weapons, it is the UAV's usurpation of the powers of God that Muslim tribespeople condemn as not only dishonourable but blasphemous. A military expert, Douglas Barrie, reacted in the House of Lords with the surprising argument that UAVs are not risk free, while declining to substantiate this statement by giving examples of UAV operators who had so far suffered any injuries. Ahmed argued that even if UAVs were to be discontinued tomorrow in the Pakistan tribal areas, the violence in Waziristan – where he was the government's political agent from 1978 to 1980 – would not stop. His book is not just about UAVs.

The book's immediate reception may be inhibited by its poetic title. The drone is a material technology that becomes a metaphor for the current age of globalization: something which comes from nowhere, destroys your life and goes away. The thistle 'captures the essence of tribal societies', an image borrowed from Tolstoy's posthumous novel *Hadji Murad*, about a Caucasian Avar leader's struggles under the yoke of imperial Russia. Thistles are prickly, tenacious and survive even when crushed. 'Man has conquered everything', writes Tolstoy's narrator, 'and destroyed millions of plants, yet this one won't submit'. Ahmed notes that others before him have drawn an analogy between the recalcitrant Scots, who chose the thistle as their national emblem, and other thistle-like tribal societies such as the Pakhtun, Somali and Kurd.

The tribal groups discussed in his book are characterized by egalitarianism, hospitality, a strong sense of justice, a commitment to freedom, a tribal lineage system defined by common ancestors and clans, a martial tradition, and a highly developed code of honour and revenge. The exclusively domestic sphere allocated to women is unacceptable today and Ahmed does not defend it, but he insists that the transition towards gender equality has to be negotiated sensitively through the tribal structures and their relationships with religious authority and with national governments. After an exceptionally varied career as a diplomat, sought-after authority on contemporary Islam, and interfaith campaigner (also a spare-time poet and playwright), Ahmed has reverted to his roots as an anthropologist: the author of *Millennium and Charisma among Pathans* (1976), one of the late Ernest Gellner's favourite interlocutors, and promoter of the concept of an 'Islamic anthropology' against Richard Tapper's sharp caveats (Tapper 1995).[1] Disturbed by the wide acceptance of the 'clash of civilizations' thesis and George W. Bush's foreign policy, largely continued by President Obama, Ahmed decided to examine the interstices between states, beginning with a return visit to Waziristan. He identifies four historical stages. First, a thousand years, when emirates were largely left on their own: an equilibrium between tribal and Muslim values. Second, the imposition of colonial boundaries in the eighteenth and nineteenth centuries, with elements of ethnocide. Third, after World War II, the launching of independent nations, whose central governments tended to treat peripheral groups as badly as their colonial masters had. And, lastly, the post-9/11 period when the United States declared the 'war on terror', which continues as a reality although the phrase itself has been dropped by the US government.

Tribal Islam, contrary to popular misunderstandings, is antithetical to Wahhabi–Salafi literalism, being typically grounded in oral folk traditions, emulation of the Prophet, and veneration of intercessionary spiritual figures or saints. It has also accommodated pre-Islamic and non-Islamic customs such as facing the sun rather than Mecca to pray (the Asir of Saudi Arabia) or trial by ordeal (the Bugti of Baluchistan, or the Bedouin of the Sinai and Negev). Bin Laden was primarily a demented tribal leader from Yemen, refusing to renounce the code of honour and revenge that is at odds with clear religious injunctions against suicide and the murder of innocents. Yemen was also the ethnic affiliation of most of the Al-Qaeda activists, especially from the south-western Saudi province of Asir, which was annexed by Saudi Arabia in 1934 after bitter fighting.

Two of the discussants in London – Owen Bennett-Jones at the House of Lords and Gilbert Achcar at SOAS – reproached Ahmed for apparently praising benighted tribal practices and some American commentators have assumed that he is anti-American. But the former objection misunderstands the anthropological approach of trying to project oneself into other frames of mind, while the latter ignores the fact that Ahmed finds much to admire in the United States, especially the heritage of the Founding Fathers – as is evident from his book *Journey into America: The challenge of Islam* (Ahmed 2010).

The sorry conclusion of *The Thistle and the Drone* is that brutal revenge attacks from the periphery will continue: groups such as the Taliban see them as a way to communicate the pain that they are experiencing. Drones and central government invasions will not work. Ahmed remains committed to interfaith dialogue as a means to encourage respect for peripheral peoples – including non-Muslim minorities such as the Tamils in Sri Lanka and the Nagas and Adivasi in India. But, there are also more pragmatic suggestions in his final chapter 'How to win the war on terror': with Aceh in Indonesia, Mindanao in the Philippines and Albanians in Macedonia cited, with qualifications, as cases of moves towards core–periphery reconciliation.

Note

1 This exchange has been reprinted in Kreinath 2012.

16

Yusuf al-Qaradawi

This chapter was originally the entry on Yusuf al-Qaradawi in the *Oxford Encyclopedia of Islam and Politics* (Oxford, 2014). A collection of articles edited by Gräf and Skovgaard-Petersen (2009) may be recommended for further reading.

Since the encyclopedia went to press, tensions between Qaradawi and the al-Sisi government in Egypt were heightened after that government declared the Muslim Brotherhood a terrorist organization. In December 2014, Interpol issued a warrant for Qaradawi's arrest, upon Egypt's request, and the International Islamic Council expelled a group that he led, the International Union of Islamic Scholars.

The charges against Qaradawi, for which he was about to be tried *in absentia* in Egypt, were of 'agreement, incitement and assistance to commit intentional murder, helping prisoners to escape, arson, vandalism and theft' (Ahramonline 2014). Qaradawi strongly rejected these accusations.

The International Union of Islamic Scholars had released a statement in July 2014 denouncing the recent declaration of a 'caliphate' by ISIS as 'null and void', since the leader of the Muslim *umma* should be a representative of the nation as a result of worldwide Shura (consultation), rather than self-appointed. The governments of Saudi Arabia and the United Arab Emirates, while regarding ISIS as the greater evil, became strongly opposed to the Muslim Brotherhood, treating it as a terrorist organization, by contrast with Qatar, which Qaradawi had adopted as his home and which was much more indulgent towards the Muslim Brotherhood. After the accession of Salman bin Abdulaziz al-Saud as king of Saudi Arabia in January 2015, it seemed that the kingdom's hostility towards the Muslim Brotherhood was somewhat abating.

Jacob Høigilt's study of Qaradawi's rhetoric, cited here, reveals how little freedom of thought Qaradawi is concerned to allow his readers. This style of exposition has had wide currency in Islamic education worldwide. (But Høigilt's analysis should stimulate reflection on the relationship between doctrine and individual reasoning, which can be traced in all organized ideologies.)

There is no reason to doubt the sincerity of Qaradawi's commitment to preaching the principles of Islamic charity: he inspired followers to open their wallets for the relief of suffering as a religious duty. But, as was noted in *The Charitable Crescent*, 'The career of this key figure illustrates an interpenetration between different fields: religious militancy, intellectual expertise in Islamic law and zakat, business and social work, considered as essential for the revival of Islam' (Benthall and Bellion-Jourdan 2003: 42). The idea of charity as a protected sphere, ring-fenced from politics and religion (see Chapter 9), would be alien to his philosophy.

***

Yusuf al-Qaradawi is an Egyptian-born theologian and preacher, who resides in Qatar. Qaradawi is regularly voted among the world's foremost public intellectuals and has a large following throughout the world, but he has also been an extremely polarizing figure throughout his career. He was born in Saft at-Turab, Upper Egypt, in 1926. His family background was modest and his father died when he was two. Beginning his education in a village Qur'anic school, he went on to study Islam and the Arabic language, achieving a doctorate at Al-Azhar in 1974 for his dissertation on zakat. He was strongly influenced by Hassan al-Banna (1906–49) and Muhammad al-Ghazali (1917–96), while acknowledging a special debt to the great Sufi scholar Abu Hamid al-Ghazali (d. 1111). His political activities led to his arrest several times during the reign of King Farouk and after the 1952 revolution. He has always been close to the Muslim Brothers, and later twice declined an invitation to become their supreme leader. Since 1961 he has resided in Qatar, founding several Islamic institutions in that state and using it as a base for the spread of his intellectual influence all over the Muslim world. His major study, *Fiqh al-zakāt* (Qaradawi n.d.) provided the main theological basis for the formation of modern Islamic charitable organizations. He has built up connections with many key Islamic institutions in different spheres – academic, financial, judicial, educational, and charitable – not only in Muslim-majority countries but in Britain, Ireland, and Switzerland. His career has embodied his doctrinal commitment to Islam as a comprehensive way of life (*shumūlīyyat al-islām*).

He has succeeded in becoming the most influential religious authority in the Sunni Muslim world, not only through the publication of over 120 books but also by his use of the media, including the Arabic and English website IslamOnline, founded in 1999. Since 1970 he has hosted his own programme, *Hadī al-Islām* (Guidance of Islam), on Qatar's national television and after the foundation of the Al Jazeera television channel in 1996 he has been the mainstay of its religious programme *Sharia and Life*, winning a huge global audience. Though Arabic is his only language, he is an impressively gifted orator.

One of Qaradawi's guiding principles is *wasaṭīyah*, or centrism, which he calls 'the soul of Islam', aiming to reconcile the intellectual conflict of the twentieth century between renewal (*tajdīd*) and conservatism, but always within current Islamic orthodoxy. He criticizes, on the one hand, those interpreters of religious texts who try to accommodate them to secular ideologies and, on the other, those who dwell on the letter rather than the meaning of the texts and are subservient to the four classical Sunni schools. This tendency was evident in his early book *al-Ḥalāl wa-al-ḥarām fī al-islām* (1960; English translation *The Lawful and the Prohibited in Islam*, 2003), translated into more than twenty languages, which sought to free Islamic jurisprudence (*fiqh*) from the pedantry and negativity of the old jurists. His authority extends throughout the Islamic world and he has even been ascribed the status of *marjiʿīyah*, an 'authoritative reference', which is a Shia concept when applied to persons. Whereas his youthful ambition was to be the Sheikh al-Azhar in Egypt, a political appointment, he is seen by many followers as the sheikh of the entire *umma* (Muslim nation).

Controversy

Qaradawi's endorsement of a middle way has not protected him from sharp controversy. Indeed, the polemics surrounding his name are paradigmatic of the crisis of authority in Islam today. From the Salafi perspective (though he is respected by some Salafi tendencies), he has been criticized for arguing that 'offensive' jihad has been made obsolete by the new media, which allow the message of Islam to be disseminated peacefully, and also on the grounds that he is too lenient towards infidels. But liberal and secular Muslims take issue with him vigorously, especially on the questions of religious freedom, gender, violence and Judaism. Study of the positions he has taken on such issues reveals many ambiguities.

On religious freedom, Qaradawi condemns apostasy as a capital offence under Sharia, but insists that the punishment should be inflicted only by the Islamic state and only if the offender publicizes the act. He urges dialogue with other religions and has defended the rights of the Coptic minority in Egypt. He has rejected the classical division of the world into *dār al-islām* and *dār al-ḥarb* (domain of war), sketching a theory of *fiqh al-aqallīyāt*, or 'law of Muslim minorities', which would facilitate integration of Muslims in non-Muslim societies such as Europe without abandoning what are seen as the essentials of the religion. On blasphemy he has been emphatic, intervening, for instance, in the Danish cartoon crisis of 2005–6 to call for a 'day of anger' against the Danish and Norwegian governments, but swiftly condemning the violence that ensued.

On gender issues, Qaradawi stresses the complementarity between male and female, sidestepping the question of gender equality and proclaiming that women have a 'natural disposition' (*bi ḥukm al-fiṭrah*) to domesticity, wifehood and motherhood. But he also encourages women to fulfil their potential in education and public life. He supports women's right to vote and stand for election, and even to engage in paramilitary operations in the Palestinian cause. Such emancipatory steps are validated, for Qaradawi, by their contribution to the collective interest and only secondarily by their implications for the individual. He is intransigent in abominating homosexuality and in defending the practice of wife beating (albeit only lightly and when reasoning has failed).

Qaradawi is strongly opposed to Al-Qaeda style violent extremism and immediately condemned the 11 September 2001 attacks on the United States. He has also dismissed as extremist the teaching of Sayyid Qutb (1906–66), during the final, radical stage of his life, when he preached violence against infidels and morally corrupt Muslims alike. But the position for which Qaradawi is most attacked in the West has been his doctrine of 'defensive jihad', according to which when Muslims are under attack – as in Israel, Chechnya, or Kashmir – resistance is obligatory and suicide bombing legitimate. He grants this permission only within the territories in dispute, but in the case of Israel he defends Palestinian attacks on civilians, including children, on the grounds that the entire Israeli society is militarized. This position reflects widespread opinion in the Arab world, but is contradicted by many other *ulama*. It is doubtless the principal reason why he was banned from entering the United States in 1999, the United Kingdom in 2008, and France in 2012. Qaradawi's image as a conciliator, deserved in some other contexts, comes under greatest strain when, on occasion, he has praised Hitler for his treatment of the Jews.

Qaradawi's rhetoric

In a study of Islamist rhetoric, Jacob Høigilt has illuminatingly analyzed the literary style of Qaradawi's publications dating back to 1998. Qaradawi has 'a pyramidal vision of the Islamic field' (Høigilt 2011: 64). At the base are the ordinary people, *al-nās*; above them is a layer of religiously aware Muslims; he is at the apex as the final judge of things Islamic. Abstaining from detailed rebuttals of other *ulama*'s interpretations, he adopts a measured, impersonal tone, respectful of the Arabic rhetorical tradition and coloured by allusions to the great thinkers and poets of the classical Islamic age. It is not Muslims who act, but a personified Islam that ordains and performs the Good – opposed by extremists, conservatives, secularists, and imperialists. All who fall outside the school of *wasaṭīyah* are disqualified. Høigilt concludes that the result is to boost Qaradawi's own authority while disempowering the reader.

Since the 'Arab awakening'

In February 2011, Qaradawi returned to Egypt – for the first time after he was banned from leading the Friday prayers there thirty years before – and preached in Tahrir Square, Cairo, to an assembly numbered in hundreds of thousands. He has been hailed by many as a great reformist religious leader and was likened by Ken Livingstone, the former Mayor of London, to Pope John XXIII. Controversy continued to erupt, however, with regard to his alleged double standards. Though he gave his approval to the anti-government forces in Egypt, Libya and Syria, he withheld it those in Bahrain, dismissing them as sectarian, although the Shia constitute a majority of the population. His critics charge that this view reflects the bias of the petromonarchies, including Qatar, his adopted country.

In 2013, Qaradawi denounced the Lebanese Hizbullah and the Iranian Shia government for their support of the Bashar al-Assad regime in Syria. More consistently with his previous positions, he called on the Egyptian people to oppose the July 2013 military coup and the deposition of President Mohamed Morsi.

17

Religion and violence

This review of David Martin's *Religion and Power: No logos without mythos* (Ashgate, 2014) and Karen Armstrong's *Fields of Blood: Religion and the history of violence* (Bodley Head, 2014) was published in the *Times Literary Supplement* (*TLS*) on 10 December 2014, under the heading 'Poplars in the marsh'.

Two very different authors reach a similar conclusion, that it is a fallacy to regard religions as having a special propensity towards violence, and they both accept that violent resistance is an inevitable response to policies that oppress large populations.

Since publication of her book, Karen Armstrong has published a more nuanced commentary on current Islamist violence, writing that after the Iranian Revolution of 1989, the USA gave 'tacit support to the Saudis' project of countering Shia radicalism by Wahhabising the entire Muslim world', thus undermining the long tradition of Islamic pluralism and eventually facilitating the rise of ISIS, which has come back to haunt the Kingdom (Armstrong 2014b).

As regards the ideology of ISIS or the 'Islamic State' that is touched on towards the end of this chapter, the political scientist Steve Niva has recently argued that this is a new amalgam of Salafi-Wahhabism with 'twentieth century communist and leftist traditions of revolutionary warfare, updated for the information age'. Niva draws on Naomi Klein's theory of the 'shock doctrine': that unpopular policies are often imposed on a public disorientated by a massive collective shock. According to this interpretation, the Bush administration deliberately collapsed the Iraqi state and society in 2003 with a view to creating a corporate utopia, but in fact it created a 'ghoulish dystopia', opening the way to the jihadi strategic doctrine of 'management of savagery' (Niva 2015).

I conclude with some brief reflections on some of the obstacles that all non-violent movements are confronted with.

***

'In religion as in science,' writes David Martin in *Religion and Power: No logos without mythos* (2014), 'you cannot have the perfume without the mustard gas'. He reminds those who blame religion for inciting violence that the problem of violence is much deeper, endemic to the human species, because group solidarity always implies the exclusion of outsiders and hence potential conflict over resources. Karen Armstrong makes a similar case in *Fields of Blood: Religion and the history of violence* (2014), but adducing the now rather dated theory of the triune human brain, its selfish reptilian substrate coexisting uneasily with limbic empathy and neocortical rationality. Both authors allude to Cain's murder of Abel in Genesis 4, but whereas Martin takes it to illustrate a general propensity to violence, Armstrong makes a connection between Cain's reply to Yahweh, 'Am I my brother's keeper?', and his later role as founder of the world's first city. She sees urban civilization as having denied the sense of responsibility for all other human beings that is embedded in human nature. Both books challenge what Martin calls the 'most favoured' ideological narrative: that there is a problematic connection between religion and violence. Armstrong sets out to refute the claim that 'religion has been the cause of all the major wars in history', which she has heard espoused by 'American commentators and psychiatrists, London taxi drivers and Oxford academics'.

Armstrong begins and ends her book with the charge that an essentialized 'religion' has been treated as a scapegoat for much broader ills and misdeeds, and Martin says much the same. Both are opposed to militant atheism. Both trace the historical regularity with which irenic teaching has been appropriated by what Martin calls 'the struggle for dominance and its associated codes of honour and face'. They also have in common an acceptance that the boundaries between the religious and the secular are porous. For much contemporary scholarship, 'religion as such is a dubious catch-all category' (Martin). 'For about fifty years now it has been clear in the academy that there is no universal way to define religion' (Armstrong). Hospitals, art galleries and concert halls are among the institutions that 'take over from religion', as can 'the mobilising power of mass rituals and the icons of sacred nationalism' (Martin). 'Secularism did not so much displace religion as create alternative religious enthusiasms' (Armstrong). Both authors draw attention to the grievances of what Martin calls 'the two-thirds world', and both go some way to empathize with those who are pushed towards violent protests against the Western powers that prop up corrupt regimes.

Each author has experienced a Christian vocation as well as studying religion as a layperson, but in a different sequence. Martin is one of the world's leading sociologists of religion and became an Anglican priest in his fifties. (His memoir, *The Education of David Martin: The making of an unlikely sociologist*, was reviewed in the *TLS* of 21 February 2014.) For seven years in her youth, Armstrong was a member of a Catholic order of sisters, the Society of the Holy Child Jesus, and she has since become a prolific historian and commentator on comparative religion. Martin's experience of ministry has evidently been fulfilling; Armstrong's experience of her convent was miserable.

Martin is determined to show that sociology is both affiliated to all the humanities and a distinctive scientific practice requiring conceptual rigour, historical contextualization and a tentative approach. He sets a high standard for less experienced social scientists to emulate, while also absorbing the results of recent scholarship. His principal argument is against the relegation of religion to a private domain, supposedly beyond the rational scrutiny that informs debate in the 'public sphere' as defined by Jürgen Habermas. Martin's strategy is to show how much the images and narratives that govern politics have in common with those that govern religion.

Martin has no difficulty in establishing this point with regard to the leading pseudo-religions of the twentieth century, Marxism-Leninism and Nazism, but he brings his case closer to home when he argues: 'There are times when politics takes on the shape of a phantasmagoric drama. Its ritual performances are a form of stylised role-play requiring a willing suspension of disbelief in order to keep the show on the road'. Barack Obama, for instance, acquired messianic status during the 2008 election as the one who would realize the 'American dream', and he quickly took note that he was carrying a dangerous religious freight. In recent British politics, Tony Blair was hailed as a saviour of the British nation in 1997, but widely disdained ten years later. Religion and politics alike, 'whether we speak of the politics of nation or of ideology, have a pervasive mythic structure marked by retrospective and prospective visions, and by ways of identifying the prime suspects standing in the way of recovering the idyllic past and reaching forward to the promised world of authentic being'.

For Martin, the social world is a unity, in which power, wealth, aesthetics and the erotic all interpenetrate. What cries out for explanation is not war, which is a legacy from our evolutionary past, but the tradition of non-violence to be found in the original teaching of the Buddha and Jesus. The radical preaching of the Sermon on the Mount and the subversive symbolism of Jesus washing his disciples' feet remained as submerged elements in Christianity even when they were appropriated by warrior kings and lords. These elements are an often unacknowledged historical foundation of the humanist morality that is now deployed against Christianity by its critics.

At some points in his book, Martin sets out, following accepted practice in the sociology of religion, to 'bracket' truth values: that is, to separate them mentally from descriptive analysis. But he also seems to be impelled to escape from the confines of social science into a more proclamatory mode, where analogical thinking comes naturally. For instance, he echoes the Catholic social anthropologist Mary Douglas in praising the condensation of multiple meanings in the Eucharist.

Since 1978, Martin has gradually refined the 'general theory of secularization' that he advanced in a book of that name, partly in response to what has been called the 'standard model', which saw religion as losing social significance and retreating to the private realm. Martin has preferred to emphasize variable histories in different regions with different confessional cultures, each affected by epoch-making events such as wars and revolutions. In the case of a nation such as Ukraine bordering rival empires, the history of its religio-political tensions as expertly outlined by Martin is so complex that one may wonder what is left of a 'general theory'. It is certain that secularization theory will have its place in histories of sociology, but Martin's acknowledgement that secularization is both a descriptive and a prescriptive concept, and that the distinction between the religious and the secular is always open to question, might suggest that the whole theoretical debate is ready to be given a rest.

Theories in social science tend to expire sooner or later. Martin, however, is also the sociologist who brought to academic attention the phenomenon of transnational Pentecostalism, a form of 'voluntarism' that challenges territorial religion but has also helped to stimulate charismatic manifestations in most of the mainstream Churches. Here Martin has been at odds with those intellectuals who prefer to idealize folk cultures. ('Béla Bartók would not have been interested in collecting Evangelical choruses and turning them into quartets: Gypsies yes, Pentecostals no; and definitely not today's Pentecostal gypsies.') The rapid expansion of Pentecostalism in sub-Saharan Africa and Latin America has made his ethnography impossible to ignore. There is much in Martin's new book to ensure its permanence on reading lists, in particular evidence of his insatiably enquiring mind, though some of the terms he uses, such as 'axial angles of transcendence' and 'socio-logic', require at least a second reading before they become clear.

Martin applies literary critical skill to impale some of the statements made by famous critics of religion. He argues that Richard Dawkins' claim that 'the meme for blind faith secures its own perpetuation by the simple unconscious expedient of discouraging rational enquiry' (from *The Selfish Gene*) has nothing empirical about it. On the contrary, it relies on the meme as a *deus ex machina*. But when Martin is understandably provoked by A. C. Grayling's dismissal of biblical writers as 'ignorant goatherds', it may not be the most effective tactic to call Grayling a bullyboy. Given that many philosophers would consider it impossible to disprove naturalistic interpretations of life and the cosmos, Martin is on stronger ground when as a sociologist he explains and defends the specific methods of social science, and when as a Christian he tacitly allows his own life to serve as an example.

If Martin's *Religion and Power* seems at times overladen with theory, Karen Armstrong's *Fields of Blood* reverts time and again to a single theoretical concept, that of 'structural violence'. It was coined by the Norwegian sociologist John Galtung in the late 1960s and refers to any impairment of human life chances that is induced by forms of social organization, even under ostensibly benevolent regimes. Armstrong cites with approval Walter Benjamin's well-known aphorism, 'There is no document of civilization that is not at the same time a document of barbarism', and the Trappist monk Thomas Merton's challenge to all of us who have benefited from surpluses extracted from labour, that we are implicated in the suffering inflicted for over 5,000 years on the vast majority of men and women. The problem with structural violence as an explanation is that it can be applied to all social arrangements that have developed in history, with the exception of some strictly egalitarian hunter-gatherer societies. It is as all-purpose and imprecise as a monkey wrench.

Yet Armstrong has written an assured and convincing world-historical panorama of the interactions of religions and violence, starting with the agrarian empires of the Middle East, China, India and Europe, and continuing through the early modern period and the Enlightenment up to the present day when the new media can both draw out our compassion for distant suffering and also activate feelings of anger and vengeance. She writes lucidly and as far as I can judge with very few factual errors. (But though it has been argued, by others as well as Armstrong, that Samson in Judges 16 was the prototype of a kamikaze or suicide bomber, saying 'Let me die with the Philistines', she overlooks that Milton in *Samson Agonistes* wrote that he was 'self-kill'd / Not willingly, but tangled in the fold / Of dire necessity'.)

Perhaps the sharpest arrow in Armstrong's quiver is her insistence on the seductive glamour of warfare, especially for young men, and equally on 'the moment in warfare when the horrifying reality breaks through the glamour'. She seizes on this moment in the ancient Mesopotamian *Epic of Gilgamesh*, when the gods punish the eponymous king and his friend Enkidu for their foolhardy aggression: Enkidu falls sick and dies, whereupon Gilgamesh is stricken with grief and rejects the heroic, martial ideal. In Homer's *Iliad*, despite the overriding emphasis on heroism, the third casualty in the Trojan war is Simoeisios, a beautiful youth who should have known the tenderness of family life but is killed by the Greek warrior Ajax. In an exquisite vignette, he is likened to a poplar in a marsh that is felled by a chariot maker and lies hardening on the riverbank.

Later, in the third century BC (and in history recorded on rock edicts, as opposed to early literature), King Ashoka, who ruled over most of India and had acquired a reputation for cruelty, underwent a conversion experience having witnessed the huge suffering after the imperial army put down a Kalingan rebellion. 'The sensory realities of warfare', Armstrong writes, 'broke through the carapace of cultivated heartlessness that makes warfare possible'. He enjoined a moral code of compassion, mercy, honesty and consideration for living creatures. Yet he also recognized that as head of state he could not renounce force. 'As society developed and weaponry became more deadly, the empire, founded and maintained by violence, would paradoxically become the most effective way of keeping the peace.'

At times, Armstrong deploys the 'structural violence' argument to urge the reader to understand the motivation behind subversive physical violence. But she accepts the coercive urban state as an ineluctable reality: 'the best that prophets and sages have been able to do is provide an alternative'. In most pre-modern cultures, she writes (no doubt with a measure of exaggeration), everyday life was seen as a pale shadow of a transcendent reality. We still today yearn for transcendence, but this craving can lead not only to good outcomes but also to narcotics, the cult of celebrity, and warfare – 'one of the oldest triggers of ecstatic experience'. Alert to these dangers, but unwilling to concede to any single religion a monopoly on the truth, Armstrong might have yielded to a New Age spiritual eclecticism. She pins her faith instead on the 'Golden Rule' of ethical reciprocity and compassion, 'do as you would be done by', that is to be found in almost all religious and philosophical traditions.

Wide respect for Armstrong's earlier publications and for her interfaith activism has sometimes been qualified by the suggestion that she is overindulgent towards Islam. Her discussion of the relationship between Islam and violence in *Fields of Blood*, which went to press before the military successes of ISIS (the 'Islamic State') in the summer of 2014, deserves to be examined closely. She sees all fundamentalist movements as defiant self-assertions of identity against a more powerful 'Other'. Protestant fundamentalism emerged in the United States in the early twentieth century as a reaction to the trauma of modern warfare and to the aggressive disdain of the secularist establishment, and it succeeded in becoming an influential voice in American politics. 'It would not resort to violence, largely because American Protestants did not suffer as greatly as did, for example, the Muslims of the Middle East.' This is a speculation that cannot count as evidence, but there is merit in her thesis that all fundamentalisms are essentially defensive, not necessarily lashing out into violence.

Islamist movements, however, do confront Armstrong with a conceptual difficulty. She asserts that 'a religious tradition is never a single, unchanging essence that impels people to act in a uniform way [but] a template that can be modified and altered radically to serve a variety of ends'. We cannot point to an 'essential' Christianity that has promoted identical courses of action. Yet in her chapter on 'global jihad' she seems ready to dissociate an essentialized Islam from jihadi violence, on the grounds that most of the young perpetrators are religiously uneducated. Her view is favoured by the preponderance of mainstream Muslims who abhor jihadism and by Western politicians who for good reasons want to dampen anti-Muslim prejudice. But it downplays the sometimes sophisticated exploitation of Scripture by jihadi ideologues, and in particular their reinterpretation of the literalist teachings of the fourteenth century scholar Ibn Taymiyyah, a forerunner of Wahhabism.

A chilling book published online in 2004, under the pseudonym Abu Bakr Naji, *Management of Savagery: The most critical stage through which the* umma *will pass*, has probably influenced the leaders of ISIS. It is thought to have been written by an Al-Qaeda propaganda chief who was killed in a US airstrike in 2008. A kind of jihadi *Mein Kampf*, it suggested taking advantage of the loss of America's 'media halo' of invincibility to promote the attrition of state authority in the Middle East, a transitional period of extreme violence, the formation of a caliphate, and territorial gains throughout the region. ISIS's priorities may well include prising the Wahhabi religious movement away from the Al Saud dynasty with which it has had a symbiotic relationship since the eighteenth century – a project which, if successful, could have immense consequences for the stability of the region. It cannot be predicted whether Shia and Sunni Muslim governments will find common ground, assisted by Western military power, to destroy ISIS, or whether its territorial claims and intemperate reworking of Wahhabism will continue to gather sporadic support as a defence against Shia domination.

David Martin and Karen Armstrong both set store by the potential of non-violence as a legacy of religious traditions. History suggests that non-violent campaigns are likely to be most successful when conducted against authorities that are amenable to compromise, also that some of the most important proponents of non-violence – Jesus, M. K. Gandhi, Martin Luther King – have met with violent deaths. It is worth asking, too, whether non-violence could ever acquire the colourful glamour that military recruiters, for both governments and rebels, have always banked on. The anthropologist Emiko Ohnuki-Tierney has shown in *Kamikaze: Cherry blossoms and nationalisms* (2002) how the cherry blossom, the traditional emblem of Japanese nationalism, was militarized in 1944–5 to represent the *tokkōtai* suicide pilots who were 'volunteered' to fall from the skies for their emperor: they wore the pink flowers on their uniforms and a single blossom was painted on their aeroplanes. Hamas suicide bombers have been depicted as carried to paradise by green birds. Whenever ISIS claims new territory, it hoists its black flag, incorporating the Seal of the Prophet Muhammad. If we set on one side the complex Christian semiotics of the Crucifixion, Gandhi's white *dhoti* is perhaps the nearest that a non-violent movement has come to achieving a symbolic éclat comparable to the glamour of militarism.[1]

Note

1 I addressed this question in more detail in 'Waiting for a Muslim Gandhi' (Benthall 2004).

Afterword

Troubled times

The level of turbulence in the Middle East is higher than at any time since the Suez Crisis of 1956, especially aggravated by ISIS's 'management of savagery' (Chapter 17).[1] Since the consequences of alliances may not be visible to the various parties, there is a risk of escalation as in 1914. In August 2013, the political analyst Edward Luttwak voiced the opinion that a prolonged stalemate in the Syrian civil war was the only outcome that would not be damaging to American interests. He added that this option was 'tragic' (Luttwak 2013). It has never been acknowledged as US government policy, but it appears to be the de facto strategy, since the alternative would be to defeat both Bashar al-Assad and the extremists fighting his regime, which would require an American invasion. Meanwhile, the new regime in Saudi Arabia, following the succession of King Salman to the throne in January 2015, seems almost as hostile to Iran and Shia Islam as it is to ISIS and has shifted from the kingdom's traditional caution into a new phase of nationalism and military adventurism with unforeseeable political and humanitarian consequences.

The Syrian war in particular has been too complex and too prolonged to hold the international media's sustained attention. In June 2015, when there was no sign of an end to hostilities, UNHCR and the UN Office for the Coordination of Humanitarian Affairs (OCHA) were reporting that more than 3.9 million registered Syrian refugees were living in neighbouring countries, such as Jordan and Lebanon; 6.5 million children were affected by the crisis; some 12 million people inside Syria were in need of humanitarian aid. There were serious shortfalls in funding for UN emergency operations.

Islamic charities

It seems that Islamic Relief Worldwide was one of the few international agencies – in common with Médecins Sans Frontières – to still be working within Syria and it has continued to demonstrate the ability of an Islamic charity to work in extremely difficult conditions despite political impediments of the kind described in this book. Even so, its 'winterization' programme in 2014–15, which managed to protect some 60,000 internally displaced persons from the cold, could have been abundantly multiplied if the generosity of Muslim donors had been allowed to translate more freely into practical humanitarian aid.

The total expenditure of Islamic Relief Worldwide, including all its affiliates, was declared as £155 million for 2013. This is an impressive figure, but is dwarfed by the private wealth of the super rich and by the annual budget of the UK's Department for International Development, which is £10–11 billion. The funding available for Islamic Relief and similar charities could be vastly increased if an efficient international system for organizing zakat were to be introduced. However, already Islamic Relief is poised to grow into a truly transnational NGO. This results in administrative problems comparable to those already experienced by Médecins Sans Frontières, Oxfam and Save the Children, as they have grown from national to global institutions.[2] With this increase in scale will no doubt come the public controversies that beset all aid agencies, which is a sign of health for trenchant debate is one of the NGO sector's strengths. Some criticisms of the aid industry are indeed devastating, but world politics would be in an even worse state than at present without practical manifestations of the 'will to improve'.[3]

Muslim charities are already as diverse as their non-Muslim counterparts. There is scope for many different aid strategies today, including massive injections of resources to respond to emergencies such as the Syrian and Iraqi refugee crises and the Yemen air war; cooperation with governments to eradicate abuses of power and stimulate business enterprise; and working at a local level to fortify grass-roots organizations, including women's groups and zakat committees.

As this book goes to press, the scale of trans-Mediterranean irregular migration and its consequences were finally becoming evident to all – with a parallel in South East Asia where the new 'boat people' in desperate search of safe havens were from the Rakhine State of Myanmar and from Bangladesh. Islamic NGOs have a potentially important contribution to make in helping to make life more tolerable for victims of conflict, oppression and economic stagnation in their home countries – a large proportion of whom are Muslims – so that they are less motivated to take huge risks in the hands of traffickers. Advocacy for disadvantaged groups, such as that engaged in by Interpal on behalf of Palestinians and by WAMY (see Chapter 9) on behalf of the Rohingya, will have its place in the repertoire – a more difficult and politically sensitive path to follow than simply raising funds and disbursing emergency aid. Another challenge for Islamic charities will be providing services for the myriad 'camps' of refugees and other migrants which have become a permanent feature worldwide. Some 150 international NGOs and 400 national NGOs, it has been estimated, have contracts with the camps administered by UNHCR alone (Agier 2014: 22); and Islamic NGOs can argue that they have a special vocation, though

laden with political and ethical complications, to care for the Muslims whom ill for-
tune has condemned to live in these 'non-places'.

Islamic humanism

This book has argued that the precedents of Islamic Relief Worldwide in Britain and
Muhammadiyah in Indonesia as successful institutions have a bearing beyond the
sphere of charities and aid. They could inspire those Muslims who are committed
to independent new thinking. A commitment to broad-based institution building
as strong as Sheikh Qaradawi's (Chapter 16), together with use of communication
media equally skilful as his but updated to take advantage of the new technologies,
will be needed if reinterpretations of Islamic doctrine, more compatible than his
with the spirit of free enquiry, are to compete effectively with the traditionalist views.

Notes

1 See Ruthven 2015.
2 Secours Islamique (France) was closely affiliated with Islamic Relief when I undertook the
  fieldwork in Mali described in Chapter 2 (administered from the head office in Birmingham),
  but it has since split off and is no longer a member of the Islamic Relief 'family'.
3 The phrase is borrowed from *Religion and the Politics of Development* (Fountain et al. 2015: 26).

References

Abdul Rahman, As'ad, 2008a, 'Zakat panel revamp plan raises eyebrows', *Gulf News*, 14 June.

Abdul Rahman, As'ad, 2008b, 'Those who sow the wind are likely to harvest the tempest', *Gulf News*, 28 June.

Abid, Sufyan, 2013, 'Contesting Islamic reformisms and multiple interpretations of being a "true Muslim": Everyday life experiences and religious practices of Birmingham Muslims', unpublished paper, South Asian Anthropologists' Group conference, University of Sussex, 11 September.

Abuarqub, Mamoun, 2010, 'Islamic Relief: Faith and identity in practice', *Ontrac* 46, 7.

ACLU, 2009, *Blocking Faith, Freezing Charity: Chilling Muslim charitable giving in the 'war on terrorism' financing* (New York: American Civil Liberties Union).

Agier, Michel, 2010, 'Humanity as an identity and its political effects (a note on camps and humanitarian government)', *Humanity* 1: 1, 29–45.

Agier, Michel (ed.), 2014, *Un monde de camps* (Paris: La Découverte).

Ahmad, Imtiaz (ed.), 1981, *Ritual and Religion among Muslims in India* (Delhi: CManohar).

Ahmed, Akbar S., 1984, 'Defining Islamic anthropology', *RAIN* 65, 2–4.

Ahmed, Akbar S. 2010, *Journey into America: The challenge of Islam* (Washington, DC: Brookings Institution Press).

Ahmed, Akbar S. 2013, *The Thistle and the Drone: How America's war on terror became a global war on tribal Islam* (Washington, DC: Brookings Institution Press).

Ahramonline, 2014, 'Qaradawi group expelled from International Islamic Council', 9 December.

Ali Khan *see* Khan, Ghazanfar Ali.

Armstrong, Karen, 2014a, *Fields of Blood: Religion and the history of violence* (London: Bodley Head).

Armstrong, Karen, 2014b, 'Wahhabism to ISIS: How Saudi Arabia exported the main source of global terrorism', *New Statesman*, 27 November.

Azad, Hasan, 2014, 'Tariq Ramadan and the reconfiguration of Islamic authority on Web 2.0', *Al-Jazeera 'Opinion'*, 2 September. Available at: www.aljazeera.com/indepth/opinion/2014/09/tariq-ramadan-reconfiguration-is-20149214173222672.html.

Baran, Zeyno, 2004, 'Understanding Sufism and its potential role in U.S. policy', WORDE [The World Organization for Resource Development and Education], March. Available at: www.worde.org/publications/commentary/empowering_asj__sufi_muslim_networks/understanding-sufism-and-its-potential-role-in-u-s-policy/.

Barnett, Michael and Janice Stein (eds), 2012, *Sacred Aid: Faith and humanitarianism* (New York: Oxford University Press).

Barthe, Benjamin, 2007, 'A Naplouse, la police palestinienne harcèle le Hamas', *Le Monde*, 28 September.

Bayly, Susan, 1989, *Saints, Goddesses and Kings* (Cambridge: Cambridge University Press).

Beaman, Lori (ed.), 2012, *Reasonable Accommodation: Managing religious diversity* (Vancouver: University of British Columbia Press).

Beatty, Andrew, 1999, *Varieties of Javanese Religion: An anthropological account* (Cambridge University Press).

Bellion-Jourdan, Jérôme, 2003, 'The Balkan case: Transnational Islamic networks in Bosnia-Herzegovina', in Jonathan Benthall and Jérôme Bellion-Jourdan (eds), *The Charitable Crescent: Politics of aid in the Muslim world* (London: I. B. Tauris), 128–52.

ben Néfissa, Sarah, 1995, 'Associations égyptiennes: une liberalisation sous contrôle', *Monde Arabe* 150, Oct–Dec., 40–7.

Benedetti, Carlo, 2006, 'Islamic and Christian inspired relief NGOs: Between tactical collaboration and practical diffidence', *Journal of International Development* 18: 6, 849–59.

Bennett, Jon et al., 2006, 'Coordination of international humanitarian assistance in tsunami-affected countries: evaluation findings: Indonesia' (Tsunami Evaluation Coalition). Available at: www.sida.se/contentassets/4a691a64e0f9430f8abcf55c3250dc99/coordination-of-international-humanitarian-assistance-in-tsunami-affected-countries_3143.pdf.

de Benoist, J. R., 1998, *Le Mali* (Paris: L'Harmattan).

Benthall, Jonathan, 1993, *Disasters, Relief and the Media* (London: I.B. Tauris); new edition 2009 (Wantage: S. Kingston).

Benthall, Jonathan, 1995, 'Missionaries and human rights', *Anthropology Today* 11: 1, 1–3.

Benthall, Jonathan, 1996, 'The religious provenances of anthropologists', *Anthropology Today* 12: 4, 1–2.

Benthall, Jonathan, 2004, 'Waiting for a Muslim Gandhi? Islam and non-violence', *Daily Star* (Beirut), 21 August. (Reprinted in *Islam and Muslim Societies* (New Delhi) 1: 1, 201–3.)

Benthall, Jonathan, 2006a, 'L'humanitarisme islamique', in *Cultures et Conflits 60*, special issue *L'action humanitaire: normes et pratique*, (Paris: L'Harmattan), 103–22.

Benthall, Jonathan, 2006b, 'Islamic aid in a North Malian enclave', *Anthropology Today* 22: 4, August, 20–1. (Republished here as Chapter 2.)

Benthall, Jonathan, 2007a, 'The overreaction against Islamic charities', *ISIM Review* (Leiden) 20: 1, 6–7. Available at: https://openaccess.leidenuniv.nl/handle/1887/17206.

Benthall, Jonathan, 2007b, 'Islamic charities, Faith-Based Organizations, and the international aid system', in Jon Alterman and Karin von Hippel (eds), *Understanding Islamic Charities* (Washington, DC: CSIS Press), 1–14. (Republished here as Chapter 1.)

Benthall, Jonathan, 2008a, 'The Palestinian zakat committees 1993–2007 and their contested interpretations', PSIO Occasional Paper, 1/2008 (Geneva: Graduate Institute of International and Development Studies). (Republished here as Chapter 4.)

Benthall, Jonathan, 2008b, 'Islamic aid in Southern Mali today', in *Islam au sud du Sahara* 1 (new series) (Paris: Les Indes Savantes), 165–74.

Benthall, Jonathan, 2008c, 'Have Islamic agencies a privileged access in majority Muslim areas? The case of post-tsunami reconstruction in Aceh [Indonesia]', *Journal of Humanitarian Assistance*, 26 June. Available at: https://sites.tufts.edu/jha/archives/153. (Republished here as Chapter 3.)

Benthall, Jonathan, 2008d, *Returning to Religion: Why a secular age is haunted by faith* (London: I. B. Tauris).

Benthall, Jonathan, 2009, 'Islamic Relief Worldwide', in *The Palgrave Dictionary of Transnational History* (Basingstoke: Palgrave Macmillan), 605–6.

Benthall, Jonathan, 2010–11, 'An unholy tangle: Boim versus the Holy Land Foundation', *UCLA Journal of Islamic and Near Eastern Law* 10, 1–10. (Republished here as Chapter 6.)

Benthall, Jonathan, 2011, 'Islamic humanitarianism in adversarial context', in Erica Bornstein and Peter Redfield (eds), *Forces of Compassion: Humanitarianism between ethics and politics* (Santa Fe: SAR Press), 95–121.

Benthall, Jonathan, 2012a, 'Diapraxis rules OK', *Anthropology Today* 28: 1, February, 1–2.

Benthall, Jonathan, 2012b, '"Cultural proximity" and the conjuncture of Islam with modern humanitarianism', in Michael Barnett and Janice Stein (eds), *Sacred Aid: Faith and humanitarianism* (New York: Oxford University Press), 65–89.

Benthall, Jonathan, 2012c, 'Charity', in Didier Fassin (ed.), *A Companion to Moral Anthropology* (Chichester: Wiley-Blackwell), 279–375.

Benthall, Jonathan, 2015, 'Building a reform movement: Could Muslims emulate nineteenth century Judaism?', in Luke Herrington, Alasdair McKay and Jeffrey Haynes (eds), *Nations Under God: The geopolitics of faith in the twenty-first century* (Bristol: E-International Relations Publishing) 246–55. Available at: www.e-ir.info/publications.

Benthall, Jonathan and Jérôme Bellion-Jourdan, 2003, *The Charitable Crescent: Politics of aid in the Muslim world* (London and New York: I. B. Tauris). (New paperback edition 2009.)

Benzine, Rachid and Luca Sebastiani, 2006, 'The new paths of modern Islam', *Eurozine* [online magazine], 18 April. Available at: www.eurozine.com/articles/2006-04-18-ben-zine-en.html.

Bilgrami, Akeel, 2014, *Secularism, Identity, and Enchantment* (Cambridge, MA: Harvard University Press).

Binder, Andrea and Claudia Meier, 2011, 'Opportunity knocks: why non-Western donors enter humanitarianism and how to make the best of it', *International Review of the Red Cross* 93: 884, December, 1135–49.

Bitter, Jean-Nicolas, 2003, *Les dieux embusqués: Une approche pragmatique de la dimension religieuse des conflits* (Geneva: Librairie Droz).

Blackburn, Simon, 2010, 'Review of Tariq Ramadan's The Quest for Meaning: Developing a philosophy of pluralism', *Times Literary Supplement*, 24 December.

Boisard, Marcel, 1979, *L'humanisme de l'islam* (Paris: Albin Michel). (Translated as *Humanism in Islam* (Indianapolis: American Trust Publications), 1988.)

Bokhari, Yusra, Nasim Chowdhury and Robert Lacey, 2014, 'A good day to bury a bad charity: The rise and fall of the Al-Haramain Islamic Foundation', in Robert Lacey and Jonathan Benthall (eds), *Gulf Charities and Islamic Philanthropy in the 'Age of Terror' and Beyond* (Berlin: Gerlach Press), 199–229.

Bornstein, Erica, 2012, *Disquieting Gifts: Humanitarianism in New Delhi* (Palo Alto, CA: Stanford University Press).

Bourdieu, Pierre, 2003 [1997], *Méditations pascaliennes* (Paris: Seuil).

Bowen, John, 1991, *Sumatran Politics and Poetics* (Newhaven: Yale University Press).

Bowen, John, 1996, '"Religion in the proper sense of the word": Law and civil society in Islamicist discourse', *Anthropology Today* 12: 4, August, 12–14.

Brenner, Louis, 2000, *Controlling Knowledge: Religion, power and schooling in a West African Muslim society* (London: Hurst).

Brett, Michael and Elizabeth Fentress, 1996, *The Berbers* (Oxford: Blackwell).

Broucek, James, 2014, 'Colonialism and the Muslim world', in *The Oxford Encyclopedia of Islam and Politics* (New York: Oxford University Press), vol. 1, 195–207.

Brown, Nathan J. 2003, 'Palestinian civil society in theory and practice', paper for annual meeting of Structure of Government Section, International Political Science Association, Washington, DC, May.

Brown, Nathan J. and Adel Omar Sharif, 2002, 'Judicial independence in the Arab world: A study presented to the program of Arab governance of the United Nations Development Program' (Washington, DC: United Nations Development Programme). Available at: www.undp-pogar.org/publications/judiciary/sherif/jud-independence.pdf.

de Bruijn, Mirjam and Rijk van Dijk, 2009, 'Questioning social security in the study of religion in Africa: The ambiguous meaning of the gift in African Pentecostalism and Islam', in Carolin Leutloff-Grandits, Anja Peleikis and Tatjana Thelen (eds), *Social Security in Religious Networks* (Oxford: Berghahn), 105–27.

Brunschvig, Robert, 1986 [1942–47], 'Ibn Abdelh'akam et Ia conquête de l'Afrique du nord', in *Etudes sur l 'islam classique et l 'Afrique du nord* (London: Variorum Editions). (Reprinted from 1942–47 journal article.)

Burhani, Ahmad Najib, 2013, 'Liberal and conservative discourses in the Muhammadiyah: The struggle for the face of reformist Islam in Indonesia', in Martin van Bruinessen (ed.), *Contemporary Developments in Indonesian Islam: Explaining the 'Conservative Turn'* (Singapore: ISEAS), 105–44.

Burke, Kenneth, 1945, *A Grammar of Motives* (New York: Prentice-Hall).

Burke, Kenneth, 1966, *Language as Symbolic Action: Essays on life, literature, and method* (Berkeley: University of California Press).

Burr, J. Millard and Robert O. Collins, 2006, *Alms for Jihad: Charity and terrorism in the Islamic world* (New York: Cambridge University Press).

Candland, Christopher, forthcoming, *The Politics of Muslim Charity in the Islamic Republic of Pakistan*, unpublished manuscript.

Candland, Christopher and Raza Rehman Khan Qazi, 2012, 'Civil conflict, natural disasters and partisan welfare associations in the Islamic Republic of Pakistan, in Sara Ashencaen Crabtree, Jonathan Parker and Azlinda Azman (eds), *The Cup, the Gun, and the Crescent: Social welfare and civil unrest in Muslim societies* (London: Whiting and Birch), 103–19.

Cannell, Fenella, 2006, 'Introduction', in Fenella Cannell (ed.), *The Anthropology of Christianity* (Durham: Duke University Press), 1–50.

Chaliand, Gérard and Arnaud Blin, 2004, *Histoire du terrorisme: de l'Antiquité à Al Qaida* (Paris: Bayard).

Challand, Benoît, 2009, *Palestinian Civil Society: Foreign donors and the power to promote and exclude* (London: Routledge).

Charity Commission, 2009, 'Inquiry Report: Palestinian Relief and Development Fund (Interpal)' (London: Charity Commission).

Ciment, James, 1997, *Algeria: The Fundamentalist Challenge* (New York: Facts on File).

Clark, Janine, 2004, *Islam, Charity, and Activism: Middle-class networks and social welfare in Egypt, Jordan, and Yemen* (Bloomington: Indiana University Press).

Clarke, Gerard and Michael Jennings (eds), 2008, *Development, Civil Society and Faith-Based Organizations: Bridging the sacred and the secular* (Basingstoke: Palgrave Macmillan).

Cook, Michael, 2014, *Ancient Religions, Modern Politics: The Islamic case in comparative perspective* (Princeton: Princeton University Press).

Corboz, Elvire, 2015, *Guardians of Shi'ism: Sacred authority and transnational family networks* (Edinburgh: Edinburgh University Press).

De Cordier, Bruno, 2007 'Shiite aid organizations in Tajikistan', *ISIM Review* 19, 10–11.

De Cordier, Bruno, 2009a, 'Faith-based aid, globalisation and the humanitarian frontline: an analysis of Western-based Muslim aid organisations', *Disasters* 33: 4, 608–28.

De Cordier, Bruno, 2009b, 'The 'humanitarian frontline', development and relief, and religion: What context, which threats and which opportunities?' *Third World Quarterly* 30: 4, 663–84.

da Silva, Jo, 2010, 'Lessons from Aceh: Key considerations in post-disaster reconstruction' (Arup). Available at: http://publications.arup.com/Publications/L/Lessons_from_Aceh.aspx.

Danish Immigration Service, 2011, 'Rohingya Refugees in Bangladesh and Thailand'. Available at: www.nyidanmark.dk/NR/rdonlyres/B08D8B44-5322-4C2F-9604-44F6C340167A/0/FactfindingrapportRohingya180411.pdf.

Darmaputera, Eka, 1982, 'Pancasila and the search for identity and modernity in Indonesian society', doctoral thesis, University of Michigan.

Das, Veena, 1984, 'For a folk-theology and theological anthropology of Islam', *Contributions to Indian Sociology* 18: 2, 293–305.

Davidson, Andrew, 1996, *In the Shadow of History* (New Brunswick: Transaction Publishers).

Davies, Katherine, 2012, 'Continuity, change and contest: Meanings of "humanitarian" from the "religion of humanity" to the Kosovo war', HPG Working Paper (London: Overseas Development Institute).

Delaney, Carol, 1998, *Abraham on Trial* (Princeton: Princeton University Press).

Delmar-Morgan, Alex and Peter Oborne, 2014a, 'Why is the Muslim charity Interpal being blacklisted as a terrorist organization?', *The Telegraph*, 26 November.

Delmar-Morgan, Alex and Peter Oborne, 2014b, 'The continuing war against Islamic charities', *The Telegraph*, 2 December.

Dickinson, Elizabeth, 2013, 'Playing with fire: Why private Gulf financing for Syria's extremist rebels risks igniting sectarian conflict at home', Saban Centre for Middle East Policy, Analysis paper 16 (Washington, DC: Brookings Institution).

Donini, Antonio (ed.), 2012, *The Golden Fleece: Manipulation and independence in humanitarian action* (Sterling, VA: Kumarian Press).

Dorsey, James M., 2015, 'How Qatar is its own worst enemy', *International Journal for the History of Sport* 32: 3, February, 422–39.

Douglas, Mary, 1966, *Purity and Danger: An analysis of concepts of pollution and taboo* (London: Routledge). (Reprinted several times with revisions.)

Douglas, Mary, 1980, *Evans-Pritchard* (London: Fontana).

Douglas, Mary, 1993, *In the Wilderness: The doctrine of defilement in the Book of Numbers* (Sheffield: JSOT Press).

Doyle, Charles, 2010, 'Terrorist material support: an overview of U.S.C. [United States Code] 2339A and 2339B' (Congressional Research Service). Available at: http://fas.org/sgp/crs/natsec/R41333.pdf.

Duffield, Mark, 2001, *Global Governance and the New Wars: The merging of development and security* (London: Zed Books).

Duriez, Bruno, François Mabille and Kathy Rousselet (eds), 2007, *Les ONG confessionnelles: Religion et action internationale* (Paris: L'Harmattan).

Dwyer, Kevin, 1997, 'Beyond a boundary? "Universal human rights" and the Middle East', *Anthropology Today* 13: 6, December, 13–18.

Eaton, Richard M., 1993, *The Rise of Islam and the Bengal Frontier* (Washington, DC: Smithsonian Institution Press).

Edhi, Abdul Sattar, 1996, *Edhi, An Autobiography: A mirror to the blind.* As narrated to Tehmina Durrani (Islamabad: National Bureau of Publication).

Emon, Anver M., 2012, *Religious Pluralism and Islamic Law: Dhimmis and others in the empire of law* (Oxford: Oxford University Press).

Evans-Pritchard, E. E., 1960, 'Introduction', in *Robert Hertz, Death and The Right Hand* (Aberdeen: Cohen and West), 9–24.

Ezz Eldin, Hussam Yousef, 2011, 'Towards an international metric for relief activity', *Egatha* 1: 4, 38–9.

Ezz Eldin, Hussam Yousef, 2012, 'Using artificial intelligence tools to increase the effectiveness of relief organizations', *Egatha* 2: 6, 30–1.

Fanany, Ismet and Rebecca Fanany, 2014, 'Religion and post-disaster development', in David Tittensor and Matthew Clarke (eds), *Islam and Development: Exploring the invisible aid economy* (London: Ashgate), 153–72.

Fardon, Richard, 1999, *Mary Douglas: An intellectual biography* (London: Routledge).

Fassin, Didier, 2012, *Humanitarian Reason: A moral history of the present* (Berkeley: University of California Press).

Fattal, Antoine, 1958, *Le statut légal des non-musulmans en pays d'islam* (Beirut: Imprimerie Catholique).

Fauzia, Amelia, 2013, *Faith and the State: A history of Islamic philanthropy in Indonesia* (Leiden: Brill).

Fisher, H. J., 1973, 'Conversion reconsidered: Some historical aspects of religious conversion in Black Africa', *Africa* 43, 27–40.

Fitzgerald, Timothy, 2007, *Discourse on Civility and Barbarity: A critical history of religion and related categories* (New York: Oxford University Press).

FitzGibbon, Francis, 2015, 'Low-hanging fruit', *London Review of Books*, 22 January, 13–14.

Flanigan, S. T., 2010, *For the Love of God: NGOs and religious identity in a violent world* (Sterling, VA: Kumarian Press).

Fountain, Philip, 2013a, 'The myth of religious NGOs: Development studies and the return of religion', in *International Development Policy: Religion and Development* (Geneva: The Graduate Institute), 9–30.

Fountain, Philip, 2013b, 'On having faith in the MDGs [Millennium Development Goals]: A response to Katherine Marshall', in *International Development Policy: Religion and Development* (Geneva: The Graduate Institute), 41–8.

Fountain, Philip, Robin Bush and R. Michael Feener (eds), 2015, *Religion and the Politics of Development* (Basingstoke: Palgrave Macmillan).

Fox, James J., 2001, 'In memoriam Professor Koentjaraningrat', *Bijdragen tot de taal-, land- en volkenkunde* 157: 2, 239–45.

Friedmann, Yohanan, 1972, 'The Temple of Multan: A note on early Muslim attitudes to idolatry', *Israel Oriental Studies* 2: 176–82.

Friedmann, Yohanan, 1975, 'Medieval Muslim view of Indian religions', *Journal of the American Oriental Society* 95: 214–21.

Friedmann, Yohanan, 1998, 'Classification of believers in Sunni Muslim law and tradition', *Jerusalem Papers in Arabic and Islam* 22: 163–95.

Friedmann, Yohanan, 2003, *Tolerance and Coercion in Islam: Interfaith relations in the Muslim tradition* (Cambridge: Cambridge University Press).

Gaborieau, Marc, 1985, 'From Al-Beruni to Jinnah: Idiom, ritual and ideology of the Hindu-Muslim confrontation in South Asia', *Anthropology Today* 1: 3, June, 7–14.

Galeotti, Anna Elisabetta, 2002, *Toleration as Recognition* (Cambridge: Cambridge University Press).

Gauvain, Richard, 2013, *Salafi Ritual Purity in the Presence of God* (London: Routledge).

Geertz, Clifford, 1960, *The Religion of Java* (Glencoe: Free Press).

Gellner, Ernest, 1988, *Plough, Sword and Book* (London: Collins Harvill).

Ghandour, Abdul-Rahman, 2002, *Jihad humanitaire: Enquête sur les ONG islamiques* (Paris: Flammarion).

Gill, Rebecca, 2013, *Calculating Compassion: Humanity and relief in war, Britain 1870–1914* (Manchester: Manchester University Press).

Giuffrida, Alessandra, 2005a, 'Métamorphoses des relations de dépendance chez les Kel Antessar du cercle de Goundam', *Cahiers d'études africaines* 45: 3–4 (179–180), 805–29.

Giuffrida, Alessandra, 2005b, 'Clerics, rebels and refugees: Mobility strategies and networks among the Kel Antessar', *Journal of North African Studies*, 10: 3–4, 529–43.

De Goede, Marieke, 2012, *Speculative Security: The politics of pursuing terrorist monies* (Minneapolis: University of Minnesota Press).

Gopal, Krishna 1995 [1972], 'Piety and politics in Indian Islam', in T. N. Madan (ed.), *Muslim Communities of South Asia* (New Delhi: Manohar), 363–404. (Reprinted from *Contributions to Indian Sociology* 6, 142–71.)

Gräf, Bettina and Jakob Skovgaard-Petersen (eds), 2009, *Global Mufti: The phenomenon of Yusuf al-Qaradawi* (London: Hurst).

Grano, Daniel A. and Kenneth S. Zagacki, 2011, 'The paradox of purity and post-Katrina guilt', *Quarterly Journal of Speech* 97: 2, 210–23.

Grim, Brian J. and Roger Finke, 2011, *The Price of Freedom Denied: Religious persecution and conflict in the twenty-first century* (Cambridge: Cambridge University Press).

Guinane, Kay and Suraj K. Sazawal, 2010, 'Supreme Court's Humanitarian Law Project Ruling Fails the Common Sense Test', Charity and Security Network [blog], 29 June. Available at: www.charityandsecurity.org/blog/Supreme_Court_Humanitarian_Law_Project_Ruling_Fails_Common_Sense_Test.

Gutelius, David, 2006, 'War on terror and social networks in Mali', *ISIM Review* 17: 38–9. Available at: https://openaccess.leidenuniv.nl/handle/1887/17066.

Haj, Samira, 2008, *Reconfiguring Islamic Tradition: Reform, rationality and modernity* (Stanford: Stanford University Press).

Halbertal, Moshe and Avishai Margalit, 1992, *Idolatry* (Cambridge, MA: Harvard University Press).

Hamel, Ian, 2007, *La vérité sur Tariq Ramadan: Sa famille, ses réseaux, sa stratégie* (Lausanne: Favre).

Hann, Chris, 2000, 'Problems with the (de)privatization of religion', *Anthropology Today* 16: 6, December, 14–20.

Harrington, James C., 2011, *Wrestling with Free Speech, Religious Freedom, and Democracy in Turkey: The political trials and time of Fethullah Gülen* (Lanham, MD: University Press of America).

Hauslohner, Abigail, 2014, 'Yemeni 'global terrorist' says he has counterterrorism advice for Washington', *Washington Post*, 16 February.

Hawting, G. R., 1999, *The Idea of Idolatry and the Emergence of Islam: From polemic to history* (Cambridge: Cambridge University Press).

Hefner, Richard W., 1985, *Hindu Javanese* (Princeton: Princeton University Press).

Hidayatullah, Aysha A., 2014, *Feminist Edges of the Qur'an* (New York: Oxford University Press).

Hirsi Ali, Ayaan, 2010, *Nomad: From Islam to America: A personal journey through the Clash of Civilizations* (Glencoe: Free Press).

Hirsi Ali, Ayaan, 2015, *Heretic: Why Islamic needs a reformation now* (New York: Harper).

Høigilt, Jacob, 2011, *Islamist Rhetoric: Language and culture in contemporary Egypt* (London: Routledge).

Hosoya, Sachiko, 2014, 'Care, redemption, and the afterlife: Spiritual experiences of bathing volunteers in a charity care center in Iran', in Robert Lacey and Jonathan Benthall (eds), *Gulf Charities and Islamic Philanthropy in the 'Age of Terror' and Beyond* (Berlin: Gerlach Press), 353–73.

Hroub, Khaled, 2000, *Hamas: Political thought and practice* (Washington, DC: Institute for Palestine Studies).

Hroub, Khaled, 2006, *Hamas: A beginner's guide* (London: Pluto Press).

Husein, Rahmawati, 2012, 'Extending transnational network: A case study of Muhammadiyah collaboration with various actors in major disaster response', paper given at International Conference on Muhammadiyah, University of Muhammadiyah Malang, 29 November–2 December.

Hutchinson, Sharon, 1996, *Nuer Dilemmas* (Berkeley: University of California Press).

ICG [International Crisis Group], 2003, 'Islamic social welfare activism in the Occupied Palestinian Territories: A legitimate target?', *Middle East Report* 13.

Israeli, Raphael, 1993, *Muslim Fundamentalism in Israel* (London: Brassey's).

Jackson, Peter, 1999, *The Delhi Sultanate* (Cambridge: Cambridge University Press).

Jakarta Post, 2007, 'BRR: criticized, praised for its Aceh work', 11 April.

James, Clive, 2011, 'Islamic law' [letter], *Times Literary Supplement*, 4 February.

Jerusalem Post, 2005, 'IDF kills Hamas commander who murdered US teen. Hinawi, described as a "ticking bomb", was refurbishing terror infrastructure in the Nablus area', 15 November.

Juul Petersen, Marie, 2014, 'Sacralized or secularized aid? Positioning Gulf-based Muslim charities', in Robert Lacey and Jonathan Benthall (eds), *Gulf Charities and Islamic Philanthropy in the 'Age of Terror' and Beyond* (Berlin: Gerlach Press), 25–52.

Juul Petersen, Marie, 2015, *For Humanity or for the Ummah? Aid and Islam in transnational Muslim NGOs* (London: Hurst).

Kaag, Mayke, 2014, 'Gulf charities in Africa', in Robert Lacey and Jonathan Benthall (eds), *Gulf Charities and Islamic Philanthropy in the 'Age of Terror' and Beyond* (Berlin: Gerlach Press), 79–94.

Kabir, H., 1969, *Muslim Politics and Other Essays* (Calcutta: Mukhopadhya).

Katz, Marion Holmes, 2002, *Body of Text: The emergence of the Sunnī law of ritual purity* (New York: SUNY Press).

Keatinge, Tom, 2014, '*Uncharitable behaviour*' (London: Demos). Available at: www.demos.co.uk/files/DEMOSuncharitablebehaviourREPORT.pdf?1419986873.

Kennedy, Hugh, 2014, 'To and from the taxman', review of Petra M. Sijpesteijn, *Shaping a Muslim State: The world of a mid-eighth-century Egyptian official* (Oxford, 2013), in *Times Literary Supplement*, 28 November.

Kepel, Gilles, 2002, *Jihad: The trail of political Islam* (London: I. B. Tauris).

Khan, Ajaz Ahmed, 2012, 'Religious obligation or altruistic giving? Muslims and charitable donations', in Michael Barnett and Janice Stein (eds), *Sacred Aid: Faith and humanitarianism* (New York: Oxford University Press), 90–114.

Khan, Ghazanfar Ali, 2012, 'WAMY seeks further measures to help Myanmar Muslims', *Arab News*, 26 August. Available at: www.arabnews.com/saudi-arabia/wamy-seeks-further-measures-help-myanmar-muslims.

Kilani, Mondher, 2012, 'Is a peripheral anthropology possible? The issue of universalism', *Kroeber Anthropological Society Papers* 101, 98–105.

Kohlmann, Evan F., 2004, *Al-Qaida's Jihad in Europe: The Afghan–Bosnian network* (Oxford: Berg).

Kohlmann, Evan F., 2006, 'The role of Islamic charities in international terrorist recruitment and financing', DIIS Working Paper 2006/7 (Copenhagen: Danish Institute for International Studies).

Kor, Zahide Tuba, 2011, *Witnesses of the Freedom Flotilla: Interviews with passengers* (Istanbul: İHHKİTAP).

Kreinath, Jens (ed.), 2012, *The Anthropology of Islam Reader* (London: Routledge).

Kropf, Annika, 2014, 'The Gulf States as multilateral donors: The special case of the OPEC Fund for International Development (OFID)', in Robert Lacey and Jonathan Benthall (eds), *Gulf Charities and Islamic Philanthropy in the 'Age of Terror' and Beyond* (Berlin: Gerlach Press), 119–44.

Kuran, Timur, 2004, *Islam and Mammon: The economic predicaments of Islamism* (Princeton: Princeton University Press).

Kuru, Ahmet T., 2011, review of Brian J. Grim and Roger Finke (eds), The Price of Freedom Denied: Religious persecution and conflict in the twenty-first century (Cambridge, 2011), in *Middle East Policy* 18: 2, Summer. Available at: http://www.mepc.org/journal/middle-east-policy-archives/price-freedom-denied.

Lacey, Robert and Jonathan Benthall, 2014, 'Introduction', in Robert Lacey and Jonathan Benthall (eds), *Gulf Charities and Islamic Philanthropy in the 'Age of Terror' and Beyond* (Berlin: Gerlach Press), 285–305.

Laidlaw, James, 2000, 'A free gift makes no friends', *Journal of the Royal Anthropological Institute* 6: 4, 617–34.

Lamb, Kate, 2014, 'Banda Aceh: Where community spirit has gone but peace has lasted', *The Guardian*, 27 January.

Lambek, Michael, 1993, *Knowledge and Practice in Mayotte* (Toronto: University of Toronto Press).

Lambek, Michael, 2000, 'Localising Islamic performance in Mayotte', in David Parkin and S. C. Headley (eds), *Islamic Prayer across the Indian Ocean* (Richmond: Curzon), 63–97.

Lamptey, Jerusha Tanner, 2014, *Never Wholly Other: A Muslima theology of religious pluralism* (New York: Oxford University Press)

Latief, Hilman, 2012, 'Islamic Charities and Social Activism: Welfare, dakwah and politics in Indonesia', doctoral thesis, University of Utrecht. Available at: www.academia.edu/1978143/Islamic_Charities_and_Social_Activism_Welfare_Dakwah_and_Politics_in_Indonesia.

Leach, Edmund, 2000a [1965], 'The nature of war', in *The Essential Edmund Leach* (New Haven: Yale University Press), vol. 1, 343–57.

Leach, Edmund, 2000b [1977], 'Anthropos', in *The Essential Edmund Leach* (New Haven: Yale University Press), vol. 2, 324–79. (Reprinted from Italian encyclopaedia article.)

Legrain, Jean-François, 2006, 'Le Hamas et le Fatah: doivent-ils dissoudre l'Autorité palestinienne?', *Le Figaro*, 23 November.

Le Monde, 2006, 'Il faut cesser de boycotter Hamas', interview with Michel Sabbagh, 17 May.

Letsch, Constanze, 2014, 'Turkey issues arrest warrant for Erdoğan rival Fethullah Gülen', *The Guardian*, 19 December.

Letts, James W., 1996, 'Emic/etic distinctions', in *Encyclopedia of Cultural Anthropology* (New York: Henry Holt and Co.), vol. 2, 382–3.

Lévi-Strauss, Claude, 1988, *The Jealous Potter*, trans. Bénédicte Chorier (Chicago: Chicago University Press).

Levitt, Matthew, 2006, *Hamas: Politics, charity, and terrorism in the service of jihad* (New Haven: Yale University Press).

Levy, Gideon, 2008, 'Twilight zone: When charity ends at home', *Haaretz*, 15 March.

Lewis, Bernard, 1984, *The Jews of Islam* (London: Routledge and Kegan Paul).

Lewis, Bernard, 1988, *The Political Language of Islam* (Chicago: University of Chicago Press).

Lievre, V. and J.-Y. Loude, 1990, *Le chamanisme des Kalash du Pakistan* (Lyon: Editions du CNRS).

Liogier, Raphaël, 2007, 'L'ONG, agent institutionnel optimal du champ religieux individuo-globalisé', in B. Duriez, François Mabille and Kathy Rousselet (eds), *Les ONG confessionnelles: Religion et action internationale* (Paris: L'Harmattan), 263–76.

Lister, Charles, 2014, 'Profiling the Islamic State', Analysis Paper 13 (Doha: Brookings Doha Center).

Lode, Kåre, 1997, 'Civil society takes responsibility: Popular involvement in the peace process in Mali' (Oslo: International Peace Research Institute). Available at: www.prio.no/page/pre-view/preview/9429/38063.html.

Lundblad, Lars Gunnar, 2008, 'Islamic welfare, discourse and practise: The institutionalization of *zakat* in Palestine', in N. Naguib and I. M. Okkenhaug (eds), *Interpreting Welfare and Relief in the Middle East* (Leiden: Brill), 195–216.

Lundblad, Lars Gunnar, 2011, *Islamic Welfare in Palestine: Meanings and practices: Processes of institutionalization and politicization of zakat, the third pillar of Islam* (Saarbrücken: Lambert Academic Publishing).

Luttwak, Edward N., 2013, 'In Syria, America Loses if either side wins', *New York Times* Sunday Review, 24 August.

McGreal, Chris, 2006, 'Israel accuses British-funded Islamic charity of being front for terrorists', *The Guardian*, 31 May.

Madan, T. N., 1981, 'Religious ideology and social structure: The Muslims and Hindus of Kashmir', in I. Ahmad (ed.), *Ritual and Religion among Muslims in India* (New Delhi: Manohar).

Mahmood, Sara, 2006, 'Secularism, hermeneutics and empire: The politics of Islamic reformation', *Public Culture* 18: 2, 23–47.

Malka, Haim, 2007, 'Hamas: resistance and transformation of Palestinian society', in Jon Alterman and Karin van Hippel (eds), *Understanding Islamic Charities* (Washington, DC: Center for Strategic and International Studies Press), 98–126.

Marshall, Katherine, 2011a, 'Journey towards faith development partnerships: The challenge and the potential', in Catherine Cornille and Glenn Willis (eds), *The World Market and Interreligious Dialogue* (Eugene, OR: Cascade Books), 190–210.

Marshall, Katherine, 2011b, 'Development and faith institutions: gulfs and bridges', in Gerrie ter Haar (ed.), *Religion and Development: Ways of transforming the world* (New York: Columbia University Press), 27–54.

Marshall, Katherine, 2013, 'Revisiting the religious revival in development: A critique of Philip Fountain', in *International Development Policy: Religion and Development* (Geneva: The Graduate Institute), 31–40.

Martin, David, 2014, *Religion and Power: No logos without mythos* (London: Ashgate).

Masters, Bruce, 2001, *Christians and Jews in the Ottoman Arab world* (Cambridge: Cambridge University Press).

Matthiesen, Toby, 2015, *The Other Saudis: Shiism, dissent and sectarianism* (Cambridge: Cambridge University Press).

Mauss, Marcel, 1990 [1925], *The Gift: The form and reason for exchange in archaic societies* (New York: Norton).

Meddeb, Abdelwahab, 2003, *Islam and its Discontents* (London: Heinemann).

Melvinger, A., 1986, 'Al-Madjūs', in *Encyclopaedia of Islam*, 2nd edition, vol. 5 (Leiden: Brill).

Metcalfe-Hough, Victoria, Tom Keatinge and Sara Pantuliano, 2015, 'UK humanitarian aid in the age of counter-terrorism: Perceptions and reality' (London: ODI Humanitarian Policy Group).

Milton-Edwards, Beverley, 1996, *Islamic Politics in Palestine* (London: Tauris Academic).

Mitter, Partha, 1987, 'Rammohun Roy and the new language of monotheism', *History and Anthropology* 3, 177–208.

Moad, Edward, 2014, 'Sufism', in *The Oxford Encyclopedia of Islam and Politics* (New York: Oxford University Press), vol. 2, 451–6.

Mohamed, Abdul Fatah S., 2014, 'The Qatar Authority for Charitable Activities (QACA) from commencement to dissolution', in Robert Lacey and Jonathan Benthall (eds), *Gulf Charities and Islamic Philanthropy in the 'Age of Terror' and Beyond* (Berlin: Gerlach Press), 259–83.

Montagu, Caroline, 2010, 'Civil society and the voluntary sector in Saudi Arabia', *The Middle East Journal* 64: 1, 67–83.

Moussa, Jasmine, 2014, 'Ancient origins, modern actors: defining Arabic meanings of humanitarianism' (London: ODI Humanitarian Policy Group.)

Nakamura, Mitsuo, 2012, *The Crescent Arises over the Banyan Tree: A study of the Muhammadiyah movement in a Central Javanese town, c. 1910s–2010* (Singapore: ISAES).

New York Times, 2010, Editorial: 'A Bruise on the First Amendment', 21 June. Available at: www.nytimes.com/2010/06/22/opinion/22tue1.html?_r=0.

Niva, Steve, 2015, 'The ISIS shock doctrine', The Immanent Frame, SSRC [blog]. Available at: http://blogs.ssrc.org/tif/2015/02/20/the-isis-shock-doctrine/#comment-2676245.

Nizami, K.A., 2002, *Religion and Politics in India during the Thirteenth Century* (New Delhi: Oxford University Press).

Orrú, Marco and Amy Wang, 1992, 'Durkheim, Religion, and Buddhism', *Journal for the Scientific Study of Religion* 31: 1, March, 47–61.

Oxby, Clare, 1996, 'Tuareg identity crisis', *Anthropology Today* 12: 5, October, 21.

Oxfam International, 2009, 'In the wake of the tsunami: An evaluation of Oxfam International's response to the 2004 Indian Ocean Tsunami'. Available at: www.oxfam.org/sites/www.oxfam.org/files/file_attachments/oxfam-international-tsunami-evaluation-summary_3.pdf.

Pall, Zoltan, 2014, 'Kuwaiti Salafism and its Growing Influence in the Levant' (Washington, DC: Carnegie Endowment for International Peace).

Palmer, Victoria, 2011, 'Analysing "cultural proximity": Islamic Relief Worldwide and Rohingya refugees in Bangladesh', *Development in Practice* 21: 1, February, 96–108.

Parkes, Peter, 2000, 'Enclaved knowledge: Indigent and indignant representations of environmental management and development among the Kalasha of northern Pakistan', in Alan Bicker, Roy Ellen and Peter Parkes (eds), *Indigenous Environmental Knowledge and its Transformations* (Amsterdam: Harwood Academic), 249–89.

Parkin, David, 2000, 'Inside and outside the mosque: A master trope', in David Parkin and S. C. Headley (eds), *Islamic Prayer across the Indian Ocean* (Richmond: Curzon), 1–22.

Peel, J. D. Y., 2000, *Religious Encounter and the Making of the Yoruba* (Bloomington: Indiana University Press).

Perreau-Saussine, Émile, 2012, *Catholicism and Democracy: An Essay in the history of political thought* (Princeton: Princeton University Press).

Posner, Richard, 2006, 'Hamas, Palestine and the Economics of Democracy', The Becker–Posner Blog, January 29. Available at: www.becker-posner-blog.com/2006/01/index.html.

Price, Matthew, 2014, 'Audit 'clears Islamic Relief' of terror funding claim', BBC News online, 12 December. Available at: www.bbc.co.uk/news/uk-30443693.

al-Qaradawi, Yusuf, 2003, *The Lawful and the Prohibited in Islam* (London: Birr Foundation). (English translation; published in Arabic in 1960.)

al-Qaradawi, Yusuf, n.d., *Fiqh Al Zakah: A comparative study of zakah, regulations and philosophy in the light of Qur'an and Sunnah*, trans. Monzer Kahf (Jeddah: Scientific Publishing

Centre, King Abdulaziz University). Available at: http://monzer.kahf.com/books/english/fiqhalzakahvol1.pdf.

Rakodi, Carole, 2007, 'Understanding the roles of religions in development: the approach of the Religions and Development Research Programme', RaD Working Paper 9 (Birmingham: University of Birmingham).

Ramadan, Tariq, 2003, *Les Musulmans d'occident et l'avenir de l'islam* (Paris: Sindbad).

Ramadan, Tariq, 2012, *The Arab Awakening: Islam and the new Middle East* (London: Allen Lane).

Ramage, D. E., 1995, *Politics in Indonesia: Democracy, Islam and the ideology of tolerance* (London: Routledge).

Rappaport, Roy, 1999, *Ritual and Religion in the Making of Humanity* (Cambridge: Cambridge University Press).

Rasmussen, Susan, 1992, 'Ritual specialists, ambiguity and power in Tuareg society', *Man* (new series) 27, 105–28.

Ratcliffe, John, 2007, 'Local Islamic response to the 2004 Indian Ocean tsunami and 2005 Kashmir earthquake', in Jon Alterman and Karin von Hippel (eds), *Understanding Islamic Charities* (Washington: CSIS Press).

Redfield, Peter, 2013 *Life in Crisis: The ethical journey of Doctors Without Borders* (Berkeley: University of California Press).

Reid, Anthony (ed.), 2006, *Verandah of Violence: The background to the Aceh problem*, (Singapore: Singapore University Press).

Refugees International, 2012, 'Rohingya in Bangladesh' [field report], 30 October.

Renard, John, 2011, *Islam and Christianity: Theological themes in comparative perspective* (Berkeley: University of California Press).

Ringgren, Helmer, 1962, 'The pure religion', *Oriens* 15, 93–6.

Robinson, Francis, 2000, 'Islam and Muslim society in South Asia', in *Islam and Muslim history in South Asia* (Oxford: Oxford University Press), 44–65.

Rokib, Mohammad, 2012, 'The Importance of Faith-Based Organizations in Shaping Natural Disaster: Case Study of Muhammadiyah', paper given at International Conference on Muhammadiyah, University of Muhammadiyah Malang, 29 November–2 December.

Rosen, Armin, 2015a, 'Here's how ISIS abuses humanitarian aid', *Business Insider UK*, 3 February.

Rosen, Armin, 2015b, 'Aiding ISIS victims without helping the jihadists is a difficult task', *Business Insider UK*, 12 February.

Rosen, Lawrence, 2007, 'Orientalism revisited: Edward Said's unfinished critique', *Boston Review*, 1 January.

Rosen, Lawrence, 2008, *Varieties of Muslim Experience: Encounters with Arab political and cultural life* (Chicago: University of Chicago Press).

Rowe, Laura B., 2009, 'Ending terrorism with civil remedies: Boim v. Holy Land Foundation and the proper foundation of liability', *Seventh Circuit Review* 4: 2, Spring, 372–427. Available at: www.kentlaw.iit.edu/Documents/Academic%20Programs/7CR/v4-2/rowe.pdf.

Roy, Olivier, 2004, *Globalised Islam: The search for a new ummah* (London: Hurst).

Russell, Gerard, 2014, *Heirs to Forgotten Kingdoms* (London: Simon and Schuster).

Ruthven, Malise, 2013a, *Encounters with Islam* (London: I. B. Tauris).

Ruthven, Malise, 2013b, 'Terror: The hidden source', *New York Review of Books*, 24 October.

Ruthven, Malise, 2015, 'Inside the Islamic State', *New York Review of Books*, 9 July.

Sanankoua, Bintou and Louis Brenner (eds), 1991, *L'enseignement islamique au Mali* (Bamako: Jamana).

Schaeublin, Emanuel, 2009, 'Role and governance of Islamic charitable institutions: The West Bank zakat committees (1977–2009) in the local context', CCDP Working Paper 5 (Geneva: Graduate Institute). Available at: http://graduateinstitute.ch/home/research/centresandprogrammes/ccdp/publications/publications-workingpapers.html.

Schaeublin, Emanuel, 2012, 'Role and governance of Islamic charitable institutions: Gaza zakat organizations (1973–2011) in the local context', CCDP Working Paper 9 (Geneva: Graduate Institute). Available at: http://graduateinstitute.ch/home/research/centresandprogrammes/ccdp/publications/publications-workingpapers.html.

Schmidt, Francis, 1987, 'Foreword: Polytheisms: degeneration or progress', in F. Schmidt (ed.), *The Inconceivable Polytheism: History and anthropology*, vol. 3, 1–60.

Seaman, John, 1990, 'Disaster epidemiology: Or why most international disaster relief is ineffective', *Injury* 21, 5–8.

Shortt, Rupert, 2012, *Christianophobia* (London: Rider Books).

Siddiqui, Mona, 2013, *Christians, Muslims, and Jesus* (New Haven: Yale University Press).

Sijpesteijn, Petra M., 2013, *Shaping a Muslim State: The world of a mid-eighth-century Egyptian official* (Oxford: Oxford University Press).

Simkhada, S. R. and David Warner (eds), 2006, *Religion, Politics, Conflict and Humanitarian Action: Faith-Based Organizations as political, humanitarian or religious actors* (Geneva: Graduate School of International Studies).

Singer, Amy, 2008, *Charity in Islamic Societies* (Cambridge: Cambridge University Press).

Sipress, Alan, 2005, 'Christian group never had custody of orphans: WorldHelp partner in Indonesia says no steps were taken to obtain 300 children', *Washington Post* Foreign Service Saturday, 15 January.

Sirry, Mun'im, 2014, *Scriptural Polemics: The Qur'ān and other religions* (New York: Oxford University Press).

Smith, Jonathan Z. 1982, *Imagining Religion: From Babylon to Jonestown* (Chicago: University of Chicago Press).

Soares, Benjamin F., 2006, 'Islam in Mali in the neoliberal era', *African Affairs* 105: 418, 77–95.

Soares, Benjamin F. and René Otayek (eds), 2007, *Islam and Muslim Politics in Africa* (Basingstoke: Palgrave Macmillan).

'Staff Monograph', 2004, 'Monograph on Terrorist Financing: Staff report to the National Commission on Terrorist Attacks upon the United States'. Available at: www.9-11commission.gov/staff_statements/911_TerrFin_Monograph.pdf.

Stanner, W. E. H., 1967, 'Reflections on Durkheim and aboriginal religion', in Maurice Freedman (ed.), *Social Organization* (London: Cass), 217–40.

Stirk, Chloe, 2015, 'An Act of Faith: Humanitarian financing and zakat' [briefing paper] (Bristol: Global Humanitarian Assistance).

Stirrat, Jock, 2006, 'Competitive humanitarianism: Relief and the tsunami in Sri Lanka', *Anthropology Today* 22: 5, October, 11–16.

Sullivan, Denis J., 1992, *Private Voluntary Organizations in Egypt: Islamic development, private initiative and state control* (Gainesville: University Press of Florida).

Svoboda, Eva, 2014, 'Aid and the Islamic State', IRIN/HPG Crisis Brief (London: Overseas Development Institute and IRIN News).

Taibi, Mohamed, 1995, *Etudes sur la tolérance* (Tunis: Institut Arabe des Droits de l'Homme).

Tamimi, Azzam, 2007, *Hamas: Unwritten chapters* (London: Hurst).

Tapper, Richard, 1995, ' "Islamic anthropology" and the "anthropology of Islam"', *Anthropological Quarterly* 68: 3, 185–93.

Telford, John and John Cosgrave, 2007, 'The international humanitarian system and the 2004 Indian Ocean earthquake and tsunamis', *Disasters* 31: 1, March, 1–28.

Thelen, Tatjana, Carolin Leutloff-Grandits and Anja Peleikis, 2009, 'Social security in religious networks: An introduction', in Carolin Leutloff-Grandits, Anja Peleikis and Tatjana Thelen (eds), *Social Security in Religious Networks* (Oxford: Berghahn), 1–19.

Tittensor, David and Matthew Clarke (eds), 2014, *Islam and Development: Exploring the invisible aid economy* (London: Ashgate).

Toobin, Jeffrey, 2007, *The Nine: Inside the secret world of the Supreme Court* (New York: Doubleday).

Tritton, A. S., 1930, *The Caliphs and their Non-Muslim Subjects* (London: Humphrey Milford/ Oxford University Press).

Tvedt, Terje, 2002, 'Development NGOs: Actors in a global civil society or in a new international social system?', *Voluntas* 13: 4, December, 363–75.

Tvedt, Terje, Paul Opuku-Mensah and T. Ronnow, 2006, 'Religious NGOs and the International Aid System: An Analysis of Roles and Relationships with Special Focus on the European Arena', draft research proposal, Bergen/Oslo, December.

Urvoy, Dominique, 1996, *Les penseurs libres de l'islam classique* (Paris: Albin Michel).

van Bruinessen, Martin, 2012, 'Indonesian Muslims and their place in the larger world of Islam', in Anthony Reid (ed.), *Indonesia Rising: The repositioning of Asia's third giant* (Singapore: ISEAS), 117–40.

van der Veer, Peter, 1994, *Religious Nationalism: Hindus and Muslims in India* (Berkeley: University of California Press).

Vatican (Pontifical Council for Culture, Pontifical Council for Interreligious Dialogue), n.d., 'Jesus Christ the Bearer of the Water of Life: A Christian reflection on the "New Age"'. Available at: www.vatican.va/roman_curia/pontifical_councils/interelg/documents/rc_pc_interelg_doc_20030203_new-age_en.html.

Vignato, Silvia, 2000, *Au nom de l'hindouisme* (Paris: L'Harmattan).

de Waal, Alex, 2002, 'Anthropology and the Aid Encounter', in Jeremy MacClancy (ed.), *Exotic No More: Anthropology on the front line* (Chicago: University of Chicago Press), 251–69.

Wansbrough, John, 1978, *The Sectarian Milieu: Content and composition of Islamic salvation history* (Oxford: Oxford University Press).

Warrick, Joby and Tik Root, 2013, 'Islamic charity officials gave millions to Al-Qaeda, U.S. says', *Washington Post*, 22 December.

Washington Post, 2001, 'White House Freezes Suspected Terror Assets', 4 December. Available at: www.washingtonpost.com/wp-srv/nation/specials/attacked/transcripts/bushtext_120401.html.

Washington Post, 2010, Editorial: 'The Supreme Court goes too far in the name of fighting terrorism', 22 June. Available at: www.washingtonpost.com/wp-dyn/content/article/2010/06/21/AR2010062104267.html.

Weaver, Sarah Jane, 2006, 'Work continues in Southeast Asia: Church partners with major organizations to serve victims', LDS *Church News*, 27 May.

Weiss, Efrat, 2008, 'Israel versus Hamas' "Union of Good"', *Israel Times*, 7 July.

Weissbrodt, David and Nathaniel Nesbitt, 2010, 'The role of the United States Supreme Court in interpreting and developing Humanitarian Law', University of Minnesota Law School, Legal Studies Research Paper Series, Research Paper 10–31. Available at: http://papers.ssrn.com/sol3/papers.cfm?abstract_id=1655047.

Wöndu, Steven and Ann Lesch, 2000, *Battle for Peace in Sudan: An analysis of the Abuja Conference, 1992–1993* (Lanham: University Press of America).

Yabi, Gilles O., 2012, 'Mali's crisis: pitfalls and pathways', *openDemocracy*, 18 April. Available at: www. opendemocracy.net/gilles-olakounl%C3%A9-yabi/malis-crisis-pitfalls-and-pathways.

Yalman, Nur, 1967, *Under the Bo Tree* (Chicago: University of Chicago Press).

Yalman, Nur, 1996, 'Lévi-Strauss in wonderland: Playing chess with unusual cats', *American Ethnologist* 23: 4, 901–3.

Yalman, Nur, 2004, Interview by Alan Macfarlane in his 'Ancestors' series, 14 June. Available at: http://www.alanmacfarlane.com/ancestors/yalman.htm.

Ye'or, Bat [Gisèle Littman], 1994, *Juifs et chrétiens sous l'Islam* (Paris: Berg International).

Yilmaz, Murat, 2011, 'On track of good: Latin America', *Humanitarian Relief* 47, October–December.

Index